In SCHOOL of CHRIST

DAVID GOODING

BOOKS BY DAVID GOODING

According to Luke
An Unshakeable Kingdom
True to the Faith

In the
SCHOOL
of
CHRIST

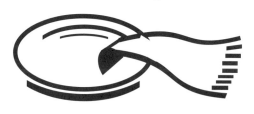

DAVID GOODING

A Study of Christ's Teaching on Holiness
John 13-17

GOSPEL FOLIO PRESS
P.O. Box 2041, Grand Rapids, MI 49501-2041
Available in the UK from
JOHN RITCHIE LTD., Kilmarnock, Scotland

Published by GOSPEL FOLIO PRESS
P.O. Box 2041, Grand Rapids, MI 49501-2041

Cover design by J. B. Nicholson, Jr.

ISBN 1-882701-19-4

Printed in the United States of America

Contents

Author's Preface

This little book was originally written to meet the needs of Russian readers, many of whom had little or no opportunity to study Scripture in any consecutive or intensive way. Naturally, this readership has determined both the style and the level at which the book has been written.

Indulgent and friendly editors of Gospel Folio Press have persuaded me that the book, even as it stands, would be of use to a wider Christian public. I am happy, therefore, to bow to their judgment, and I thank them sincerely for all their expertise involved in its production. Their cover design is particularly worthy of praise.

I pray God's blessing on this and all their other publications.

DAVID GOODING
Belfast
November 1995

Historical Note

Nearly twenty centuries ago, Jesus Christ was crucified in Jerusalem during Pontius Pilate's tenure there as Procurator of the Roman occupying power.

It was the time of the Jewish festival of Passover, and just before His betrayal by a traitor and His arrest by the authorities—which led to His death—Jesus invited His disciples to join Him at a borrowed house in Jerusalem in order to celebrate the Passover. He used the occasion to teach them many memorable lessons concerning the very heart of the Christian faith, the nature of their ongoing relationship with Him, and the transformation of their characters and personalities so that they would progressively reflect His glory.

When the time came to leave the house, He still had not finished His teaching and so, as they made their way through the darkened streets of Jerusalem which were filled with hostility to Him, He continued the lessons, telling them how He would empower them to bear clear witness to Him in a world that would often hate them too.

Jesus was the teacher, the disciples were His pupils. It was the school of Christ. Our purpose in this book is to join Jesus' disciples in His school and learn the lessons with them.

Introduction:
At the School Door

Undeniably our world is full of beauty, from sunlight on virgin snow to the flowers of spring and summer, from the bloom on the face of a newly-wed bride to the noble lines of character which life has sculpted on the face of her grandmother.

But the world is even more beautiful than at first appears and certainly than we have any right to expect. Astonishingly so. Put an insect's wing under a microscope and it is seen to be a marvel of construction. Talk to a physicist who has just discovered how some vast complex system in the universe works, and he will tell you that the mathematics which describe it are not only self-evidently correct: they are astonishingly elegant and beautiful.

And the world is also full of pleasures and joys, some of them deep and profound like those of satisfying personal relationships, and others, like fragrances, which are not vital to life, and seem to exist just for the purpose of giving us additional and unexpected pleasure.

But that said, there is no denying that our world is also full of ugliness and sorrow, much of it totally unnecessary. Why must otherwise intelligent and supposedly civilized nations slaughter each other? Why must rich business men cheat in order to amass even more millions than they already have? Why do so many children eventually break their parents' hearts? And why are some women so cruelly and destructively jealous, some men so ruthlessly selfish, aggressive, and unfaithful?

Sooner or later, our bitter and frustrating experience—concerning the way ugly human behavior destroys what could have been beautiful and joyful—will set all kinds of questions running in our heads. Why isn't the whole of life beautiful and joyful? Why do all of us sometimes hurt even those we love best? What is wrong with our world and with us men and women? Is there, after all, as the Bible says there is, another world where all is beautiful and no ugliness is allowed to spoil it? And if so, have we any realistic hope of getting there one day? Or is that only a fairy tale for children, a make-believe world whose illusions encourage people to put up with life's injustices instead of struggling to eliminate them? If so, we should certainly get rid of these illusions and concentrate on improving people's behavior and making the world a more beautiful and joyful place. But how? The Bible says that there is a power available to change us so that we can live beautiful and joyful lives in this world, not only in heaven. Is it true? If so, how does it work?

In this connection it would be interesting to allow some of the original followers of Jesus Christ to tell us what first attracted them to Him. Peter, the Galilean fisherman, for instance (who later became the Apostle Peter), was a tough, strong, practical man, used to the hardships of making a living out of fishing the often dangerous waters of the sea of Tiberias. He was not, we may suspect, a man much given to sentimentality, or to religion either. Jesus "called us," he explains, "by His own glory and virtue" (2 Pet. 1:3). It was the sheer splendor and beauty of Christ's character that attracted Peter: His strength yet His gentleness, His moral purity yet His extraordinary love and kindness and patience with broken and sinful people; His blazing anger against all injustice perpetrated on other people, and yet His readiness to forgive without retaliation the suffering inflicted on Him personally. So powerful was the attractiveness of Jesus' character and behavior that Peter eventually left his fishing, and followed Jesus; and the opportunity this gave him of observing Jesus closely in all kinds of situations convinced him that, yes, there was a heaven, and that the majesty and glory of Jesus' character were of unearthly origin.

The same impression was made on Peter's fellow-fisherman, John, who also later became an Apostle. "We beheld His glory," says John (Jn. 1:14), "the glory as of the only begotten with (God) the Father."

10

And then over these manly, practical fishermen there stole a profound experience. They found they could no longer be content with what they now felt was their former sinful behavior. They were filled with a longing not only to be with Jesus, but to live like Him as well. To be, in fact, what the Bible calls "holy." And far from them feeling that their longing to live and behave like Him was an unrealistic daydream for practical men like they were, Jesus assured them that their longing could be fulfilled. Admittedly, after a comparatively short time, the world at large showed what they thought of Jesus' character and way of life by crucifying Him. Ugliness once more seemed to have triumphed over beauty. But He rose again from the dead, say His apostles; and His resurrection unleashed—both for them and for all who sincerely believe on Christ to this present day—the power to live a truly Christian and holy life in the rough and tumble, the realities and practicalities of this workaday world.

But here we meet a difficulty. For many people the term "holy" is decidedly unattractive. It seems to them to be itself a negative thing, which denies all that is pleasurable in life. Holy people would be pale-faced recluses, only half-alive; and holiness would be not only beyond the reach, but altogether beyond the inclination, of normal full-blooded people.

Admittedly, holiness does have a negative side to it; but then so, for instance, does surgery. The positive aim of surgery is to make people physically well and strong. But for that very reason surgery has a very negative attitude to germs and cancerous growths. In the same way, the positive aim of holiness is to make people morally pure, strong, and beautiful, with a beauty like that of the Creator Himself. But for that reason it understandably has a negative attitude to everything that would dishonor the Creator, degrade us His creatures, or defile, corrupt, and destroy life's lovely things. Of course, holiness will be against some things that appear at the time to be pleasurable. To the teen-age drug-addict, the next fix of cocaine seems the only attractive and pleasurable thing in the world. He cannot see what the outsider can see that, however pleasurable it may seem, the drugs are destroying his brain. Similarly, revenge can seem very sweet; but it not only wounds its victim, it damages the very soul of the man who indulges in it.

We, therefore, need Christ to teach us what true beauty, true

11

pleasure, true holiness are, and how we too may become holy like He was on earth and now is in heaven. It is His teaching on this topic that we are now invited to attend.

OUR FELLOW STUDENTS

So let's come and meet the students who attended the course of lessons on holiness when Christ first gave them, and which are now recorded for us in the Gospel of John, chapters 13-17. The fact that they were all apostles might make us think that we should find ourselves out of place in a class like this; and that Christ's teaching on holiness is suitable only for religious experts. But that would be far from the truth. None of the apostles had been trained in the theological schools of the day; none was highly educated. And as for their being experts, Christ had Himself described them as theological and intellectual babies (Lk. 10:21). Indeed, as we hear them questioning Christ in the course of His teaching, we shall probably conclude that they were just as slow to see the point as we sometimes are.

They were in fact a varied group of men. Several of them were, like Peter, fishermen by trade: tough, courageous, practical, workers who knew just how hard it was to make a living and support a family. Peter himself was an eager, lovable man, always ready with a comment or response, tending to lead and speak for the rest, but impetuous—apt to speak and act first, and then to think afterwards. Matthew, by contrast, was a cool, calculating type. Before responding to Christ's call, he had made a lot of money as a tax collector, working for the hated Romans. At his conversion he gave up this socially unacceptable business, but he was used to keeping detailed and well-ordered records, and used his ability eventually to write a record of the life of Christ, the Gospel of Matthew.

John and James were ambitious go-getters. They did not care how hard they worked or what they sacrificed if only they could secure the top posts in Christ's kingdom (Mk. 10:35-45). Their ambition was not a hundred percent healthy, and their sense of justice could sometimes be sadly mixed with spiteful revenge (Lk. 9:51-56). Philip, we know from the records, was a gentle, easily approachable person (Jn. 12:21); Thomas, a hard-headed man who was not afraid openly to express his doubts and difficulties in believing (Jn. 11:16; 20:24-29); and Simon the Zealot had, before his conversion, been a right-wing political activist, the very opposite of what Matthew the collaborator had been. Others were quiet people: we never hear them say anything— though they were nonetheless serious students for that. Then there was one shadowy figure. He held the group's common purse; but he was not a genuine disciple, and in the end was exposed as a traitor.

And we, whatever our personalities and characters, and whatever our past political, cultural or social background, could comfortably find ourselves as fellow students with men like these in the school of Christ.

THE SCHOOL

Actually not all the lessons were taught in the same place. And there were reasons for this. There are two sides to holiness. The first is love and devotion to the Divine Persons of the Trinity, holding fellowship with them and allowing them to show us Their love for us and to teach us Their will and desire for us; making Them a home in our hearts now here on earth, as They will one day make us a home with them in heaven. This part of the course Christ taught, appropriately enough, in the quiet seclusion of a private guest-room where He and His apostles had met to celebrate the Jewish Passover. And as they reclined in Oriental fashion around the meal table in intimate, heart-to-heart fellowship, Christ showed them that holiness is not primarily a question of keeping rules and regulations (though there are plenty of commandments to keep) but a question of our response of love to the love of God shown us through His Son, Jesus Christ.

But there is another side to holiness, for true holiness will not lead us to run away from life and shut ourselves off from the world as spiritual recluses. True holiness will take Christ's disciples out into the world with all its sin and hostility against God. And there they will be expected to witness boldly for Christ, living lives that glorify God, demonstrating His holiness, rebuking sin, but embodying and displaying God's love for all His creatures however sinful they may be. To teach this side of holiness Christ led His disciples out of the cosy seclusion of the guest-room, down into the streets of Jerusalem where the night air was laced with the hatred of His enemies who were already plotting with the traitor Judas to destroy Him. And there, along the streets of the city on His way to Gethsemane where He was arrested and taken away to be crucified, Christ, appropriately enough, taught this second side to holiness.

THE LESSONS

This much may be said at once: we shall not find Christ's teachings on holiness to be full of sophisticated, abstract concepts which only a trained philosopher or theologian could understand. They will be as simple as Christ's divine wisdom can make them. It is a mark of the Creator's genius that He can communicate to the minds and hearts of the humblest of His people.

And though the lessons contain a large amount of detail, the major elements in both parts of the course are few and straightforward. They can be set out simply like this:

INSIDE THE CHRISTIAN COMMUNITY (chs. 13-14)	OUTSIDE IN THE WORLD (chs. 15-16)
I. THE ENACTED PARABLE OF THE FOOT-WASHING: God's basic provision for making us holy (13:1-20)	I. THE PARABLE OF THE VINE AND THE BRANCHES: God's basic provision for developing our witness in the world (15:1-17)
II. CHRIST'S EXPOSURE OF JUDAS' TREACHERY: Showing us what the basic principle of holiness (and of unholiness) is (13:21-32)	II. CHRIST'S EXPOSURE OF THE WORLD'S HATRED: Helping us to understand the world's hostility to our witness (15:18-27)
III. CHRIST'S GOING AWAY: Its purpose and implications for the perfecting of our holiness (13:33-14:31)	III. CHRIST'S GOING AWAY: Its necessity and implications for our victory over the world (16:1-33)

14

THE TWO SIDES OF HOLINESS

Even the detail will be easy to follow and understand when we find that much of what is taught in the first part of the course is repeated in the second (as can be seen from the lists on pp. 128-131).

No, the main difficulty, many will feel, is not in following and understanding Christ's teaching on holiness, but in carrying it out in practice. Their concept of a 'saint' is someone who by rigorous religious disciplines and almost superhuman abstinence has, after many years, attained to an extraordinarily advanced level of saintliness; and they instinctively feel in their own hearts that they could not possibly carry such a burden themselves.

But this idea of how you become a saint is badly distorted. Listen to the terms in which Christ elsewhere phrases His invitation to His school:

"Come unto Me, all you who are weary and burdened, and I will give you rest. Take My yoke upon you and learn from Me, for I am gentle and humble in heart, and you will find rest for your souls. For My yoke is easy and My burden is light" (Mt. 11:28-30).

True, Christ will expect His followers to keep His commandments and to work hard at putting them into practice. But the reason why His yoke is easy and His burden is light will become clear in the coming lessons. It is that every necessary major step forward in the development of holiness is achieved not by what we do for Christ but what He does for us, not by our effort but by His power. To start with, Christ does not simply call on us to live a Christ-like life: He first implants within us His very own life, so that we then have the potential and wherewithal to live a Christ-like life. After all, it would be no good telling someone to write a symphony unless they had first been given special musical talent. So we shall find that Christ's very first lesson on holiness will be this: that He has the power to implant within us the life of the Holy Spirit without which we could not begin to be holy (ch. 13).

Thereafter, He certainly asks us to make Him a home in our hearts here on earth; but not before He has announced that He is going to prepare a home for us in His Father's house, and has promised to come again and take us there (ch. 14).

He will, of course, expect us to show the fruit of the Spirit, love, joy, peace and so forth, in the way we live. But not by our own unaided effort. We are not the Vine-stock that creates this fruit: He is. We are only expected to be branches that receive from Him the life, grace, and endurance that make fruit-bearing possible (ch. 15).

Yes, Christ's followers are required to witness boldly for Christ in this hostile world. But the chief responsibility for conducting this witness is not theirs: the Holy Spirit, sent by the Father in Christ's name, carries the main burden of this worldwide task. Christ's followers are but the Holy Spirit's junior partners (ch. 16).

On terms like these, then, anyone can become holy. Let's proceed at once to enter Christ's school.

THE COURSE: PART ONE

A. The Cleansing of the Disciples

Preview

In this session we shall be taught:
God's basic provision for making us holy and beautiful people.
This provision is designed to deliver us from our sinful attitudes and from the defects in our characters which the Bible calls, in figurative language, "spots, wrinkles, and blemishes."

It consists of:

1. *The regeneration performed within by the Holy Spirit.*
    • it is referred to metaphorically (not literally) as a once-for-all, bathing-all-over, spiritual experience.
    • it is itself an indispensable, initial, spiritual experience.
    • it gives new life, new desires, and new powers.
    • without it, true holiness is impossible.
    • once experienced, it never needs to be repeated.

2. *The cleansing and renewal of heart, mind, and action by the Lord Jesus.*
    • it is referred to metaphorically (not literally) as a constantly repeated washing of the feet.
    • it is itself a process that needs constantly to be gone through in order to maintain practical fellowship with the Lord Jesus.

1
The Setting and Timing of the Course

"It was just before the Passover Feast. Jesus knew that the time had come for Him to leave this world and go to the Father. Having loved His own who were in the world, He now showed them the full extent of His love" (13:1).

The original setting of the course of lessons which we are about to study was poignant indeed. For three years Christ had lived, worked and travelled with the twelve men that were His apostles; and they all (except one) had loved Him, served Him, and sacrificed home comforts and worldly wealth in order to follow Him. And now, very abruptly (or so it would seem) He was going to leave them! What should they make of it?

He had told them several times before that He must leave them. But, like us, they did not take in what in any case they did not want to hear; and they soon forgot what He said. This night He would have to tell them again at length and in unmistakably clear language: He must leave them! He must go! The news would devastate and bewilder them. And when a few hours later they saw the violent death by which He left them, they would be overwhelmed with shock, sorrow, fear, and a very troubled sense of having been deserted. Admittedly their shock would not last long. Three days later, they would be transformed by His resurrection. But even so, a mere forty days after that, He would ascend into heaven and leave them once more. This time, permanently.

Then why, we ask, did He have to leave them? It is a question that concerns us today as much as it concerned the original disciples. If Jesus was, and is, the Son of God, sent by God into the world to save us men and women, He could have stayed here as long as He liked. Why then did He stay such a short while? The time He spent with His disciples, teaching them, preaching to the crowds and doing miracles, was only a little more than three years! Could He not have helped them more, convinced and saved more people, if only He had stayed with them longer? Why must He leave His disciples so soon?

Let's get this at least clear, to start with: it was not because He had lost interest in them, or because His love for them had waned. "Having loved His own who were in the world," says John (13:1), "He loved them to the end," that is, to the uttermost.

Nor was it that He was being thrown out of the world against His will by His enemies as the weak victim of their hatred, powerless to help His disciples any longer. No! He was leaving the world deliberately in order "to go to the Father" (13:1). From now on He would be raised by God to the position of supreme power over the universe, "seated at God's right hand in heaven far above all rule, and authority, and power, and dominion, and every name that is named, not only in this world, but also in that which is to come" (Eph. 1:20-21). His going was not a forced exile nor even a tactical retreat.

Even so, we ask again, Why must He leave His disciples so soon? The answer is this: He was determined to make His disciples holy, and the only way He could do that was to leave them . That sounds strange at first; but it is true, and in this course we shall learn why. He could have stayed longer with them and have given them, for example, much more teaching on ethics than He gave them in the Sermon on the Mount. That, perhaps, would have helped them to a fuller grasp of what God's standards of holiness are; but by itself it would never have turned them into holy men, for it could not have given them the power to live up to the standards. The only way He could make available to them the power necessary first to become holy and then to lead a holy life, was by Himself going away.

We must get this clear in our minds. Christ was not like a tennis-player who struggles valiantly all through a tennis tournament, but loses the last match, and so goes home. He was not even like the champion who wins the last match, and then, with the tournament over, retires. For Christ, going home to the Father was itself part of the tournament, an indispensable part of the process and provision for making His disciples holy. And not only His disciples then, but all His disciples ever since.

This, therefore, was the major lesson that He would teach His apostles in His school of holiness during the last hours before He left them.

THE TEACHER'S CONFIDENCE

"The evening meal was being served, and the devil had already prompted Judas Iscariot, son of Simon, to betray Jesus. Jesus knew that the Father had put all things under His power, and that He had come from God and was returning to God" (13:2-3).

So Jesus was intending to make His disciples holy! But must we not ask, "What realistic hope had He of success?" After all, these were men whom He had personally chosen and called to follow Him, and He had spent three solid, busy years teaching and training them, encouraging them with His own friendship and example. Yet look at them now! Here they were gathered to eat a last meal together before He died. But the room in which they met was borrowed, and there was no servant in attendance to perform the simple courtesy (customary in the Middle East at the time) of washing each guest's feet before the meal. Yet not one of the disciples had the sensitivity or the grace to perform this courtesy for the Lord Jesus, let alone for the other disciples; and our Lord was obliged to do it Himself (13:5-12). How selfish and self-centered these men were. Just like us, in fact.

Not only so. On this most sacred occasion, when friendship's ties might have been expected to be at their strongest, one of the disciples, Judas Iscariot, was actually finalizing in his mind the details of his plan to betray Christ. Before the night was out he would have sold Christ to His death for thirty pieces of silver.

A little further round the table was another disciple, Peter. He was loud in his avowal of love and loyalty to Jesus, promising to follow Him to prison and to death, if necessary. And what is more, he sincerely meant what he said. But his sincerity would avail little. A few hours later, the first hint of possible persecution would crumple his courage like a piece of paper, and he would deny Jesus three times over. The rest of the twelve were scarcely any better. When the crunch came and Jesus was arrested, they would all desert Him and run for their lives.

What hope was there of ever making men like that holy? They knew all about Jesus' ethical teaching. But where would the necessary courage come from to carry it out in an evil and hostile world? And from where would come the indispensable love and loyalty, grace and power, determination and perseverance?

Was it that Jesus had overestimated His disciples' love, loyalty and good intentions? Or underestimated the wretched selfishness, weakness and fickleness of the human heart? No! He knew His disciples through and through. He knew that Judas was planning to betray Him (13:11), and that Peter would deny Him (13:36-38). And what is more, He was aware that behind Judas' perfidy and Peter's weakness there was a more sinister power, using both of them to defeat in advance, if it could, all Jesus' intentions. For it was Satan himself who had put it into Judas' heart to betray Jesus (13:2). And now, at this strategic moment, He had positioned Judas opposite Jesus at the table to taunt Jesus with this imminent, and apparently disastrous, defection. And it was Satan who would panic the apostles into deserting Jesus, when He was arrested, and reduce Peter to a lying coward at Jesus' trial (Lk. 22:31-32).

Jesus knew it all. He had no illusions about the supposed strength of His disciples' characters. But—and here is the point —knowing everything about them, He nevertheless set Himself to turn them into genuinely holy men, real everyday saints. Undeterred by their weakness and the strength of the opposition, He set about teaching them His course on holiness.

But how could He be so confident? John tells us (13:3). The Lord Jesus was at this very moment aware of two things. First, the Father had given all things into His hand. That is, God had given Him supreme and ultimate power: nothing was outside of His control. To take one example: "No one," Christ had earlier said, "takes My life from Me, but I lay it down of Myself. I have authority to lay it down, and I have authority to take it again. This command I have received from My Father" (Jn. 10:18).

Secondly, Jesus was aware that He had come forth from God

and was going to the Father (13:3). This had always been the intended sweep of His mission to our world. He came with all the authority of God behind Him: but not to stay! His mission would not be complete until He returned to the Father. Nothing would stop Him from achieving that goal.

Satan, in an attempt to thwart Christ and bring His mission to an end, was engineering Christ's betrayal and crucifixion. Misguidedly enough! For the sufferings of the cross were to be the very means by which Christ would provide forgiveness for all who believed on Him, and so set them free to embark on a life of holiness. Satan, in his attempt to destroy Christ's influence over men and women, was working to have Christ slung out of this world by a brutal execution. But Christ's departure out of this world by resurrection and ascension to the Father would liberate the very power which His disciples needed to live a holy life, and make it available to them. Satan's attempt to thwart Christ's intention to turn His disciples (and millions like them) into genuinely holy people, would ultimately have the effect of furthering that intention. No opposition would be strong enough or clever enough to defeat Christ's purpose.

In this confidence, Jesus rose from the table to give His disciples the first lesson in His course on holiness. And His confidence eventually became the source of their own confidence that they would one day most certainly attain to the glory of God. Listen to the Apostle Paul: *"And we know that in all things God works for the good of those who love Him, who have been called according to His purpose. For those God foreknew He also predestined to be conformed to the likeness of His Son, that He might be the firstborn among many brothers. And those He predestined, He also called; those He called, He also justified; those He justified, He also glorified....For I am convinced that neither death nor life, neither angels nor demons, neither the present nor the future, nor any powers, neither height nor depth, nor anything else in all creation, will be able to separate us from the love of God that is in Christ Jesus our Lord"* (Rom. 8:28-30; 38-39). Confidence like this sets a believer's heart singing.

But now, before we begin the first lesson, let us pause for a moment to take in the school's atmosphere.

THE ATMOSPHERE IN THE SCHOOL

A child going to school for the first time, or a student entering a university, might well feel apprehensive. Will the course be very difficult? And what will the teachers be like? Sympathetic, helpful and patient? Or austere, distant and demanding? And will they really care whether their students pass or fail?

Even more so, an invitation to attend a course of lessons at which Christ is to be each student's personal teacher might seem to many people dauntingly unattractive. Their concept of Christ is that of the glorified Son of God, the Almighty Ruler of the Universe, surrounded by serried ranks of angels, patriarchs and saints, majestic but utterly remote from ordinary mortal, weak men and women. So remote indeed that they might well prefer not to have to deal with Him directly, but to approach Him, if at all, through one or two intermediaries.

How different in fact was the atmosphere in the Upper Room when Christ, just before He died, gave His disciples this course of lessons on holiness. The first half of the course was given during an evening meal as He and His students sat together round a table, and ate as they talked. Indeed it was more informal and intimate than even the word 'sat' might suggest. Being Easterners, they reclined full length on thin mats round a low table, supporting themselves on their left elbow and leaving the right hand and arm free to reach for and take the food. And when one of the disciples who was reclining next to Jesus wanted to ask Him a question, he simply and naturally leaned back onto Jesus' breast and looked up into His face (13:25). Nor was any of them afraid to interrupt Him and tell Him, if he did not understand what He said (14:5-10, 22-23). Once Peter even protested at something Jesus did. It was foolish of him, no doubt; but the fact that he was not afraid to do it shows how completely at ease they felt in the presence of the Lord. That in turn reveals what a gracious and approachable Teacher He was.

Since then, of course, He has ascended into heaven; but at heart Jesus is no different now than He was in the Upper Room. "Jesus Christ is the same yesterday, today and forever," says the Bible (Heb. 13:8); and as we now attempt to follow the lessons He taught His disciples in the Upper Room, we may bring our questions to Him directly in prayer every bit as freely as they did then in their direct conversation with Him.

2

The Washing of Regeneration

"*Now before the feast of the Passover, Jesus knowing that His hour was come that He should depart out of this world unto the Father, having loved His own which were in the world, He loved them unto the end. And during supper, the devil having already put into the heart of Judas Iscariot, Simon's son, to betray Him, Jesus, knowing that the Father had given all things into His hands, and that He came forth from God, and goeth unto God, riseth from supper, and layeth aside His garments; and He took a towel, and girded Himself. Then He poureth water into the bason, and began to wash the disciples' feet, and to wipe them with the towel wherewith He was girded. So He cometh to Simon Peter. He saith unto Him, Lord, dost Thou wash my feet? Jesus answered and said unto him, What I do thou knowest not now; but thou shalt understand hereafter. Peter saith unto Him, Thou shalt never wash my feet. Jesus answered him, If I wash thee not, thou hast no part with Me. Simon Peter saith unto Him, Lord, not my feet only, but also my hands and my head. Jesus saith to him, He that is bathed needeth not save to wash his feet, but is clean every whit: and ye are clean, but not all. For He knew him that should betray Him; therefore said He, Ye are not all clean*"

(Jn. 13:1-11).

"'A person who has bathed all over, only needs to wash his feet; otherwise he is completely clean. And you are clean, but not all.' For He knew the one that was about to betray Him; which is why He said, 'You are not all clean'" (Jn. 13:10-11).

It was only to be expected that our Lord should begin His teaching on holiness with a lesson on the need for cleansing. All of us have been defiled by innumerable sinful attitudes and sinful acts; and it is obvious that if ever we are going to be holy, we shall need cleansing, and constant cleansing at that. And it is nothing to be surprised at either, that the Lord Jesus, being the perfect teacher that He was, should enforce the need for moral and spiritual cleansing by a physical object lesson or parable, by washing His disciples' feet in water.

But suddenly, in reply to a remark by Peter, our Lord stated a basic principle of spiritual cleansing, the startling magnificence of which leaps out of the page and irresistibly arrests us: "He who has been bathed all over, only needs thereafter to wash his feet; otherwise he is completely clean."

Completely clean? How can anyone be completely clean, morally and spiritually, while still on earth? Perhaps, then He was referring to the future: all believers will eventually be completely clean when at last they get home to heaven? But no, Christ was not referring to the future. His disciples were obviously not yet in heaven. In spite of that, Christ said to them, "And you *are* clean." They had been "bathed all over." They were totally clean; from now on they would only need to wash their feet.

WHAT THE ENACTED PARABLE CAN TELL US

Let's look first, therefore, to see what the enacted parable can tell us about this "bathing all over."

First, it is a spiritual cleansing (13:10-11). This is obvious from our Lord's remark to His disciples, "And you are clean, *but not all.*" The Gospel explains why Christ added "but not all." He was referring to Judas. Judas was about to betray Him, and our Lord knew it. The other disciples had been "bathed all over" and were clean. But Judas was not clean, because he had not been "bathed all over." By that our Lord cannot have meant that Judas had not taken a literal bath recently. He was referring to the fact that though Judas was an apostle he had never experienced spiritual cleansing; he was not a genuine disciple and never had been (Jn. 6:70-71). The "bathing all over," then, is a spiritual cleansing, with spiritual, not literal, water. Judas may have been baptized; but he had not been bathed all over in the spiritual sense.

Second, the bathing all over is the initial cleansing. In the enacted parable of the foot-washing, Peter at first objected to having the Lord wash his feet. Then he went to the other extreme and wanted the Lord to wash not only his feet but his hands and his head as well. And it was that that drew the Lord's response: he who has been bathed all over, only needs to wash his feet; otherwise he is completely clean (or, clean all over). Obviously, then, the bathing comes first, and makes a man clean all over; and this is why he subsequently needs only to wash his feet. So also in the spiritual reality to which the parable points, the bathing all over comes first: it is a disciple's initial cleansing. What answers to the foot-washing in the parable is a subsequent and lesser (though still very important) cleansing.

Third, the bathing-all-over is a once-for-all cleansing. The enacted parable is based on the Oriental custom of the day. Invited to a banquet, a man would bathe all over in his own house (or in the public baths) before setting out for his host's house. As he walked to the banquet, however, his feet would get covered with dust or mud; and when he arrived, a servant would wash his feet before he entered the banqueting hall. But the servant would not repeat the bathing all over: there would be no need for that. In real life the man would, of course, eventually take another bath; but within the parable, the bathing is once for all, it is not repeated; and the same is true of the great reality to which it points.

So now we must consult the rest of the New Testament to discover what this bathing all over in the parable represents in reality. As we do so, let's remember it must satisfy these three conditions: it must be a spiritual cleansing; it must be an initial cleansing; and it must be a once-for-all cleansing.

THE BATHING ALL OVER IS
THE WASHING OF REGENERATION

Some people have thought that by the bathing-all-over Christ was referring to the fact that He can cleanse our consciences from the guilt of our sins, because when He died on the cross and poured out His blood, He paid the penalty of our sins. Now, of course, it is wonderfully true that the moment we put our trust in Christ, God assures us that the blood of Jesus Christ, His Son, cleanses us from all sin (1 Jn. 1:7); and so thorough and complete is that cleansing that God can promise us: "Their sins and iniquities I will remember no more" (Heb. 10:17). But when our Lord wanted to symbolize the fact that through His blood we have the cleansing and forgiveness of our sins, He filled a cup with wine (not water), gave it to His disciples and told them to *drink* it—not bathe themselves in it (Mt. 26:27-28). The symbol He used in the enacted parable in John 13, however, was not wine, representing His blood, but water. It points, then, to that other magnificent, once-for-all, cleansing which Christ offers to all who come to Him in true repentance and faith: the washing of regeneration.

WHAT THE WASHING OF REGENERATION IS
AND WHAT IT DOES

But what in practical terms is this "washing of regeneration?" What actual experience in a person's life does it represent?

We can find the answer in Paul's letter to Titus in the New Testament, where he not only goes over the theory of it in detail, but backs up the theory by relating his own personal experience of the process.

Titus, you should understand, was one of Paul's fellow missionaries, and had helped Paul to preach the gospel and to found churches of believers in the island of Crete. But in those far-off days Cretans were notoriously bad characters. "Even one of their own prophets," Paul observes to Titus, "has admitted that Cretans are always liars, evil brutes, lazy gluttons." What, then, could and should be done to help people of that kind?

First of all, they would need forgiveness for all the actual sins that they had committed; and upon their repentance and faith, the blood of Christ would be sufficient to cleanse their consciences from the guilt of sin. But, clearly, forgiving the actual sins of people like this would not be enough. Indeed, to forgive their sins and yet to do nothing about their evil characters would be a disaster. It would, in fact, be a caricature of the gospel. For God is not only interested in forgiving the guilt of our sins: He is also concerned to deliver us from the power and habit of sinning, and to deal with the wrong and evil attitudes of our hearts from which these sinful actions spring. He is concerned, in other words, not merely to forgive the results, but also to deal with the causes.

But how could that be done? Well, certainly it would not be done overnight. The Bible never pretends that the moment we put our faith in Christ He makes us sinlessly perfect. None of us shall be sinlessly perfect until we reach heaven. But, on the other hand, Christ does not leave us simply to try to do our best to improve ourselves. He has a basic provision for us, which Paul now explains to Titus.

He begins as follows: "Remind them," he says, "to be subject to rulers and authorities, to be obedient, to be ready to do whatever is good, to slander no one, to be peaceable and considerate, and to show true humility towards all men."

But that, you might think, was a very tall order. Indeed, almost an impossibility for people who were naturally "liars," who could never tell the truth about anything; "evil beasts" who would bite and tear you to pieces at the slightest provocation; and "lazy gluttons" who were always wanting to fill their own stomachs without ever doing a stroke of work either for themselves or for others. "But don't lose heart," says Paul to Titus, "for remember that at one time we too were foolish, disobedient, deceived and enslaved by all kinds of passions and pleasures. We lived in malice and envy, being hated and hating one another. But then God saved us" (3:3). "How?" says someone, "and by what means and method?"

Perhaps we think we have the answer to the question without looking further to see exactly what Paul says. We say to ourselves: God saved Paul and Titus through the blood and sacrifice of Christ. And that, of course, is true. Through the blood and sacrifice of Christ, God was able to give Paul and Titus complete forgiveness and to cleanse their conscience from the guilt of sin. But that is not the answer that Paul gives Titus here, because Paul is not thinking of the guilt of their sins. He is thinking of all those ugly features that distorted their personalities; of all those blots, blemishes and wrinkles that disfigured their characters before they became Christians. And it was not the blood of

Christ that dealt with those blots and blemishes. What was it then? Listen to the answer Paul actually gives: "But when the kindness and love of God our Saviour appeared, He saved us, not because of the righteous things we had done, but because of His mercy. He saved us through the washing of regeneration and renewal by the Holy Spirit, whom He poured out on us richly through Jesus Christ our Saviour."

THE DOUBLE FUNCTION OF
THE WASHING OF REGENERATION

The very description of this initial experience of salvation introduces two ideas. In the first place it is a washing, a cleansing away of evil and polluted things. In the second place it is regeneration, the positive implanting of a new life, and a new order of living. The Holy Spirit washes us by bringing us to see the wrong and evil in our sinful attitudes and desires. He makes us feel their uncleanness, and leads us to repent of them and repudiate them. More deeply than that, He brings us to see that, in spite of all our efforts to improve ourselves, we cannot eradicate these evil powers within us: we need a Saviour. We cry out in the secret of our hearts: O wretched man that I am! Who shall deliver me? For all too often the good things I want to do, I don't do; and the bad things I don't want to do, I do (Rom. 7:15-25). And He brings us to the point where we are prepared for all the changes of lifestyle that we must be willing to accept, if we receive Christ from now on as Saviour and Lord of our lives.

But then Christ does not leave it there; He does not leave us simply with these newfound desires to lead a holy life. Nor does He simply exhort us from now on to try to do good works and to lead a Christian life. His provision for making us holy is much more radical than that. He implants within us the very life of the Holy Spirit of God, an utterly new and spotlessly clean life that we never possessed before, a new life with new powers and new desires and new abilities to lead a life pleasing to God, since it is the life of the Spirit of God Himself. That does not mean that when a person first trusts the Saviour and receives the new life of the Spirit of God, that person immediately becomes sinlessly perfect, and that all sin is forthwith eradicated from that person's life; but it does mean that there is now within that person a life that has the power to rise up and overcome the wrong desires and attitudes of his sinful heart. It is as though one planted an acorn inside a sepulcher. It would not improve the corpse that lay rotting inside; but from that acorn and amidst all that corruption there would grow up a new life, vigorous, strong, perfectly clean, and beautiful, that was not there before.

So is it with Christ's provision for making us holy. He does not expect us to try to achieve holiness by our own strength; nor is it that He simply gives us a little help from time to time in our struggles to be holy. He has something far more wonderful for us than that. He begins the whole process of making us holy by giving us the gift of the new life of the Holy Spirit within. That life is perfectly pure, since it is the life of God Himself. It is incorruptible. It will never decay. It lasts eternally. "You have purified your souls," says Peter to his fellow-Christians "...having been begotten again, not of corruptible seed, but of incorruptible, through the Word of God that lives and abides for ever" (1 Pet. 1:22-23). "If anyone is in Christ," says Paul, "there is a new creation. The old things have passed away; behold, they have become new" (2 Cor. 5:17).

And once we have experienced this washing of regeneration, once we have received this gift of new life, the experience never needs to be repeated. As in the physical realm, so in the spiritual, one can only be born once. Said our Lord, "He who has been bathed all over, only needs thereafter to wash his feet, for he or she is completely clean."

Completely clean! This is so wonderful, that had Christ not said it, we could not have believed it. But He has said it, and it is no exaggeration. We may, therefore, rejoice and take confidence from His assurance. The biggest part of the process of our being made holy has been forever accomplished once we trust Christ.

A MISTAKE TO AVOID

Elsewhere in the New Testament the Apostle Peter, in his kind but firm manner, reminds us that it is by failing to understand, and then by failing to experience, this personal, internal, spiritual regeneration, that some people who profess to be Christians eventually get themselves into trouble. He too uses a vivid illustration to illustrate what he means (2 Pet. 2:17-22). He reminds us of the ancient Greek fable entitled, "The sow that took a bath." An old sow had been watching the ladies of the city attend the public baths. It had seen them emerge all pink and beautiful in their flowing dresses; and it decided to follow their example and try to be a lady itself. So it went to the baths and had itself scrubbed all over, and came out all pink and smelling of scent. Then it dressed itself up in a beautiful dress and put a jewel in its snout and pranced up the main street on its hind legs, doing its best to behave like ladies behave. And, for a while, it more or less succeeded—until, coming across a pool of dirty, muddy water, it forgot all about trying to be a lady, dived into the water and wallowed in the mud. That, of course, ruined its whole attempt to act like a lady.

The important thing to notice is why its attempt failed. It failed because the sow made the mistake of thinking that in order to be a lady it had simply to try to do the things that ladies do. So it got itself cleaned up outside, but alas it had never been changed inside. If the old sow were to have any hope of ever becoming a lady, the first essential would be that it would have to be changed inside and receive the life and nature of a lady. In other words, to be born again. Without that internal regeneration, all hopes of behaving as a lady would be in vain.

Now Peter tells the story to remind us that it is possible to make a similar mistake. Many people do. They decide they would like to be Christians; so they watch how Christians behave, and notice that Christians sing hymns, say prayers, go to church, are kind to the poor, and so forth. And so they imagine that if they try hard enough to do these things, they will eventually reach the stage when they might be justified in calling themselves Christians. For a while they manage to clean up their lives and to achieve an outward moral reformation; and this they imagine is genuine progress in holiness. But outward reformation is not the same thing as inner regeneration. In fact, never having received the life of God's Spirit within, never having been born again of the Spirit of God, they have never actually begun the path of true holiness, and are in danger of eventually coming to disaster.

THE WASHING IS NOT CHRISTIAN BAPTISM

We owe it to ourselves, therefore, to be clear in our minds that the washing of regeneration, the once-for-all bathing-all-over, is not Christian baptism, nor is it effected through Christian baptism, important as that symbolic ordinance is. There is no power or magic in the water of baptism. It is only a symbol. Some Jews in the time of Christ had already seen this. The great (non-Christian) Jewish historian, Josephus (born 37/38 AD) was the son of a Jewish priest. Yet when he comments on the baptism practiced by John the Baptist, whom he regarded as a God-sent prophet, he remarks that for this symbolic rite to have any significance "the soul must be already (i.e. *before* baptism) thoroughly cleansed by righteousness" (*Antiquities of the Jews,* 18:117).

Our Lord Himself, of course, made it abundantly clear to the Pharisees of His day that ceremonial washing is at best only a token and cannot itself cleanse away moral and spiritual defilement. The Pharisees were meticulous in their practice of ceremonial ablutions. They would never dream of eating a meal without first rigorously washing their hands right up to the elbow, and that not merely to clean away any literal dirt or germs that might be clinging to their skin, but in order to cleanse themselves from ceremonial defilement contracted through touching things that pagan, idolatrous Gentiles had touched. And so when they saw Christ's disciples eating their food without first performing this kind of ceremonial washing, they protested to the Lord Jesus, and He replied by pointing out the practical futility of this religious ritual. "It is not that which goes into a man's mouth that defiles him," He said, "but that which comes out of a man's mouth...for the things which come out of a man's mouth come out of his heart, and it is they that defile him; for out of the heart come evil thoughts, murders, adulteries, fornications, thefts, false witness, slanderings. These are the things which defile a man" (Mt. 15:1-20). It would be mere play-acting to pretend that some ceremonial water sprinkled on our bodies can, by some kind of magic, cleanse the moral pollution of our hearts.

When, therefore, the Bible says, as it does in Ephesians 5:25-27, that Christ cleanses the Church by the washing of water, the term "water" is an obvious metaphor; but a metaphor for what? Here John the Baptist can help us. When the crowds came to him in response to his preaching, he baptized them in the literal water of the River Jordan as a public token of their repentance. But it was only a token. It did not *make* them holy. Only Christ could do that. Listen, then, to John the Baptist proclaiming to the people how Christ could make them holy. First he said, "Behold the Lamb of God, who takes away the sin of the world" (Jn. 1:29). Takes it away, of course, by His blood poured out at Calvary. Then secondly he said, "I baptized you with water; He shall baptize you with the Holy Spirit" (Mk. 1:8). Here then, is the double cleansing of sin. First, the blood of Christ to cleanse our consciences from the guilt of sin and to secure for us justification before God; and secondly, the cleansing by water, a metaphor for the power of the Holy Spirit, to cleanse us from the defilement of sin to give us new life, and to make us holy.

THE HOW OF PERSONAL REGENERATION

If, then, the washing of regeneration is not effected by baptism, how is it effected? Let's look to see how Peter understood it. When Christ came to wash his feet, you remember, he first objected, then going to the other extreme, he asks for not only his feet, but his hands and his head to be washed. Obviously, at the time, he had not understood that the bathing-all-over does not need to be repeated, or else he had forgotten about it. "What I do you do not know now, but you will understand later on," said Christ (13:7). And, sure enough, after Pentecost, Peter came to understand it perfectly.

He was, for instance, sent on one occasion to preach the gospel to some Gentiles. As these Gentiles listened to him preaching the gospel, they believed, received the Holy Spirit, and then on that ground were baptized (Acts 10). Subsequently, Peter had to explain to his fellow apostles and elders just how the spiritual cleansing of these Gentiles took place: He said, "God who knows the heart bore them witness, giving them the Holy Spirit...*cleansing their hearts by faith*" (Acts 15:8-9). Personal faith in the Lord Jesus, then, is the indispensable condition for the washing of regeneration.

AN ACTUAL CASE HISTORY

No better analogy could be found to illustrate this process than that which our Lord cited to Nicodemus, when Nicodemus asked how this new birth is brought about (Jn. 3:9-16). Nicodemus' ancestors sinned on one occasion against God so seriously, that God in His justice sent a plague of poisonous snakes among them. Many people were bitten and were dying. Then God in His mercy provided a way of recovery for them. He told Moses to make a snake of bronze, erect it on a pole, and proclaim that every one who fastened his eyes on the serpent would be given new life. Many did so, and found that it worked. That was faith in action (Num. 21:4-9).

But simply looking at the bronze snake must at first have seemed a strange thing to be asked to do in order to receive life. What made them do it? The plain answer is *repentance*. They were dying under God's condemnation. No other means of healing was available. They could not save themselves. All hope of living long enough to improve themselves, and thus merit release from the penalty of their sin, was futile: they would be dead within a few hours. They faced the facts. Abandoning hope in everything else, they took God at His word, looked to the serpent—and in that moment they received new life.

"Even so," said Christ as He applied the analogy to the spiritual level, "must the Son of Man be lifted up on the cross, that whoever believes may in Him have eternal life" (Jn. 3:14-15).

And this brings us back to our Lord's first lesson in His course on holiness. "Someone who has been bathed all over is already completely clean. All he now needs to do is constantly to rinse his feet." In our next chapter, we must study what this constant rinsing of the feet means in practice, why it is necessary, and how it is done. But for the moment let us sit back and contemplate the first and bigger part of this double operation: the bathing all over once and for all. If we have indeed put our faith in Christ and have been born from above, then Christ Himself tells us with divine authority that in God's sight we are already completely clean: we have been bathed all over. The operation will never need to be repeated. Its effect can never be undone. The biggest part in the process of our sanctification has already taken place. It is all entirely of God's grace: we may safely rejoice and be exceeding glad.

ADDITIONAL NOTE

Many people have thought that when our Lord remarked, "He who has been bathed all over...is completely clean," He was referring to the cleansing of our sins by the blood of His atoning sacrifice. But there are several reasons why He must have been referring to cleansing not by blood but by water.

In the Bible there are two major cleansings provided by God for His people and it is important to understand the difference between the two.

Let's start, then, with the Old Testament. In the Tabernacle (Ex. 25-30) and again in the Temple (1 Ki. 6-7) there stood in the court two major vessels: first, the big bronze altar, and second, the laver (or, sea). Both offered symbolic cleansing for people who wished to approach God: the altar cleansing by blood, the laver cleansing by water. At the laver there was a once-for-all bathing-all-over in water: when Israel's priests were inducted, they were bathed all over in water between the altar and the door of the tabernacle, precisely were the laver stood (Ex. 29:4; 40:11-15, 30). They were only inducted once; the ceremony was not repeated. This bathing-all-over was once-and-for-all. Subsequently they frequently had to wash their hands and feet at the laver whenever they did service in the Tabernacle (Ex. 30:17-21).

Similarly, the New Testament speaks both of cleansing by blood and cleansing by water. John, for instance, in his first epistle declares that "the *blood* of Jesus Christ, God's Son, cleanses us from all sin" (1 Jn. 1:7). Paul, on the other hand, remarks: "Christ also loved the Church, and gave Himself up for her, so that He might sanctify her, having cleansed her by the washing of water with the word, that He might present the Church to Himself all glorious, not having spot or wrinkle or any such thing; but that she should be holy and without blemish" (Eph. 5:25-27).

The question is: to which kind of cleansing was Christ referring when He talked of being bathed all over (Jn. 13)?

First, we should notice that it was in the context of washing His disciples' feet in water that our Lord pointed out that their initial bathing-all-over did not need to be repeated. Unless there were strong reasons to the contrary, one would naturally assume that the bathing was in water, just like the foot-washing. Moreover in the Bible no one's body is ever bathed all over in blood, either literally in Israel's temple-rituals, or metaphorically. The apostles in the Upper Room would have had no reason to suppose that our Lord was referring to bathing all over in the blood of His atoning death.

Secondly, we should notice how the writer to the Hebrews (10:22) describes the cleansing which God has provided us with to make it possible for us to enter the Most Holy Place of His presence: "Let us draw near with a true heart in fullness of faith," having the following:

1. "our hearts sprinkled from an evil conscience." This sprinkling is, metaphorically, by the blood of Christ. Compare Hebrews 9:14, "How much more shall the blood of Christ...cleanse your conscience from dead works...."

2. "our body bathed all over with pure water." The word for "bathed all over" is the same as our Lord uses in John 13; "he who has been bathed all over." Notice particularly that the "bathing all-over" here in Hebrews 10:22 is explicitly said to have been done in water (not blood).

Thirdly, we should notice that in John 13-17 our Lord is concerned not so much with our justification and the forgiveness of our sins, as with our sanctification and the development of the fruit of the Holy Spirit in our characters. To this subject it is the washing of regeneration and renewing by the Holy Spirit that is particularly relevant, rather than our justification through the death and blood of Christ.

3

The Constantly Repeating Rinsings

*"Since we have these promises, dear friends, let us purify our-
selves from everything that contaminates body and spirit, perfecting holiness out of reverence for God"* (2 Cor. 7:1).

If now we have understood, or better still experienced, the
once-for-all bathing-all-over, that is the washing of regeneration,
we are ready to move on to the second lesson which our Lord
illustrated by His enacted parable. In the parable, the once-for-
all bathing had to be followed by repeated rinsing of the feet.
But what does this rinsing represent in everyday practical life?

For the answer we could do no better, surely, than to consult
the Apostle Peter once more. After all, he was the one who at
first objected to Christ washing his feet, and Christ had to warn
him: "If I do not wash you, you have no part with Me" (13:8).
Peter, if anyone, should be able to tell us what Christ meant.

Now we have already seen how Peter described what happened to his fellow Christians in present-day Turkey, when they
first believed the gospel and were "bathed all over once and for
all." Here are his words again: *"Seeing you have purified your
souls in your obedience to the truth unto unfeigned love of the
brethren, love one another from the heart fervently, having been
begotten again, not of corruptible seed, but of incorruptible, through
the Word of God which lives and abides for ever"* (1 Pet. 1:22-23).

Now that they had been purified and born again, what does Peter say they must do next? Here are his words: *"Put away...all malice, and all deceit, and hypocrisies, and envies, and all evil speakings. Like newborn babies, long for the spiritual milk which is without guile, that you may grow thereby in your salvation"* (1 Pet. 2:1-2).

Newborn babies may cry a lot and give their parents sleepless nights. But one thing they don't do: in all their innocence they do not constantly engage in malice, deceit, hypocrisy, envy, and slander! And when people are born again by the washing of regeneration, there is born within them a brand new life that was not there before. It is the life of God Himself who now has become their Father. At the first, this new life is small like a baby and needs, as a matter of urgency, positively to grow by being fed on the wholesome, life-building Word of God. But in addition, everything that is unclean and incompatible with that new life, must constantly be put away. As Peter's fellow-apostle, Paul, puts it, believers in Christ are to cleanse themselves from all defilement of flesh and spirit, perfecting holiness in the fear of God (see 2 Cor. 7:1). In other words, to use the phraseology of our Lord's parable, both Peter and Paul are telling their fellow-Christians that they need constantly to wash their feet.

But that, you may say, is more easily said than done. It certainly is! This world is a morally filthy place, and as we walk through it, we unavoidably get bespattered and soiled from time to time by the moral mud that flies up at us from all directions. What is more, the ups and downs of life, the temptations of the world, and the difficulties of personal relationships will sometimes provoke within us the same old bad attitudes and patterns of behavior that marked us in our pre-conversion days.

WHAT HAPPENS WHEN A BELIEVER SINS?

New believers can become very disturbed when they sin. And so they should! It is a sign that their conscience is beginning to function as it should. On the other hand, it is possible to jump to wrong conclusions. Some may think, for instance, that it means that they were not saved in the first place. Others may feel that they were genuinely saved to start with, but that now they have lost their salvation. How good it is, therefore, to have the steadying and authoritative word of the Lord Jesus: the person who has been bathed all over, only needs to wash his feet, otherwise he is completely clean. When believers sin, it does not mean that they have lost their salvation. Nor does it mean that they need the washing of regeneration all over again. The new God-given life brought into existence by the new birth remains. Believers, to use Christ's words, remain completely clean—apart from the feet. They, admittedly, have been defiled and must be cleansed.

But how? First, believers, if they sin, must confess their sins to the Lord; and in so doing they have the Lord's assurance of forgiveness. "If we say that we have no sin," says the New Testament (1 Jn. 2:8-9), "we deceive ourselves, and the truth is not in us. If we confess our sins, He is faithful and righteous to forgive us our sins and to cleanse us from all unrighteousness."

Then of course we need to cleanse ourselves by regularly reading God's Word. As we read, the Lord Himself, who knelt at His disciples' feet, will kneel at ours. He will lovingly but faithfully show us where our feet are defiled, where our attitudes and actions displease Him. And He will call on us to change these attitudes and put a stop to these actions and will give us the grace, courage, and strength to begin to do so. In this way He still constantly washes our feet, a lifelong, unceasing process.

THE DANGER OF UNWASHED FEET

If, on the other hand, we grow careless as believers, and do not let the Saviour constantly wash our feet, it will have sad and serious consequences. When in the course of Christ's enacted parable, Peter refused to let Christ wash his feet, Christ warned him: "If I do not wash you, you have no part with Me" (13:8). Thereupon Peter submitted to the symbolic washing of his feet. But a little while after that, when it came to the reality which the foot-washing symbolized, Peter was not prepared to submit to it. He boasted that he would be prepared to lay down his life for the Lord. The Lord kindly but firmly told him that he was not so strong as he thought. That very night, in fact, he would deny the Lord (13:37-38). The sensible thing for Peter to have done would have been there and then to admit his weakness and to ask the Lord to help him overcome it. But, as we know from the other Gospels, he would not believe or even listen to the Lord (Mt. 27:31-35), would not admit that he had this hidden flaw in his personality. The result was that, full of foolish self-confidence instead of reliance on Christ, he followed Christ into the High

Priest's court where Christ was being interrogated. And there, when he might boldly have confessed Christ and publicly have stood with Him, his weakness overcame him. Instead of having part with Christ, he denied him three times over.

Take another example. On one occasion, when Jesus was travelling through Israel preaching the gospel, He sent messengers ahead into a nearby village to book lodgings for Himself and His disciples for the night. But the people of the village were all Samaritans who for ethnic and religious reasons hated Jews; and they all refused to let Jesus and His disciples stay the night in the village. Two of Jesus' disciples, James and John, were so angry at this that they wanted to call down fire from heaven on these Samaritans. But in giving way to such desires for revenge, John and James showed themselves altogether out of fellowship with Christ who had come not to destroy men's lives but to save them. Had they continued in such an attitude toward people of other cultures and religions, they could have had no part with Christ in His evangelism and in His love even for His enemies. And so our Lord rebuked them; or to put it in other words, He "washed their feet" (Lk. 9:51-56).

Similarly, if as believers we do not allow Christ constantly to wash away our ethnic and nationalistic animosities, our outbursts of bad temper, our selfishness, dishonesty, jealousy, pride, and all other moral and spiritual uncleannesses, we shall enjoy little practical communion with Christ and little practical fellowship with Him in His mission of love to the world.

Thus, as believers who have been born again, we are assured that we shall not be condemned along with unbelievers at the Final Judgment. But that does not mean we are free to live careless and sinful lives. We are constantly to examine ourselves; and where we find in ourselves wrong attitudes and deeds, we are to judge ourselves, confess it to the Lord, and seek His pardon. And if we do so, all will be well. But if we grow careless and do not judge ourselves and "wash our feet," then the Lord in His love and faithfulness will take us in hand and discipline us so as to bring us to repentance and back to close and practical daily fellowship with Himself (see 1 Cor. 11:31-32).

A Balanced Life

And so the constant rinsing of the feet, the constant renewing by the Holy Spirit, is equally necessary as is the initial bathing all over.

Some people, as we observed earlier, make the mistake of trying to live a life of Christian holiness without ever having first experienced the once and for all bathing all over. They try to start with the second lesson and busily rinse their feet, but of course find it ultimately ineffective. Other people make the opposite mistake. Having genuinely experienced the washing of regeneration through personal faith in the Lord Jesus, they forget the need for the constant and daily rinsing of the feet and, thereafter, make no progress in the Christian life, grieve the Saviour, and are a bad testimony to the world at large. We need, therefore, to learn both lessons, and make sure that we have experienced the first and are daily applying the second.

4
Practical Footwashing

"When He had finished washing their feet, He put on His clothes and returned to His place. Do you understand what I have done for you? He asked them. You call me 'Teacher' and 'Lord,' and rightly so, for that is what I am. Now that I, your Lord and Teacher, have washed your feet, you also should wash one another's feet. I have set you an example that you should do as I have done for you. I tell you the truth, no servant is greater than his master, nor is a messenger greater than the one who sent him. Now that you know these things, you will be blessed if you do them" (Jn. 13:12-17).

If we have understood and undergone the initial spiritual experience of the once-and-for-all bathing; and if we have seen the need thereafter for the constant rinsing of the feet, and have set ourselves as believers to cleanse ourselves from all defilement of the flesh and of the spirit; we shall now be ready for the next lesson in Christ's school of holiness. Briefly put, it is this: if we would make progress in holiness, it is not enough (though very necessary, of course) to carefully and constantly cleanse our lives from the defilement of unclean attitudes and acts. We must also seek to be positive, actively engaged in serving our fellow men and women and especially our fellow-believers.

For when our Lord had washed His disciples' feet, put His clothes on again and sat down, He turned from the spiritual significance of His enacted parable to its practical implication: "If I then, the Lord and the Teacher, have washed your feet, you also ought to wash one another's feet" (13:14).

How then shall we understand this instruction? Some Christians have thought that Christ meant His people from time to time to hold a ceremony in which believers should literally wash one another's feet. But the very first Christians understood the Lord's instruction in a rather more practical way. Here, for instance, is Paul discussing by letter with his fellow Christian worker, Timothy, the custom which the early churches had of caring for and supporting the widows in their communities financially. So that this custom should not be abused by some of the younger widows who expected the church to support them in a life of idleness, Paul suggests that before a widow is enrolled for full-time maintenance by the church, they should look at her past record to see "if she has shown hospitality to visitors, if she has washed the saints' feet, if she has relieved the afflicted, if she has diligently followed every good work" (1 Tim. 5:10). In this context the phrase "washed the saints' feet" could well imply that this dear woman had literally washed the feet of her Christian visitors after the custom of those times. But the phrase could equally be used metaphorically to refer to any task of humble service to others.

In the time of our Lord, washing people's feet was normally a menial task performed by a very lowly servant or even a slave. In instructing His disciples to wash one another's feet, therefore, our Lord was telling all His followers that they must adopt the genuine heart-attitude of a servant, and be prepared to serve people in whatever practical way is necessary. For holiness is not just a theological doctrine: it involves an attitude of mind and heart that looks for opportunities to serve, and counts no task below its dignity.

THE AUTHORITY OF OUR TEACHER

But to serve other people in this way is a very demanding task. What shall drive us to it and keep us at it?

The first thing is the authority of our Teacher. "You call Me Teacher and Lord," He said as He resumed His place among them at the table; "and you say well, for so I am. If I then your Lord and Teacher..." (13:13-14). We notice at once the change in the order of the words. In thinking and speaking of Him, the disciples had been inclined to call him "Teacher" first, and "Lord" second. In speaking to them of Himself, Christ reversed the order: first "Lord" and then "Teacher." The difference may appear small, but when it comes to our attitude to Christ and His commands, the difference assumes great practical importance. All too often we come to Christ as a Teacher, hear what He has to say, and then make up our mind whether we will accept His teaching and carry it out, or not. But that is not the proper way for believers to behave in the school of Christ, nor the best way to make progress in holiness. What we should do is to come to Him first as Lord, making up our minds in advance to obey Him and to do whatever He teaches us; and then, in that spirit, to listen to Him as Teacher.

But if that is the attitude which He requires of us, does that not turn Him into somewhat of a tyrant? No! for consider next His example.

THE POWER OF CHRIST'S EXAMPLE

"I have given you an example, that you also should do as I have done to you" (13:15). A capable teacher knows that the most effective way of teaching is when theory is accompanied by practical demonstration. And so the Perfect Teacher gave His disciples an example of humble, loving, practical service, so vivid that they would immediately grasp its general significance and never forget it for the rest of their lives. But there was infinitely more to it than that. He was not simply a teacher. Indeed He was not first and foremost the Perfect Teacher. He was first and foremost their Lord. In fact, the Lord of the universe. They had no claim on Him that He should serve them, nor any right to expect Him to do it. On the contrary, it was already a grievous fault in them that they had not hastened to do their duty towards Him, their Lord, and wash His feet. That He, their Lord and Creator Incarnate should, in spite of it, divest Himself of His clothes, gird Himself with a towel like a humble servant, kneel at their feet, wash them and dry them with the towel which His own body had warmed, was astounding. When He had done this for them, how could they resent His command that they should similarly serve others? "Truly, truly, I say to you," said Christ, "a servant is not greater than his lord, neither one that is sent greater than he who sent him" (13:16).

The time would come when He would send them into the wide world as His apostles with apostolic authority. But there was a danger that their high office in the church might cause them to forget that their duty was humbly to serve their fellow-believers, and instead to think that their fellow-Christians ought to bow down before them and serve them. So they were always to remember that the Christ they represented had, like a humble servant, done the menial task of washing their feet. After that how could they become arrogant and proud and behave as if they were greater and more important than their Lord? The feel of the touch of His hands on their feet would never fade from their memory, a silent rebuke to their pride, an irrepressible and undeniable call to act as the servants of even the lowliest of men.

THE MOTIVE POWER FOR CHRISTIAN BEHAVIOR

"I have given you an example," said Christ, "that you should do *as I have done to you*...If you know these things, happy are you if you do them" (13:15, 17).

Here we have the heart-secret of Christian ethics. It is not a question simply of keeping rules and regulations. The true believer will increasingly feel impelled to treat others as Christ has treated him. Has Christ forgiven him? Then he will stand ready to forgive others. Has Christ washed his feet? He will seek to wash other people's feet. Has Christ laid down His life for him? Then he ought to lay down his life for others (1 Jn. 3:16).

That will mean serving others in practical ways; but in spiritual things as well. And at this level it becomes clear that we can help others only to the extent that we have experienced the help of Christ ourselves. Obviously I cannot help someone else to see what it means to be born again if I have never had the experience myself.

Similarly, if you notice that a fellow-believer whom you know well is behaving in a way that is unbecoming for a Christian, allowing his weaknesses to dominate him, you may feel it your Christian duty to help him recognize his faults, and to "wash his feet," so to speak. But do be careful how you go about it. You can only do effectively for him what you have first experienced Christ do for you (13:15). Remember how you too need Christ to wash your feet. Remember how He goes about it; and as you come to correct your friend, imitate His method. For if you come in some superior manner and sternly rebuke your friend for his faults, you will find that all his psychological defensive mechanisms will come into play, and he will steel his heart against you, and not allow you to proceed with your intended mission. Indeed, you may well be fortunate if he does not start accusing you, in his turn, of arrogance and pride, because your criticisms, though true, have humiliated him, and made him feel miserable and threatened and worthless.

You would do better to approach him as the Lord approached His apostles. He let them sit up on their couch, and Himself kneeled at their feet. That made them feel important, almost embarrassingly so. But it was not a mere gimmick: He meant them to feel important, for He loved them individually, and to Him they were important; so important, in spite of their present faults and failings that He was about to go to Calvary and give His life for them. Sensing that He loved them, and that in His eyes they were individually dear, they found the courage to open their hearts to His gentle teaching, and even to His rebukes. And in finding the courage to face their failings, they took the first step towards overcoming them and towards Christian maturity and holiness of life.

5

A Foot That Kicked

"I am not referring to all of you; I know those I have chosen. But this is to fulfill the scripture: 'He who shares My bread has lifted up his heel against me.' I am telling you now before it happens, so that when it does happen you will believe that I am He. I tell you the truth, whoever accepts anyone I send accepts Me; and whoever accepts Me accepts the One who sent Me" (Jn. 13:18-20).

"If you know these things," said Christ, as He drew out the practical applications of His enacted parable, "happy are you if you do them." Doing Christ's commands is not the condition which we have to fulfill in order to receive salvation and eternal life; for both these things are free gifts which God graciously bestows on us the moment we repent and trust the Saviour. But doing Christ's commandments is the necessary evidence that we have received salvation and eternal life. A baby does not have to cry in order to receive physical life. It gets life as a gift from its parents. But when a baby is born it normally cries, and its crying is the evidence that it has life. If it never cried or moved, and there was no outward evidence that it was alive, it would mean that it was still-born.

All believers in Christ are as yet imperfect. None keeps all Christ's commandments fully as they should be kept. They are like children at school: doing their best to learn, but making mistakes, getting some of the lessons wrong and not always doing too well at their practical work. And the Teacher has great patience with each one, as He did with Peter. But at this point in the course, the Lord announced that one of the disciples present at the table with Him in His school of holiness was guilty of an attitude that could only be described as follows: "The one who eats My bread has lifted up his heel against Me" (13:18). What did it mean? How serious was it? What was it evidence of?

All kicking of a fellow human being is brutal; but there are two ways of kicking a man. One is to wait until the man comes near enough, and then in full view of the man to fling your leg forward and kick him hard somewhere on the front of his body. This form of kicking is at least open and undisguised.

The other way is to approach the man, smiling all over your face and greeting him as if you loved and respected him, and then just as he has passed you, and he cannot see what you are going to do, you lift your leg up backwards and kick him with your heel. This way of kicking a man is not only brutal: its hypocrisy followed by treachery makes it doubly despicable. To treat any man like that would be shameful; to attempt to treat the Son of God like that would be unspeakably evil.

Yet at that very moment there sat one man at the table with the Lord, eating His food and pretending to be His friend, making out that he was eager to learn the lessons that Christ was teaching in His school of holiness. But the man was a fraud. He had no intention of even trying to carry out Christ's commandments. Thinking that he had impressed Christ with his outward show of interest and discipleship, he was secretly (as he thought) intending not only to disobey Christ but to betray Him.

Christ was not deceived, of course; He had long since read the man's heart. But He did not immediately identify the traitor. He was content for the moment to let it be known that He was aware that there was such a traitor present. He had earlier declared that one of the twelve disciples was not "clean," had not been "bathed all over," was not a regenerate man (13:10-11). Now He described in advance the behavior by which this professing disciple would presently demonstrate to the world at large that he was not, and never had been, a true believer. The untamed rebellion of this outwardly religious, but actually unregenerate, man would presently take advantage of what it supposed to be secrecy, and surreptitiously vent its smoldering resentment of Christ and of Christ's commandments by kicking Him as hard as it could in the back.

As I have said, Christ did not immediately indicate which one of the twelve disciples this was. For a brief while He simply allowed the announcement to lead each one present to examine himself and honestly to make sure what his own heart attitude to the Lord was. It will do us no harm at this point to examine our own hearts with that same purpose in view. It is dangerous to be outwardly religious without ever having been born again. For if people continue like that, Christ's commands will eventually provoke the resentment of their unregenerate hearts; and even if it never expresses itself openly, they will not hide it from Christ.

THE FAITH AND BEHAVIOR OF TRUE DISCIPLES

The traitor, we know, was Judas; for John who subsequently wrote the Gospel, was able to tell us, his readers, in advance (13:2) that Judas was the one who should betray Jesus.

But there was another reason why Jesus showed His disciples before the betrayal that He knew Judas through and through, and was aware that Judas would betray Him. Jesus had chosen Judas (we shall consider why presently) along with the other eleven, to be not only a disciple but an apostle. Judas had gone out preaching like the others; he even held the post of treasurer of the apostolic band. If Jesus had not shown Himself aware of what Judas was going to do before he did it, the other apostles might have concluded that Jesus had been deceived by Judas, and that He had been unable to tell the difference between a regenerate and unregenerate man, and so had misguidedly invested an unregenerate man with apostolic authority.

But it was not so, of course. "Jesus...knew all men and...did not need any one to bear witness concerning man; for He Himself knew what was in man" (2:24-25). He, therefore, warned His disciples of the coming betrayal before it happened, so that when it did happen, it would confirm, and not undermine, their faith in Him (13:19).

This fact, then, that Jesus knew in advance that Judas was a pseudo-apostle is a comfort to us as well. The New Testament epistles show us that the early Christian churches were troubled from time to time by false apostles, by preachers and office-bearers that were not even regenerate men (see 2 Cor. 11:13, 26; Gal. 2:4; 2 Pet. 2:1; 3 Jn. 9-10); and the Church at large has been plagued with such people ever since. Christ Himself warned us it would be so (Lk. 12:45-46). It has not happened because He failed to foresee and prevent it.

But at the same time Christ has indicated to us where true spiritual authority lies, and what our attitude to it must be. "Verily, verily, I tell you, he who receives whomsoever I send receives Me; and he who receives Me, receives Him who sent Me" (13:20).

Let's start at the top of this pyramid of authority. If we receive the Lord Jesus, we thereby receive God who sent Him. But how do we know that God sent Him? Jesus Himself tells us. Speaking to God about His disciples He says: "Now they know that all things whatsoever Thou hast given Me are from Thee: for the words which Thou gavest Me I have given unto them; and they received them and knew of a truth that I came forth from Thee and they believed that Thou didst send Me" (17:7-8). We know Jesus was sent by God, then, because the words He speaks to us are self-evidently the words of God.

In that same way, if anyone claims today to have been sent, or appointed, by the Lord Jesus, we can know whether the claim is true by a similar test: are the words which this claimant speaks and preaches, self-evidently in tune with the words of the Lord Jesus and His apostles in the New Testament? And the corollary of this is true as well. The mark of a true believer is this: when he reads the words of Christ's apostles in the New Testament, he will accept and obey them. For to reject the words of Christ's apostles in the New Testament is to reject Christ; and to reject Christ is to reject the Father who sent Him.

B. The Exposure of Judas' Treachery

Preview

In this session we shall be taught: *The Essence of True Holiness*

- if we are going to perfect holiness in the sight of God, we shall need to know what it is that we are aiming at.
- in Christ's exposure of Judas Iscariot's treachery we shall see an extreme example of what unholiness is at heart.
- Judas took Christ's gifts and friendship, but had no love or time for Christ Himself, and in the end was prepared to sell Christ for material advantage.
- the essence of holiness is thus seen to be an attitude of heart that is the direct opposite of that of Judas. It is love and loyalty and devotion to the Lord Jesus, to the Father and to the Holy Spirit.

6

The Essence of Holiness

"After He had said this, Jesus was troubled in spirit and testified, 'I tell you the truth, one of you is going to betray Me'"
(Jn. 13:21).

The first major lesson in Christ's school of holiness began with a powerfully symbolic object-lesson: Christ's washing of His disciples' feet. Now the second major lesson will consist of another momentous symbolic gesture: Christ's giving of the sop to Judas. The giving of that sop did two things: first, it unmistakably identified the traitor; and secondly, it vividly exposed the nature of his sin.

John's first reason for recording this event is, doubtless, that it actually happened. But the event is more than history: it carries a universal lesson that we need to learn, especially at this particular point in our course on holiness. Its relevance is this: our Lord's washing of His disciples' feet has taught us that true believers are expected to "cleanse themselves from all defilement of flesh and spirit, perfecting holiness in the fear of God" (2 Cor. 7:1). Granted, then, that we should aim at becoming ever more holy, how shall we do that unless we have a clear idea of what holiness is? And not merely what particular attitudes and acts are holy, but what the essence and heart of holiness is.

Now one way of learning what a thing is, is to be shown its

opposite. We learn, for instance, to appreciate beauty all the more by being shown ugliness. We become acutely aware of what it means to be healthy, when we lose our health and become sick. What, then is the opposite of holiness?

"Sin, of course!" says someone; and that is correct as far as it goes. But sin expresses itself in many ways. As the opposite of righteousness, for instance, sin, says the Bible (1 Jn. 3:4), is lawlessness. It is living in total disregard of God's law, as if God's law did not exist. But what is sin as the opposite of holiness?

It is this that the Lord Jesus is about to teach us. In identifying the traitor, Judas, and in vividly exposing the nature of his sin, He will show us what the very essence of unholiness is. We shall then perceive all the more clearly what its opposite, true holiness, is and what the secret is of attaining holiness.

THE ESSENCE OF UNHOLINESS

We have already heard Christ describing Judas' sin (without naming him) in the words: "One who eats My bread has lifted up his heel against Me." Now our Lord adds the even darker phrase: "One of you shall betray Me" (13:21). We know from the other Gospels that Judas betrayed the Lord for money, sold Him for thirty pieces of silver (see Mt. 26:15). We must put all these elements together to get a comprehensive view of Judas' sin.

Let's go back, then, to the phrase, "One who eats My bread," and notice the possessive adjective "*My* bread." It was not a question of thirteen men sharing a meal together in a restaurant, with each man paying his own share of the cost of the meal. On this occasion, as on many occasions in the past, Jesus was the Host who, in His loving generosity, had invited Judas as His personal guest to come and share His table. In addition to the food on His table, the Lord Jesus had bestowed on Judas several high privileges and gifts besides: He had appointed him as an apostle, and commissioned him to go out as His envoy along with the other apostles, to preach the gospel of the kingdom of God. It may even be that Judas was empowered like the other apostles to do miracles, for though Judas was never anything else than an unbeliever (and our Lord knew that, see 6:70-71), it is possible for people who are not believers to do miracles in the name of Jesus (see Mt. 7:23). In addition, Judas was trusted with the post of treasurer of the apostolic group: he held the purse which contained all the money which Jesus owned (from which purse, incidentally, Judas often misappropriated the funds, 12:6).

But far beyond these high privileges, gifts and honored duties, Christ had offered Judas His personal friendship. Christ could have treated Judas as a non-commissioned officer in an army who, important though his rank might be, would never be invited to dine with the Supreme Commander of the army, let alone with the President of the country. But no! Jesus had habitually invited Judas to His table, offering him not only His food but His personal friendship.

And Judas' sin? He had taken all Christ's gifts, accepted all the privileges, eaten the very food off Christ's table—and had no time, love or loyalty for Christ personally. Yes, he had pretended to be Christ's friend and loyal servant. But he had never loved Christ. And as for loyalty, when the opportunity came, he would not only steal Christ's money from the bag; he would sell Christ's friendship, and Christ Himself into the bargain.

THE SERIOUSNESS OF JUDAS' SIN

Now there are some things in life so sacred that one could not put a monetary value on them and anyone who was prepared to sell these things for money would be heartily despised by all right thinking people. Friendship is one of these. Loyalty is another. A man who spies on a foreign country may well be admired by his fellow-citizens for his courage and skill. But a man who is prepared to sell his own country, so long as the price is high enough, is regarded by his fellow-countryman with loathing and disgust, as guilty of the most appalling perversion of true values. If detected and caught he will normally be shot. And what would we say of a man who would sell his mother into slavery for a handsome fee?

Now for Judas to take all Christ's gifts and then to steal His money from the common purse was certainly a mean and despicable trick. But in the end, what would the loss of a few coins mean to Christ? For Judas to take all Christ's gifts, to sit as His guest, pretend friendship, eat the very food off His table, and then sell both Christ Himself and His friendship for money— that was to strike a dagger personally into Christ's very heart. Christ was no unfeeling stoic. Years later, as John recalled the scene and recorded it for us, he still could picture in his mind the distress Jesus showed as He made the announcement: "He was troubled in the spirit and testified and said: 'Truly, truly, I tell you, that one of you shall betray Me'."

But more, if Jesus had been simply an ordinary man, or even a uniquely brilliant theologian and teacher, Judas' treachery would still have been infamous. But Jesus was no ordinary man. He was the Son of God. To take Jesus' gifts and food, and then reject Him was the same as taking God's gifts and then rejecting God. To sell Jesus and His friendship was to sell God and His friendship. The dagger Judas thrust into the heart of Jesus penetrated the very heart of God.

JUDAS' HEART: A MICROCOSM OF MANKIND

Judas' behavior may seem to us extreme; but his attitude of heart is more common than you might think. Judas took Christ's gifts, but He had no time, love or loyalty for Christ personally. And multitudes take and enjoy God's gifts, but have no time, love or loyalty for God either. They treat God the Creator as Judas treated Christ. All around us spread out for our enjoyment are the good, and often delightful, gifts of Nature, our daily bread included. But there is more to life than the impersonal forces of Nature. Behind Nature there beats the throbbing heart of a personal Creator; and Nature's gifts are His loving invitations to us to seek Him and His personal friendship. Multitudes take and enjoy the gifts but have no interest in the Divine Giver. They own no debt of gratitude to Him, no love for Him, no loyalty to Him, no desire for His friendship. They ignore Him. Worse still, to get more money, better positions in society, more acceptance with the world, many are prepared to sell God's Son and to barter faith in God for worldly success. This is the very heart and essence of unholiness. To be unholy you don't have to murder, or raid a bank, or commit adultery, or torture little children. All you have to do is to take God's gifts and have no love or time for God Himself. By that process you wound the very heart of God and desacralize everything in life into the bargain.

AN ANCIENT SIN

This false, unholy, attitude of heart is the sin into which Satan originally lured Adam and Eve. Genesis (ch. 3) describes how he pointed to the tree of the knowledge of good and evil, made Eve aware that it was good for food, that is, for physical satisfaction; that it was good to look at, that is, for aesthetic satisfaction; and desirable to make one wise, that is, intellectual satisfaction; and he put to Eve the lie that it is possible to enjoy these lovely things—in a word, to enjoy life to the full—independently of God and without regard either for Him or for His Word. Adam and Eve believed the lie and inevitably it re-orientated mankind's attitude to life, to its resources and relationships. Life's benefits ceased to be regarded as gifts from the gracious hand of God, to be enjoyed in fellowship with God, drawing their hearts into ever closer friendship with God, so that when life on earth ceased and life's temporary gifts were gone, the friendship with God would continue eternally in God's heaven. Now life's benefits became an end in themselves, drawing their hearts away from God instead of to Him. Moreover their alienation from God made them afraid of God. He was someone to hide from, no longer a source of their enjoyment of life, but a threat to that enjoyment. And the poison of this false attitude to God has infiltrated the veins of every human being.

It is the world's typical sin, so much so that the Bible often uses the word "world" in a bad sense to refer to human society, organized and living on the basis of this false heart-attitude to God. We shall find many examples of this later on in this course.

Moreover, unregenerate people are not the only ones to be marked by this sin: genuine believers are still drawn to it, and need to be exhorted in the words of the Apostle John, "Love not the world, neither the things that are in the world. If any man love the world, the love of the Father is not in him. For all that is in the world, the desire of the flesh, and the desire of the eyes, and the boastful arrogance of life, is not of the Father, but is of the world" (1 Jn. 2:15-16). It is not that the beautiful things in life or even the desire for them are wrong in themselves. God, says the Bible, has given us all things richly to enjoy (1 Tim. 6:17). The damage is done when the lovely things of life (or anything else, for that matter) are allowed to steal our hearts away from God. That is worldliness and the very essence of unholiness.

Suppose a wealthy man who, when his son came of age, decided to mark his son's birthday by giving him a private airplane. And suppose the son took the gift without thanking his father, climbed into the cockpit, flew off and never returned to visit his father again throughout the rest of his life. What should we think of the son? And how would the father feel?

THE ESSENCE OF HOLINESS

If this, then, is the basic principle of unholiness, we may at once deduce that the essential nature of holiness is its exact opposite. It is not so much the keeping of a list of rules, although Christ will later on be reminding us that "if we love Him, we shall keep His commandments." At heart, true holiness is unswerving love and devotion to the Divine Persons.

Failure to grasp this has sometimes led people to the observance of all kinds of legalistic practices which have an outward show of holiness, but lack its basic principle. There are some Christians, for instance, that still wear mediaeval clothes, in the belief that to wear modern dress would be unholy. It is not for us, of course, to judge the inner state of their hearts; but we can be sure of this that it is possible to wear antiquated clothes and to keep all kinds of rigid codes of conduct, and yet at heart have little or no love for the Saviour, or active devotion to Him personally. Even preachers and theologians are not immune to this danger. It is possible to study Holy Scripture as a mere profession or hobby, and to preach the Bible for the sheer joy of the sense of power it gives the preacher over large congregations, and yet at heart to be distant from the Lord, and lacking in personal love for Him. And it is also possible for preachers—let Judas warn us—for the sake of position, career or gain, to be disloyal to Christ morally, spiritually and theologically.

If we are going to be progressively more holy, we must become ever more devoted to the Lord, love Him more dearly and serve Him more loyally. But if that is so, the most fervent believers will be the first to admit that their love for Christ is not as warm and constant as it should be. The pressures of life, its joys, sorrows and struggles, exhaust the heart's energies, distract its loyalties and cool its affections towards Christ. What can unfreeze them and renew their devotion? And Christ, who sees and knows the fickleness of our hearts and their disloyalties to Him—how will He react towards us? Denounce and reject us?

That very question drives us back to the Upper Room to watch Christ's reaction to Judas and to observe how He identified the traitor and by what means He exposed his treachery.

7

The Exposure of Man's Treachery

THE GIVING OF THE SOP TO JUDAS

"His disciples stared at one another, at a loss to know which of them He meant. One of them, the disciple whom Jesus loved, was reclining next to Him. Simon Peter motioned to this disciple and said, 'Ask Him which one He means.' Leaning back against Jesus, he asked Him, 'Lord, who is it?' Jesus answered, 'It is the one to whom I will give this piece of bread when I have dipped it in the dish.' Then, dipping the piece of bread, He gave it to Judas Iscariot, son of Simon. As soon as Judas took the bread, Satan entered into him. 'What you are about to do, do quickly,' Jesus told him, but no one at the meal understood why Jesus said this to him. Since Judas had charge of the money, some thought Jesus was telling him to buy what was needed for the Feast, or to give something to the poor. As soon as Judas had taken the bread, he went out. And it was night" (Jn. 13:22-30).

By the time that the Lord Jesus announced, "One of you shall betray Me," Judas must finally have realized that Jesus knew what he was scheming to do. But as yet none of the others in the Upper Room knew who the traitor was; and they stared at one another at a loss to know which of them Jesus was referring to.

Now one of them, the apostle whom Jesus loved, was reclining next to Jesus. Peter therefore motioned to this disciple to get him to ask Jesus which one of them He meant. So leaning back against Jesus, this disciple asked Him directly, "Lord, who is it?"

Now came the dramatic moment when Jesus must expose the traitor. How would He do it?

He could have done it by silently pointing an accusing finger at him, while Judas squirmed in his seat. But He did not choose to do it that way. He could have done it by naming Judas in the course of a withering denunciation of his treachery. That would have been terrifying.

Perhaps we can recall some of the other occasions on which our Lord was obliged to expose the sin of evil men. How awesome, for instance, must have been the sight of His flashing eyes and uplifted whip, as He drove the money-changers out of the temple (Jn. 2:14-17). How withering must have been His denunciation of certain teachers of the law and certain Pharisees: "You brood of vipers, how shall you escape the damnation of hell?" (Mt. 23:33). But the sins that moved our Lord on those occasions to such trenchant public rebuke were the desecration of God's house, the misrepresentation of God's character, the persecution of God's prophets, and the oppression of the poor under the guise of religion. Christ would not stand by and see other people spiritually damaged through the religious perversities of hypocritical men.

But now in the Upper Room it was not other people that were about to be damaged. Judas' sin was hurting Christ personally, thrusting a poisoned arrow at Christ's own heart. How, then, and in what terms, and in what tone of voice, and by what action would He expose this viper's treachery against His own person? In answer to John's question as to who the traitor was, He said, "It is the one to whom I will give this piece of bread, when I have dipped it in the dish." Then, dipping the piece of bread, He gave it to Judas Iscariot, the son of Simon.

This eloquent action was more than a convenient way of indicating who the traitor was. Judas, we remember had for the last three years been taking Christ's bread, pretending to be His friend. Now by betraying Christ, he was about to fling the bread of Christ's friendship back into His face. How would Christ react to that? By offering him once more that self-same bread!

There was no burning indignation, no vitriolic vituperation. Only the offer of the sop which said with unspoken eloquence: "Judas, you have taken the bread of My friendship, and, in spite of it, you have treacherously lifted up your heel to kick Me. Now you are about to betray Me. I know all about it. But in spite of it, before you do it, Judas, I offer you once more the bread of My friendship! Will you not accept it?"

The gesture was neither cynical nor sarcastic. Nor was it a bribe to curry favor with Judas. It was a genuine, last minute attempt to save him from his self-chosen hell. According to the unwritten laws of ancient Middle Eastern hospitality, if a host took a piece of bread, dipped it in the dish and personally handed it to one of his guests, it did not only mean that he was honoring the guest by offering him a specially tasteful morsel of food from the banquet: it meant in addition that he was pledging himself to that guest, to be his loyal friend. And we may be sure that, even at this dark and dramatic moment in Judas' pathway to hell, our Lord's offering to him of the sop was a genuine gesture, late as the time was, to urge upon Judas His friendship and love and with them the forgiveness, the pardon and the eventual glory that they implied.

JUDAS' REACTION

How Judas felt at that moment we are not told. Poor Judas! Why ever did he not cry out in the wretchedness of his heart, "Lord, I didn't know You knew; but now I see You have found me out. I am consumed with this dastardly, despicable lust for money and for power that drives me to sell and betray You. But if knowing all about it You can still offer me the sop of Your loyal friendship, then I need it above everything else. The devil himself seems to have got hold of me and is dragging me down to hell. Save me from myself. Save me from my appalling perversion." We may be sure that if Judas had so cried out, he would have found that Christ's gesture in offering him the sop was genuine indeed. Christ would have saved him and remained loyal to him forever. As it was, Judas took the sop; but once more it was a hypocritical action. He took the given sop but, utterly unrepentant, he continued with his schemes to betray the Giver.

He had made his final decision. "And now," says John, "Satan entered into him, he rose to go." What would Christ's reaction be to this further and final rejection of His friendship and salvation? There came no violent thunderbolt of denunciation. All Christ said was, as Judas passed through the door, "What you are about to do, do quickly." At the time no one at the table understood what this meant. They thought, says John, that since Judas had charge of the money, Christ was telling him to buy what was needed for the feast, or to give something to the poor. Just imagine, if you can, in what tone of voice and accompanied by what looks and bodily gestures Jesus would normally have told His disciples to give something to the poor! It was in that tone of voice that our Lord made His final comment to Judas.

Even so, John's recording of the disciples' mis-reading of Christ's words to Judas is poignant in the extreme. It recalls an incident that John has recorded a few verses earlier (12:1-8). On that occasion Mary, the sister of Lazarus, had expressed her gratitude, love and devotion to the Lord Jesus by anointing His feet with a whole flask-full of expensive perfume worth at least a whole year's wages. To Judas such extreme devotion to Christ seemed absurdly excessive, and he voiced his criticism: "Why was this perfume not sold for three hundred Roman denarii and given to the poor?" John adds that Judas did not really care for the poor. He was a thief; and since he held the common purse, if the perfume had been sold and the proceeds had been temporarily put into the purse, he might well have helped himself to some of it. But away and beyond that, what actually annoyed him was that anybody should think Jesus worthy of such extremely expensive devotion, and should love Him enough to spend so much on Him. He himself had served Jesus while it suited him, for the position, power and money he got out of it. But love Jesus personally? Why would anyone love Jesus like that? He certainly didn't; and he could not understand why anyone else should.

And now he never would understand. Had he accepted not only the sop, but what it stood for, he would have gone on to discover with ever increasing wonder what the friendship of Christ means for those who accept it. But having taken the sop, he now barricaded his heart for the last time against Christ's love and friendship. Immediately he went out, and, says John (13:30), "it was night." It was, of course, literally night-time. But the phrase points beyond mere time-table. At that moment Satan, whose suggestions Judas had earlier welcomed (13:2) as allies in his struggle to maintain his independence of Jesus, did not go away and leave Judas to his hoped-for freedom. He entered into Judas (13:27), overpowered him and made him his minion. With that, Judas went out into a night of unrelieved moral and spiritual darkness that will never know a dawn. He is but an extreme example of what the Bible warns us will happen to those who finally reject God and His Son.

"But that's terrible," says someone. "Are you really saying that God would let people go to hell, or even send them there, just for refusing to believe in and accept Jesus Christ? If so, who could respect, or believe in, a God like that? Is He not supposed to be a God of love?"

But this very objection leads us on to consider what Jesus said next when Judas had gone out.

8

The Display of God's Glory

> *"When he was gone out, Jesus said, 'Now is the Son of Man glorified and God is glorified in Him. If God is glorified in Him, then God will glorify the Son in Himself, and will glorify Him at once'"* (Jn. 13:31-32).

Let's get this straight to start with: neither Jesus' choice of Judas to be an apostle, nor His prediction that Judas would betray him, *made* Judas betray Him. Suppose, looking down from a helicopter, you saw two cars approaching each other at high speed round a blind corner, you could predict that they were bound to crash into each other. But your prediction, though true, would not *make* them crash. The crash would be the drivers' fault. And so it was with Judas. Jesus knew in advance and predicted that he would betray Him; but that did not *make* Judas betray Him or excuse him for doing it. Judas did what he did of his own free will, out of the sinfulness of his own heart.

Nor did Satan have any intention of fulfilling the Old Testament prophecies that the Messiah must die, when he infiltrated into Judas' mind the idea of betraying Jesus. He too acted out of the scheming of his own mind. To his fallen and devilish way of thinking, the betrayal of Jesus and His death on a cross could only be a disastrous defeat for Jesus. Death by crucifixion was the most opprobrious punishment known to the ancient world. The shame of it would drown the cause of Jesus in an ocean of disgrace. And so he thought it a masterful stroke of strategy when he suborned one of Jesus' chosen apostles to betray him to that public humiliation.

But how mistaken Satan was! The Son of God had come to our world on purpose to die the death of the cross! Knowing in advance that Judas would betray Him to that death, He had deliberately chosen him as an apostle. And when Judas finally left the Upper Room to go out to do his dastardly deed, Christ commanded him: "What you do, do quickly" (13:27). So far from the shame of the cross destroying the reputation of Christ, the suffering of the cross would become the greatest exhibition of the glory of God and of the Son of God that the world has ever seen or that the universe will ever see. Which is why, when Judas had gone out and Christ's crucifixion was now imminent, Christ declared: "Now is the Son of Man glorified and God is glorified in Him."

Ever since Satan had polluted mankind's heart with slanderous misrepresentations of God's character, God had been planning and working towards this moment. In due course God's own Son set foot on our rebel planet. Then came the climax when the Creator Incarnate came face to face in the Upper Room with the creature that was about to betray Him to a cross. Now the world would see what God was like! Now God's reaction to this traitor would reveal exactly what was in God's heart. Deliberately, and in full knowledge of what Judas was about to do, He offered Judas the sop of His friendship.

Magnificent though this gesture was, it formed but the prelude to the even more majestic display of God's glory at Calvary. For just as Christ's giving of the sop to Judas exposed the traitor and his evil treachery, so God's giving of His Son into the hands of mankind, exposed man's rebel hatred against God. "This is the Heir," they said; "come, let us kill Him, and the inheritance shall be ours." But even as they nailed His hands and feet to the cross, God was offering Christ to the world as the sop of His friendship, as the pledge of His forgiveness and eternal love to all who would repent and receive Him in sincerity and truth. "God was in Christ reconciling the world to Himself, not reckoning unto them their trespasses" (2 Cor. 5:19). For "God commends His love to us in that while we were yet sinners, Christ died for us...For if while we were enemies we were reconciled to God through the death of His Son, much more, being reconciled, we shall be saved through His life...." (Rom. 5:8, 10). And right down to us in our century comes God's call through Christ's apostles: "We are ambassadors therefore on behalf of Christ, as though God were intreating by us: we beseech you on behalf of Christ, be ye reconciled to God. For He has made Him to be sin for us, Him who knew no sin, that we might become the righteousness of God in Him" (2 Cor. 5:20-21).

If after that, people take all the Creator's natural gifts, but reject the sop of His friendship, they will, like Judas, go out into a night of eternal darkness where the light of God's friendship never comes and the awareness of His holiness burns like an unquenchable fire. But they will have only themselves to blame.

So when Judas had gone out, Jesus said, as we have already noticed: "Now is the Son of Man glorified and God is glorified in Him." But He added: "If God is glorified in Him, God will glorify the Son in Himself, and will glorify Him at once."

Jesus was predicting that His death on the cross would be followed by His resurrection and His elevation by God to the position of supreme power in the universe and by His appointment as the Judge and Ruler of all mankind. One day God will require every knee, in heaven, earth and hell, to bow and every tongue to confess that Jesus Christ is Lord—worthy to control and administer the wealth of the universe and to receive the submission and worshipful service of every sentient creature. And when God does so, it will be universally acknowledged that God is no tyrant. His moral right to insist on universal submission and worship will have been established not simply in the name of His almighty power, but in the name of Jesus, who humbled Himself to wash His creatures' feet, offered the sop of His friendship even to Judas and died for all mankind on the cross.

This is how the New Testament sums it up:

"...Christ Jesus: who, being in very nature God, did not consider equality with God something to be grasped, but made Himself nothing, taking the very nature of a servant, being made in human likeness.

71

And being found in appearance as a man, He humbled Himself and became obedient to death—even death on a cross! Therefore God exalted Him to the highest place and gave Him the name that is above every name, that in the name of Jesus every knee should bow, in heaven and on earth and under the earth, and every tongue confess that Jesus Christ is Lord, to the glory of God the Father" (Phil. 2:5-11).

C. The Maintenance, Development and Perfecting of Holiness

Preview

In our last session we learned that the essence of true holiness is devotion to the Divine Persons.

In this session we shall discover *the provision Christ has made to secure His people's increasing, and ultimately complete, devotion to God.*

Briefly stated, it consists of:

1. Christ's "going" to prepare a place for us in the many dwelling-places in the Father's house in heaven; and His eventual coming again to take us to Himself, that we may be permanently with Him where He is (14:1-3).

2. Meanwhile, the readiness of the Father, Son, and Holy Spirit to come and make Their dwelling-place in our hearts here on earth (14:17, 23).

The key verse will be Christ's announcement: "I am the Way, the Truth, and the Life: no one comes unto the Father, but by Me" (14:6).

This statement will then be expounded thus:

- *Christ is the Way,* not only to the Father's house in the future but to the Father Himself both in the here and now and the hereafter (14:1-15).
- *Christ reveals to us the Truth* about the Father, by praying the Father to give us the Spirit of truth as another Counselor to dwell within us and guide us into all truth (14:15-17).
- *Christ is the Life,* in that He gives us and shares with us His own eternal life by means of which we can know and enjoy fellowship with the Father (14:18-24).

9

Christ's Going Sets the New Standards

"*Little children, yet a little while I am with you. Ye shall seek Me: and as I said unto the Jews, Whither I go, ye cannot come; so now I say unto you. A new commandment I give unto you, that ye love one another; even as I have loved you, that ye also love one another. By this shall all men know that ye are My disciples, if ye have love one to another*"

(Jn. 13:33-35).

So far in the school of Christ we have learned:

1. that true holiness begins with the personal experience of regeneration effected in us once and for all by the Holy Spirit of God; and that that experience is followed by the constant cleansing performed by the Holy Spirit as He takes Christ's words and applies them to us.

2. that the essential nature and heart-principle of holiness is devotion to the Divine Persons, to the Father, the Son, and the Holy Spirit; and that this love and devotion to God must, and will, express itself also in love, devotion and self-denying service to the people of God.

Now we are to learn of that magnificent, climactic provision for the perfecting of our holiness that is to be made for us by and at the Second Coming of Christ.

John tells us in his later writing (1 Jn. 3:2) that when Christ is revealed to His people at His Second Coming and they see Him as He is, the sight of Him will finally perfect God's work within them. Instantaneously their transformation will be completed, and they shall be like Christ, for they shall see Him as He is.

But more than that, the heart of true holiness lies, as we have seen, in unswerving devotion to the Lord Jesus, in "following the Lamb whithersoever He goes" (Rev. 14:4); and, therefore, provision shall be made at the Second Coming of Christ—indeed has been and is being already made—for all believers to be permanently and eternally with Christ where He is, and never to wander in heart, mind, presence, or devotion from Him ever again.

This, then, was the major lesson that Christ would teach His disciples at this stage in the course. But before He could do so, there were some preliminary things He must inform them of; and some of them would at first seem very unpleasant.

THE NECESSITY OF CHRIST'S GOING

Obviously, Christ's Second Coming could never take place unless He first went away. So now He must tell them very plainly, and then further impress it on them, that He must go away and leave them.

Some months earlier, at the great religious Feast of Tabernacles, the Jerusalem authorities had sent officers to arrest Jesus to stop Him preaching to the crowds. To the officers' surprise Jesus replied in effect: "Don't worry! You need not arrest Me. I am going away of My own accord." What He actually said was: "Yet a little while am I with you, and then I go unto Him that sent Me. You shall seek Me, and shall not find Me; and where I am you cannot come." Our Lord was referring, of course, to His death, resurrection, and return via the ascension to His Father in heaven. But it never occurred to the officers that that was what He was referring to—for the simple reason that they had no idea that His entry into the world had been anything different from any other man's entry into the world; or that He was the Son of God come forth from the Father and sent into our world by means of the Incarnation. So not truly understanding where He had come from, they were at a complete loss to understand what He meant when He talked of returning to the One who sent Him, as also when He added that He would be going to a place where they could not come even if they tried. All they could think of was that He might be going on a lecture-tour to the Greek speaking Jews in Egypt and elsewhere. "Whither will this man go," they said, "that we shall not find Him? Will He go to the Dispersion among the Greeks and teach the Greeks?" (Jn. 7:32-36).

Such lack of understanding on the part of the officers, however, was to be expected: they were not believers. But now the Lord says to His "little children," as He called the disciples, virtually the same as He had earlier said to the officers: "Little children, yet a little while I am with you. You shall seek Me: and as I said to the Jews, Whither I go you cannot come; so now I say to you" (13:33). He was referring once more not merely to His death—they could have followed Him to death if they had been called on to do so at that time—and if they had had the courage to do so—but He was referring to His bodily resurrection and His bodily ascension into the immediate presence of God. And there they would not be able to follow Him for the time being.

CHRIST'S GOING SETS A NEW STANDARD

Now having announced His imminent departure, our Lord then had to teach His disciples what their prime duty would be during His absence: "A new commandment I give unto you, that you love one another" (13:34).

How is it new? Had not God already commanded His people centuries earlier in the Old Testament: "Thou shalt love thy neighbor as thyself" (Lev. 19:18).

The answer lies in the words which our Lord added: *"even as I have loved you, that you love one another."* It was the standard, quality, and extent of the love that was new. He had loved them while He was with them. Now He was going away, and the first stage of His going would be the cross. His death would there display a love the like of which they had never known before. He would die not only for His friends but for His enemies. He would die for them while they were still sinners. He would not love them simply as He loved Himself: He would sacrifice Himself for them.

This then was the standard that the Lord Jesus set for their love and devotion to others which was to be the mark of their developing holiness. And not only so. This would be the standard by which the world around them would judge whether they were genuine disciples of Jesus or not: "By this shall all men know that you are My disciples, if you have love one for another" (13:35).

Experts in music can sometimes be heard commenting on a young musician: "You can tell whom he trained under," for the young man's playing bears the unmistakable imprint of his teacher. And people at large still recognize true Christians by this test. They may know very little Christian doctrine or theology. But they know the kind of love Christ stood for and expressed. And if they find people who profess to be Christians persecuting each other, using the secular powers of the State to discriminate against those who differ with them on points of doctrine, and even fighting civil wars against each other and practicing genocide, the world will come to its own conclusion that such people are not Christians at all. Only those whose behavior bears some resemblance to Christ's standard of love will pass with them as genuine Christian disciples.

But if, to be practically holy, we have to love others as Christ has loved us, have we any realistic hope of ever reaching this standard? Yes, for Christ has resources for us that can enable us to follow His example. But it often happens that, before we learn to lay hold on and rely on those resources, we first have to discover the inadequacy, indeed the bankruptcy, of our own resources, as we shall now see.

10
Inadequate Followers

There follows now a lesson which it is moderately easy to agree with in theory but much more difficult to face when we discover its truth in practical experience. The lesson is this: however grateful to the Lord we may be for what He has done for us, and however determined we may be to love, obey, and follow Him, our love and determination are not enough in themselves to keep us following Him as we should. Indeed we have hidden weaknesses within us which, were we dependent solely on our own resources, would easily ruin the whole procedure completely.

Of course, every believer will unhesitatingly agree that he is still imperfect and sins from time to time; but almost unconsciously many of us assume that, given adequate determination, care, and effort, we can manage by ourselves to overcome or suppress our sins and achieve the desired standard of holiness. It just is not true. Sin has sapped our strength and damaged our moral fiber more than we think; and it can be a bitter experience when repeated failure makes us face this unpleasant and disturbing fact.

The great Apostle Paul openly confesses the feeling of utter wretchedness that came over him when he made this discovery. "With my mind," he says, "I serve the law of God;" for intellectually he saw clearly that serving God was the only sensible way of living. "I delight," he adds, "in the law of God after the inward man;" for living to please God was to him no cold, merely intellectual activity. He delighted in it: it moved him emotionally. Moreover he says, "To will is present with me;" his determination to live a holy life was driven by an iron will. But all in vain! All too often practice turned out to be the opposite of intention. "The good that I would do," he wails, "I don't do, but the evil which I would not do, that I practice" (Rom. 7:15-25). Intellect, emotion, and will, all combined, and put to the task of living a holy, Christ-like life, were found to be seriously inadequate. It was a bitter experience for Paul.

God, however, had known it from the very start; and when Paul discovered his bankruptcy, God pointed him to the provision He Himself had made so that even a bankrupt Paul might be able to follow, love, and obey the Lord Jesus as he should (Rom. 8). And so it will be with us. Using Peter as His object lesson, Christ will now point out to us our inadequacy; and if only we are prepared to take Christ seriously and believe what He says about us, we shall be ready to learn about, and then lay hold of, His provision which brings holiness realistically within our grasp.

Peter: Our Object Lesson

"Simon Peter saith unto Him, Lord, whither goest Thou? Jesus answered, Whither I go, thou canst not follow Me now; but thou shalt follow afterwards. Peter saith unto Him, Lord, why cannot I follow Thee even now? I will lay down my life for Thee. Jesus answereth, Wilt thou lay down thy life for Me? Verily, verily, I say unto thee, The cock shall not crow, till thou hast denied Me thrice" (Jn. 13:36-38).

When the Lord remarked that He was going away, and that where He was going His disciples could not come, Peter considered the matter for a few seconds and decided that our Lord was exaggerating things unnecessarily. "Lord," said Peter, "where exactly are You going?" Our Lord replied, "Where I am going you cannot follow Me now, but you will follow later."

But Peter was not satisfied, for he felt that the Lord's remarks implied a defect in his courage. "But, Lord," he said, "why can't I follow You now? I will lay down my life for You." He meant every word, for in the past years there had grown up in Peter's heart a deep and warm devotion to the Lord Jesus and, as far as he knew, he was perfectly willing to lay down his life for Him, if necessary. Certainly he was no Judas; and perhaps in Peter's way of thinking the exposure of Judas' insincerity and treachery had made him feel all the more certain that he would never treat the Lord in this despicable way, but would follow Him, if need be, to prison and to death. As far as he knew, then, his devotion to Christ was not to be doubted. The trouble was that he did not know himself anywhere near well enough. Actually, there was in Peter's personality a hidden weakness; and when, in a few hours' time, by the sinister machinations of the devil himself, circumstances exerted unbearable pressure on that weakness. Peter's devotion was going to collapse completely and Peter would deny the Lord with oaths and curses. This the Lord now had to tell him and expose to him his weakness, as earlier He had exposed Judas' treachery.

PETER'S BASIC MISTAKE

Of course, we must not confuse Peter's weakness with Judas' treachery. Peter's weakness was the weakness of a man who had been bathed all over, had experienced the regeneration of the Holy Spirit, had been made completely clean (13:10-11); Judas' treachery was the treachery, not merely of an unregenerate man, but of a man who was led by, and eventually possessed, by the devil (13:2, 10-11, 18, 27). Peter's weakness would eventually be overcome: Judas' treachery would never be reversed.

On the other hand, Peter's weakness would not be overcome automatically. The only way for any of us believers to overcome our weaknesses is first, to be made to face them and to admit they are there, and then to repent of them and to seek the Lord's grace and the power of the Holy Spirit to overcome them. Had Peter been willing, therefore, to listen to the Lord Jesus and to accept that what He said was true, Peter could have spared himself enormous anguish and sorrow. And we might wonder, if we did not know the obtuseness of our own hearts, why Peter did not reply to the Lord Jesus in the following fashion: "Lord, I cannot believe it. I am not that kind of man. I don't think that I have this weakness that You talk of; but if I have—and You know best—then please tell me now how I may overcome it, and be saved from this ugly thing that You say I am going to do." If he had said that, the Lord Jesus would most certainly have showed him how he could have avoided the oncoming fall.

But, no, Peter could not believe it about himself, not even when the Lord told him. He thought he had resources enough of courage and determination to make any sacrifice that was necessary in the course of his devotion to the Lord. The fact was, he had not. Therefore, he had to learn the hard and bitter way that the Lord knew him and his personality better than he did himself. The weakness that the Lord said He saw in him was really there, and must be brought to the surface before it could be healed. If, then, the only way to make Peter face his weakness, and thus to learn to overcome it, was to allow him to come into circumstances where he would fail, and deny the Lord, then the Lord's love was such that He would allow Peter to come into those circumstances and make that appalling discovery. For, as chapter 13 reminds us, "Having loved His own which were in the world, He loved them to the end"; and His love was determined to make Peter eventually perfectly holy, whatever the cost and the price should be.

The Certainty of Peter's Restoration

But Christ was certain, of course, that Peter would eventually be restored, and triumph. "Whither I go you cannot follow Me now," he said to Peter, "but you shall follow afterwards." And so Peter did. Though his courage left him, and he denied and deserted Christ in order to escape suffering in the High Priest's court and at the cross, he was afterwards restored, then served and followed Christ magnificently for many years, and finally, like the Lord, went home to glory via a martyr's death.

And we should not fail to notice this: when the breakdown came, as our Lord predicted, and Peter failed to follow the Lord in His suffering as he should have done, it must have been a tremendous source of encouragement and new hope for Peter to remember what the Lord said before it all happened: "You cannot follow Me now; *but you shall follow afterwards.*" All through the ups and downs of the rest of Peter's life, he would constantly have repeated the Lord's words to himself over and over again, giving them their fullest meaning. He had not yet been allowed to follow the ascending Lord bodily into the glory of the Father's presence in heaven. But there was no doubt he would one day. Christ had said he would; and His promise would not fail. And what is more, entry into the glory of the Father's presence in heaven, and the direct sight of the blessed Lord Jesus, would instantaneously complete Peter's sanctification and complete it forever beyond danger of any further collapse. This too, then, our Lord let Peter know by implication, before he fell. The certainty of this promise and the courage it gave him enabled him to face his failure, to come back, and follow the Lord devotedly for the rest of his life. And since Christ has no favorites, all who trust Him may take this same promise to themselves.

11

The Goal Secured

"Let not your heart be troubled: ye believe in God, believe also in Me. In My Father's house are many dwelling-places; if it were not so, I would have told you; for I go to prepare a place for you. And if I go and prepare a place for you, I come again, and will receive you unto Myself; that where I am, there ye may be also" (Jn. 14:1-3).

"Let not your heart be troubled," said Christ; for doubtless He had seen the look of dismay that had spread over His disciples' faces at His announcement that He was going away, and at the further announcement that Peter would deny Him. If Peter's devotion was so unreliable, was their own any better? If Peter could not be loyal to the Lord in His suffering while Christ was still bodily here on earth, would it not be a thousand times more difficult for all of them to remain loyal to Him when He was altogether gone? Would not failure then take the heart out of their devotion and fatally undermine it? And would it not destroy any hope of their being ultimately holy? Surely they had every reason for letting their hearts be troubled. After all, the sin of denying the Lord is extremely serious. The Lord Himself had earlier warned them that those who denied Him before men, He would deny before His Father in heaven (Mt. 10:33). If, therefore, someone who claimed to be a believer unrepentantly continued all his life to deny the Lord Jesus, that would be grounds for seriously doubting that he was ever a true believer at all.

How should they not be troubled?

Nonetheless Christ had no sooner announced that Peter would deny Him (13:38) than in the very next verse (14:1) and almost in the same breath, He added, "Let not your heart be troubled." He had His reasons.

First, He knew that Peter, in spite of his weakness, was a genuine believer, that his denial would be only a temporary (though serious) inconsistency, and that he would recover from his fall: Christ's prayer for Peter (Lk. 22:32) would guarantee that. And from a practical and psychological point of view it was very important that Peter and the other apostles should keep Christ's announcement of Peter's coming fall in its true perspective and proportions. The fall was certain: but so also would be the recovery.

Secondly, serious as his fall was, two or three good things, at least, would come out of it; for in the end God works all things together for good, even the mistakes, for those who love Him and repent of their failures. It would, for instance, destroy Peter's misplaced trust in his own strength, and induce in him a sober, realistic awareness of his weaknesses.

Next, it would convince him of Christ's realism. Christ had not been misled by his fervent protestations of devotion: nor, in one sense, had Christ been disappointed by his fall, for He had foreseen it happening, was expecting it, and loved him still.

Fourthly, Peter would now be ready to listen to Christ in a way he was not before he fell, and to learn to assimilate the provision that Christ was going to make for maintaining, developing, and eventually perfecting his devotion to Himself and to the Father.

And finally, in the light of all this Peter would be specially able to strengthen his fellow-believers (Lk. 22:32).

"Let not your heart be troubled," said Christ; and we do well to listen to His advice. For there are two equal and opposite mistakes that believers can make in regard to their failures. The one is to treat them lightly as if they did not matter at all—to fail to repent of them; to refuse to let the Lord Jesus 'wash their feet' and cleanse them from their defilement. That way leads to increasing failure and fruitlessness. The other mistake, however, lies at the opposite extreme. It is to allow oneself to become engrossed with oneself, one's failures and inadequacies. The mind then becomes absorbed with a sense of defeat, the spirit becomes weak, and Satan himself takes advantage of the situation and induces despair, joylessness, and further defeat. This is not true holiness! True holiness leads us to repent of, and confess, our sins and then to rest on God's assurance of forgiveness (1 Jn. 1:9); to agree with God that "in us, that is, in our flesh dwells no good thing" (Rom. 7:13). We then look away from ourselves to Christ and to the glorious provision He has made, and is making, for overcoming our weaknesses and eventually perfecting our devotion.

So with divine wisdom Christ now turned His disciples' attention away from their inadequacies and Peter's failure to the glorious future before them.

HIS PROVISION FOR THEIR
BEING PERMANENTLY WITH HIM

"Let not your heart be troubled," said Christ; for He had His eye on His disciples not as they were at this moment, but as they would be when God's program for their sanctification was complete. Holiness would not only mean their following and serving Christ devotedly now for a few years in His mission of mercy and salvation through this broken, sin-tainted, sorrow-filled world: it would mean following Christ hereafter in His ascension to heaven, there to serve God sinlessly and with perfect devotion in that heavenly temple where no veil needs to hide the immediate presence of the All-Holy God from His people.

Of that temple Christ now began to speak to them. As the Son of God, come down from heaven, He had first-hand experience of these heavenly things. But His disciples had none; nor could they know anything about them unless they were prepared to believe everything He told them with that absolute unquestioning faith that they normally placed in God. "You believe in God," He said; "then believe also in Me."

"In My Father's house," He continued, "are many dwelling-places." Once before, early on in His public ministry, Jesus had used the term 'My Father's house,' and on that occasion He had used it to refer to the temple in Jerusalem. Even that earthly house was holy, and all who served God in it, the main priests and the lesser priests (the Levites), had to be holy, that is, set apart and devoted entirely to the service of God. Nothing must be allowed to sully the sanctity of the house. And so when our Lord found the temple-courts desecrated by the unholy money-making commerce of the merchants, He drove them out, saying, "Take these things hence; make not My Father's house a house of merchandise" (2:16).

And now, in talking to His disciples of the grandeurs that awaited them, He used the term again, not now of the earthly temple, but of the heavenly, "the greater and more perfect tabernacle, not made with hands, that is to say, not of this creation" (Heb. 9:11). "In My Father's house are many dwelling-places," or rooms. Interestingly enough His Father's earthly house likewise had many rooms surrounding it, in which the priests and the Levites were accommodated, each according to the particular task that he had to do, whether it was preparing the incense or storing the wood offering for the fires on the altar, or making the showbread, or whatever it was. Each of the servants of God in that temple had a place where he might be, so to speak, at home, and there carry out the service and worship of God. And now Christ used the same phrase to describe that infinitely higher and greater and more glorious eternal temple above. That temple, too, has many rooms, where His people in their glorified bodies and their infinitely varied redeemed personalities shall, at Christ's Second Coming, enter upon their eternal, unceasing devoted service and worship of God.

THE PREPARATION OF A PLACE

"I go to prepare a place for you," said Christ; and opinions have differed as to what exactly He meant. Some have felt that He was referring to His going to the cross. His death would pay the penalty of their sins and make it possible for God to remain perfectly righteous and yet forgive and accept them (Rom. 8:24-26). And the blood of Jesus would cleanse their conscience and set them free to serve the living God (Heb. 9:14). This, of course, is all blessedly true: the death of Christ has achieved all this not only for the original disciples but for all who trust Christ.

On the other hand, if this is what Christ was referring to, we might have expected Him to say, "I go to prepare you for a place" rather than "to prepare a place for you." When Christ ascended and sat down on the right hand of the majesty on high, He was but ascending to where He was before (Jn. 6:62). As the Son of God, He resumed His rightful position; the Father "glorified Him alongside of Himself with the glory which Christ had with the Father before the world was" (Jn. 17:5). And yet it is also true that when the Man Christ Jesus ascended into heaven, it changed the face of heaven. Never before had there been in the immediate presence of God a human being with a glorified human body. What adjustments will be necessary in those glorious realms when the millions of Christ's redeemed people follow Him into the eternal tabernacle of God's presence, not as disembodied spirits, but as truly and fully human beings with glorified bodies—this we cannot tell, for we are not told. But of this we can be sure: Christ will have prepared accommodation suited to their redeemed humanity, ready to welcome all His people, including Peter who once denied him.

THE PURPOSE OF CHRIST'S COMING

Christ's phrasing is significant. He could have said, "I shall come again and take you to heaven where there will be no more crying, sorrow, or pain, and no more curse;" and that would have been perfectly true. But He expressed Himself differently, for He was thinking of His Second Coming as the event that shall finally perfect the holiness of His people. "I will come again," He said, *"and receive you unto Myself that where I am there you may be also."* Here is the first and foremost purpose for which Christ is preparing a place for us in the Father's house. It is so that one day we shall be forever with Him where He is, and never again wander from Him. Never again shall weakness lead Peter to deny Him, nor fear panic the other disciples into forsaking Him. It will be a temple from which, as Revelation 3:12 puts it, "We shall go out thence no more." Our devotion will be complete.

THE SCOPE OF CHRIST'S SECOND COMING

Christ's provision and promise embrace all true believers without exception. The Apostle Paul, describing what shall happen at Christ's Second Coming, says:

"Behold I tell you a mystery: we shall not all sleep, but we shall all be changed, in a moment, in the twinkling of an eye, at the last trump: for the trumpet shall sound, and the dead shall be raised incorruptible,

and we shall be changed. For this corruptible must put on incorruption, and this mortal must put on immortality. But when this corruptible shall have put on incorruption, and this mortal shall have put on immortality, then shall come to pass the saying that is written, Death is swallowed up in victory" (1 Cor. 15:51-54).

And again, writing to the Christians at Thessalonika, he says:

"For if we believe that Jesus died and rose again, even so them also that are fallen asleep in Jesus will God bring with Him. For this we say unto you by the word of the Lord, that we that are alive, that are left unto the coming of the Lord, shall in no wise precede them that are fallen asleep. For the Lord Himself shall descend from heaven, with a shout, with the voice of the archangel, and with the trump of God: and the dead in Christ shall rise first: then we that are alive, that are left, shall together with them be caught up in the clouds, to meet the Lord in the air: and so shall we ever be with the Lord" (1 Thess. 4:14-17).

How well Paul, inspired by the Spirit of God, had read the chief longing of the Saviour's heart. "I shall receive you unto Myself," said Christ, "that where I am, there you may be also." "And so," says Paul, "we shall ever be with the Lord."

THE SCOPE OF THE ETERNAL PRIESTHOOD

The next beautiful thing to notice is this: in the ancient earthly temple of God in Jerusalem the service of God was not performed by all the people of God. It was restricted to members of one special tribe, the tribe of Levi, who were set apart and consecrated to act as priests on behalf of the laity. Because of their ordination, they were regarded as specially holy and privileged to enter into parts of the temple where the laity were not allowed to come. But in Christ all such limitations, distinctions, and special privileges are abolished. Now all the people of God are priests. They are so here and now, as the Apostle Peter declares: "You also...are built up a spiritual house, to be a holy priesthood, to offer up spiritual sacrifices acceptable to God through Jesus Christ" (1 Pet. 2:5). All the redeemed sing their praise to Christ, along with the Apostle John, "Unto Him that loves us and loosed us from our sins by His blood; and He made us a kingdom, priests unto His God and Father; to Him be the glory and the dominion for ever and ever" (Rev. 1:5-6). And for all the redeemed in heaven the promise is given: "Therefore they are before the throne of God, and they serve Him day and night in His temple...and His servants shall do Him service, and they shall see His face, and His name shall be on their foreheads" (Rev. 7:15; 22:3-4).

Words are inadequate to express the grandeur and the magnificence of this provision of a place in the Father's house on high. Its effect will be perfect and eternal. It is something, moreover, that we do not have to provide or work out for ourselves. It is altogether the unaided work and provision of Christ. And our Lord tells us about it already while we are still on earth, not to make us careless, but for the very opposite purpose: to foster our determination to be holy. While we are still surrounded by trials and temptations, and while from time to time we still stumble and fall, we are to know that the ultimate goal is secure. We need never give up, we need never lose heart. We shall one day be conformed to the Lord Jesus. We shall one day be perfectly holy. We shall be with Him forever. There will come a day when our devotion to the Divine Persons will never again be less than complete.

12
Christ—The Way
to the Father

"And whither I go, ye know the way. Thomas saith unto Him, Lord, we know not whither Thou goest; how know we the way? Jesus saith unto him, I am the Way, and the Truth, and the Life: no one cometh unto the Father, but by Me. If ye had known Me, ye would have known My Father also: from henceforth ye know Him, and have seen Him. Philip saith unto Him, Lord, show us the Father, and it sufficeth us. Jesus saith unto him, Have I been so long time with you, and dost thou not know Me, Philip? He that hath seen Me hath seen the Father; how sayest thou, Show us the Father? Believest thou not that I am in the Father, and the Father in Me? The words that I say unto you I speak not from Myself: but the Father abiding in Me doeth His works. Believe Me that I am in the Father, and the Father in Me: or else believe Me for the very works' sake. Verily, verily, I say unto you, He that believeth on Me, the works that I do shall he do also; and greater works than these shall he do; because I go unto the Father. And whatsoever ye shall ask in My name, that will I do, that the Father may be glorified in the Son. If ye shall ask Me anything in My name, that will I do" (Jn. 14:4-14).

The first part of Christ's provision for maintaining and perfecting our devotion to God is, as we have seen, to prepare us a place in the Father's house above. But now Christ is about to expound the second part. That will be concerned with our providing the Father and the Son with a dwelling place in our hearts here below. Let us watch, then, how the Lord makes the transition from the first part of the provision to the second. "I am going," said He, "to prepare a place for you in My Father's house...and you know the way to the place where I am going" (14:4).

But at that point Thomas interrupted. "Lord," he interjected, "we do not even know where You are going; so how can we possibly know the way there?"

Before we dismiss Thomas' question as a sign of weak perception, we ought to ask honestly whether we ourselves know the way to the place where the Saviour has gone, any more than Thomas did. What is the way to the Father's house? Where is heaven, and by what road does one get there? We know, of course, that we do not reach heaven by simply rising up into the sky. No astronaut could get there even if he could survive long enough to travel billions of light years through space. Are we to think, as some have done, that heaven is a fifth or sixth dimension of our universe in addition to the four dimensions we already know about, and to which we are, for the time being, limited? Or is it altogether unconnected with our universe? The fact is, we do not know. God has not told us, and it is useless for us to speculate. The likelihood is that in our present state we would not be able to understand it, even if God tried to explain where it is and by what road and by what kind of travel one gets to it.

It is, therefore, all the more interesting that when our Lord replied to Thomas' question, he rephrased the original proposition. "I am the Way, the Truth, and the Life," He said, "no one comes—and He did not say no one comes *to the Father's house*, but—*to the Father*, except by Me" (14:6).

Is there a difference, then, says someone, between coming to the Father's house and coming to the Father? Why, yes, of course, conceptually and practically there is a very big and very important difference. On earth one can visit magnificent palaces in many countries where once kings and emperors lived. Though the kings and emperors are no longer there, one can still admire the architecture and the fabulous treasures in those great palaces; but though enjoyable, it is altogether a different experience from what it would have been had one been able to meet the kings and emperors themselves, talk, dine, and be entertained by them. Or again, you could travel to a distant city, and while there, decide to visit a friend you knew long ago—only to find when you arrived at your friend's house that your friend had gone away on a holiday. In that case, being able to look round your friend's house would not compensate you for the disappointment of not meeting your friend. In the same way, if it were possible (it isn't, of course) to come to the Father's house and never have fellowship with the Father would not only be a disappointment: it would be an eternal disaster. The very heart of unholiness in this life here on earth has been, as we learned in a previous lesson, that people have taken all the manifold gifts of the Creator, but have had little or no time for the Creator Himself, and no desire whatever to have fellowship with Him. If it were possible to go to heaven and to enjoy all the marvels of the Father's house, and yet still have little or no interest in the Father Himself, would but perpetuate and increase our calamitous unholiness.

And so Christ is not concerned simply to take us to the Father's house when He comes again. The far more important thing is that the Lord will bring us to the Father Himself. Indeed, this is so important, so absolutely essential for the maintenance and the eventual perfection of our holiness, that Christ proposes not to wait until we get to heaven before introducing us to the Father. He proposes to bring us to the Father now already in this life, or rather to bring the Father to us. So that, long before we have reached the Father's home above and meet Him there, we may know what it is to welcome and have fellowship with the Father and the Son in the home of our hearts here on earth.

Thus when Thomas said, "Lord, we do not know where you are going, so how can we know the way there?" our Lord replied: "I am the Way, and the Truth, and the Life, no one comes to the Father except by Me" (14:6). And the explanation of this great pronouncement is going to fill the large paragraph which follows.

First, "I am the Way, no one comes to the Father except through Me;" and in verses 7-14, He will explain how, and in what sense, He is Himself the Way to the Father.

Secondly, "I am the Truth, no one comes to the Father except through Me;" and in verses 15-17, He will explain how, by sending the Spirit of truth, He will help us grasp the truth about the Father.

Thirdly, "I am the Life, no one comes to the Father except through Me;" and in verses 18-24, He will explain how He imparts to us the life that we must have, if we are going to enjoy fellowship with the Father.

CHRIST THE FULL AND
SUFFICIENT WAY TO THE FATHER

Christ, then, is the only way to the Father; but, of course, we need no other since Christ is the full and sufficient way to the Father. He is that because He is the full and complete revelation of the Father. "If you had known Me," He said to Thomas, "you would have known My Father also. And from now on you know Him, and have seen Him" (14:7).

But at that point Philip interrupted. "Actually," he said, voicing what seemed to him to be a very good idea, "I was thinking, Lord, that it would make it easy for us to understand, and it would settle the matter for us once and for all, if You would show us the Father right here and now; and that would be enough."

It would seem that Philip was thinking in terms of seeing the Father in some physical sense, or by means of some direct, ecstatic vision; and that somehow if they could be given to see the Father like that, it would forever dispel all doubts. Perhaps we have also felt like that on occasions. Burdened, so we think, by the necessity of always taking everything on faith, and not being able to see God with our own two eyes, which we imagine would be the highest and most convincing proof of His existence, we too would like, if we dared, to make the same suggestion as Philip did. Indeed, various philosophers and mystics in the course of the centuries have claimed that such direct vision of God is possible for us in this life, and can be achieved if we prepare ourselves for it by various rigorous intellectual and psychological techniques.

The pagan Greek philosopher, Plotinus (AD 205-269/70), for instance, assured his disciples that God (or 'The One,' as

Plotinus called him) was completely unknowable; but that nonetheless it was possible by suitable intellectual and psychological techniques to attain to ecstatic direct vision of the One, in which the Self achieves identity with the One. Certain forms of Hinduism make the same claim. And, unfortunately, from time to time down the centuries some Christians have been tempted to think that by following these same philosophical principles and psychological techniques they could get beyond what Christ can show us about God, and, arriving at a God who is utterly unknowable, have direct vision of this unknowable God and enjoy ecstatic union with Him.

But against all such fascinating but fallacious claims stands Christ's unambiguous pronouncement: "No one comes to the Father but by Me." In our quest for God, we shall never get beyond Christ, or learn something about the Father that Christ has not, or could not, tell us. And we have no need to try. For listen to His reply to Philip: "Have I been so long time with you, and do you not know Me, Philip? He who has seen Me has seen the Father. How then can you say, 'Show us the Father'?" Christ is the image of the invisible God (Col. 1:15). He is the radiance of His glory, and the very image of His substance (Heb. 1:3). No one has seen God at any time; but the Only-begotten Son who is in the bosom of the Father, He has told Him out (Jn. 1:18).

But Christ's reply to Philip must have left an expression of incredulity or incomprehension on Philip's face, for our Lord continued: *"Do you not believe that I am in the Father, and the Father in Me? Take the words that I speak to you, and the marvellous works that I have performed. How do you suppose I do them, Philip? I am not the source of the words that I speak to you, nor of the works that I do. The source of both is the Father who dwells in Me. Believe Me, Philip, that I am in the Father, and the Father in Me, or else if you cannot simply take My word for it, believe Me on the evidence of the very works that I do."*

That must have been a wonderful moment in that wonderful evening. Thomas and Philip had been thinking of God as being a long way off in heaven; but they now discovered that the Father was, so to speak, sitting at the other side of the table in the Person of Jesus. All evening long they had been listening to Jesus' words, marvelling at their grace and their wonder. But all the while they were the Father's words they were listening to.

As they had listened, they had watched Jesus' face and its expressions of love, encouragement, and sorrow; and what in fact they had been watching was the light of the knowledge of the glory of God in the face of Jesus Christ. John had actually leaned on Jesus' bosom; and the love that throbbed in every heartbeat he heard was the love of God. And was that truly God who a few moments ago had knelt at their feet and washed them? Was God like that? Yes, precisely: "The words that I say unto you I speak not on Mine own initiative; but the Father abiding in Me does His works. He who has seen Me has seen the Father." This is what God is like. Certainly the apostles had not seen there in the Upper Room the external glories of God and Christ, as later John was privileged to see them in the revelation given him on the island of Patmos (see The Revelation), and as all God's people shall one day see them. But they had seen the Father's heart and mind, character and attitude, words and works, fully expressed. Christ had brought the Father to them. And never to all eternity, not even amidst the full blaze of God's external glory in heaven, would they discover something different in the heart of God from what Jesus had shown them. Thank God for Jesus Christ, His Son! How infinitely superior He is to those philosophers and mystics, who, when you have followed all their theories and psychological techniques, can only hold out the (quite fallacious) hope of seeing an altogether unknowable and incomprehensible God!

CHRIST—THE PATTERN FOR US

"Verily, verily, I say unto you, He that believeth on Me, the works that I do shall he do also; and greater works than these shall he do; because I go unto the Father. And whatsoever ye shall ask in My name, that will I do, that the Father may be glorified in the Son. If ye shall ask Me anything in My name, that will I do" (Jn. 14:12-14).

But there is another sense in which Christ is for us the way to the Father. Not only has He made known to us the Father who dwelled in Him by doing the works and speaking the words which the Father did and spoke through Him: but in all this He becomes a pattern for us at our lowlier level, as He now explains to the apostles.

To grasp the point clearly, let us just repeat the pattern once more. When Christ said: "The words I say to you I speak not from Myself, but the Father abiding in Me does His works," He was not representing Himself as a mindless machine, or computer, through which the Father simply expressed Himself. They were indeed the Father's words and works. Their source was the Father's initiative and power. But Christ personally and knowingly used His own lips to speak those words and His own hands did the works.

And so when Christ now says, "Verily, verily, I say to you, He who believes on Me, the works that I do shall he do also," He genuinely means that the believer will himself do the works: the believer will not be simply a machine which Christ uses. And yet at the same time it will be Christ who does those works in and through the believer. Listen to this twice repeated affirmation: "Whatever you ask (that is, of the Father) in My name, that will *I* do.... If you ask Me anything in My name, that will *I* do." In other words, the believer's relationship to Christ will, for these purposes, be patterned on that between Christ and the Father.

But then Christ added a startling thing: "The works I do shall he (the believer) do also, and greater works than these shall he do because I go unto the Father." In what sense greater? How indeed is it even possible for there to be any works greater than those which Christ did when He was here on earth? On more than one occasion He raised the dead. Could anything be greater than that?

To understand how it can be, we must pay close attention to the reason which Christ gives: "greater...*because* I go to the Father." When Christ was here on earth, He could, as we noticed earlier, only be in one place at a time. Even though He could exercise power and heal people at a distance (see Jn. 4:46-53; Lk. 7:2-10), there is no record of His ever being and speaking in two places at once. But when He went to the Father at the ascension, there was no longer any such limitation. For now thousands of believers all round the earth can simultaneously pray to the Father in the name of Christ, and Christ can put all the answers to their prayers into effect by working simultaneously through all those believers. The works will be greater than those Christ did on earth, greater numerically.

But they will be greater in quality as well. It is a great thing to be raised from the dead like Lazarus was (Jn. 11) and to receive for a while (Lazarus eventually died again) the temporary gift of physical life. It is a far greater thing to receive the imperishable gift of the Holy Spirit, and by the Spirit to be incorporated into the Body of Christ (1 Cor. 12:13). Now Christ spoke of the gift of the Holy Spirit when He was here on earth, but Scripture makes clear that the gift was not generally given until Jesus, after His ascension, baptized His people in the Holy Spirit on the Day of Pentecost. So Jesus said to the crowds at one Feast of Tabernacles: "He who believes on Me...out of his belly shall flow rivers of living water." And the Gospel writer adds: "But this spake He of the Spirit whom those who believed on Him were to receive; for the Spirit was not yet given because Jesus was not yet glorified" (that is, ascended; Jn. 7:38-39. See also Acts 1:4-5; 2:2-3).

Now no man, no Christian preacher, not even an apostle, can impart the Holy Spirit to anyone. But from Pentecost onwards the risen Lord has spoken through His servants, and as a result people have believed and thereupon received the gift of the Holy Spirit. Here, for instance, is Peter relating what happened when he was sent to preach to a Roman centurion and his friends "words by which they might be saved." "And as I began to speak, the Holy Spirit fell on them, even as on us at the beginning. And I remembered the word of the Lord, how that He said, John indeed baptized in water, but you shall be baptized in the Holy Spirit" (Acts 10:14-16). Nothing like this is ever recorded as having happened when Jesus preached here on earth. These are the "greater works" which the risen and ascended Lord has been doing through His people since Pentecost.

It goes without saying, of course, that Christ's promise to do whatever we ask the Father or Him in His name must be read strictly in this context. It is no guarantee that we shall receive whatever we decide we would like to have. Our asking must be "in His name," that is, it must be consistent with His character and declared purposes and in His interests. And when Christ does what we ask, it will always be with this purpose "that the Father may be glorified in the Son" (14:13). He will act for no other reason.

But these limitations are no restriction on the wonder of what

Christ is teaching us here. Only think what an inexpressible glory it is that the Father and the Son should take up frail vessels of mortal clay such as we are, cleanse and sanctify us, and then with our co-operation work through us to make Their glory known. As the Apostle Paul later put it: *"For we preach not ourselves, but Christ Jesus as Lord, and ourselves as your servants for Jesus' sake. Seeing it is God, that said, Light shall shine out of darkness, who shined in our hearts, to give the light of the knowledge of the glory of God in the face of Jesus Christ. But we have this treasure in earthen vessels, that the exceeding greatness of the power may be of God, and not from ourselves"* (2 Cor. 4:5-7).

13
Christ—The Truth About the Father

"I am...the Truth...no one comes unto the Father but by Me...If you love Me, ye will keep My commandments. And I will pray the Father, and He shall give you another Comforter, that He may be with you forever, even the Spirit of truth: whom the world cannot receive; for it beholdeth Him not, neither knoweth Him: ye know Him; for He abideth with you, and shall be in you" (Jn. 14:6, 15-17).

All true and efficient learning proceeds by statement, understanding, and repetition. So it is for us students in the school of Christ. Repetition is riveting on our minds that the basic principle of all true holiness is love and devotion and service to the Divine Persons; and hence if we would be holy we must be brought continually nearer to the Father.

To that end we have learned that Christ will one day return and take us to Himself bodily in the Father's house. Meanwhile, and to prepare us for that event, Christ has already brought us to the Father and the Father to us by His incarnation, His life, His ministry here on earth, His death, and resurrection. *"The Word was made flesh and tabernacled among us,"* says the Apostle John, *"and we beheld His glory, glory as of the only-begotten from the Father, full of grace and truth"* (Jn. 1:14). Seeing Him, as our Lord explained to Philip, we have seen the Father.

But if we are to be brought increasingly closer to the Father, we shall, let us say it reverently, need more than the full revelation of God in Christ. Not of course that there is anything inadequate in that revelation. Far from it. But there is a great inadequacy in our ability to comprehend that revelation.

You can see that if you picture again the eleven men who reclined round the table with our Lord in the Upper Room. Seeing Jesus, Philip and the others were seeing the Father. But they did not properly take in and understand and enjoy all they saw. And why not? Because their minds were full of their own ideas, presuppositions, false expectations, and sheer ignorance. So full indeed, that some of what Christ said and did seemed to them disappointingly puzzling, and some positively wrong; and they told Him so. If they were ever to be brought fully to the Father, they would need not only the full revelation of the Father in Christ, but something to deal with their internal intellectual and emotional blockages, to dissipate the dark clouds of their fears, doubts, and misunderstandings, so as to let the light of God's revelation in Christ shine through.

They would need something more. The unaided human spirit, however intellectually sharp, cannot take in the things of God, says Scripture (1 Cor. 2:14). Only the Spirit of God can understand the things of God. Therefore, if the disciples were ever going to know the Father, they would need the Spirit of God. This is precisely what the Lord Jesus now informs the disciples He will supply: *"I will pray the Father and He will give you another Counselor, that He may be with you forever, even the Spirit of truth."*

We notice at once the title that is here given to the Spirit: not the Spirit of God, nor the Spirit of grace, nor the Spirit of holiness—though He is of course all these things and is so called elsewhere in Scripture. But here our Lord refers to Him as the Spirit of Truth. And this resonates with what our Lord said earlier: *"I am...the Truth.... No one comes to the Father but by Me."* So now He promises to pray the Father, who in response to His prayer will send the Spirit of Truth, not only to be with His people but in them, and, by helping them to grasp the truth about the Father, to bring them ever nearer to the Father.

THE TRUTH ABOUT THE FATHER

Let's use an illustration. A friend of mine was once asked to conduct Christian education classes in a home for unwanted children run by a large city council. One day when he opened the door of the reception center and walked in, he found a nurse with a little boy of seven or eight years. As soon as he saw my friend come in, the little boy started to scream, so that the nurse had to ask my friend to go out for a moment while she pacified the child. That done, she called my friend in again and, taking off the little boy's clothes, she showed him his body scarred all over with burn-marks. The little boy explained: "My father always burns me." The fact was that his father used to come home drunk, put a poker in the fire until it was red hot and then beat the child with it. Suppose my friend had tried to tell that little boy that God wanted to be his Father. What kind of a concept would the word 'father' have evoked in the child's mind? What difficulties my friend would have had to get across to the child what God was really like, and what He means when He calls Himself our Father!

Satan, by his dastardly work in the Garden of Eden, has, to a lesser or greater degree, perverted all our concepts of what God is actually like. That is one reason why, of course, unconverted people do not come lining up to accept the gospel. Their concept of God is that, if they were to believe Him and accept His heaven, it would make their lives miserable boredom.

And then of course there are further problems. By inducing mankind to sin, Satan has filled their minds with guilt, and they fear God's justice and try to convince themselves that He does not exist; for if He does exist, He must, they fear, be against them. And that makes them feel that God must be a horrible ogre.

The believer has discovered that that is not true. God's justice must be against the sinner's sin, but God loves the sinner; and Christ died for sinners while they were still sinners. The cross of Christ declares that God's love has found a way to pardon and accept every one who sincerely repents and is prepared to be reconciled to God through His Son, Jesus Christ. So far as his acceptance with God is concerned then, the believer has perfect peace with God both now and forever.

But the problem of suffering can, and often does, still trouble believers. "Why did God have to allow this?" we ask. "Why doesn't God answer my prayers and put an end to my suffering or difficulty, whatever it may be? Surely I have not deserved all this suffering? It's unfair. Why should I, who have worked so much for the Lord, and have been prepared to sacrifice for Him, have to undergo all this pain, whereas others who are not so devoted, and indeed may not even be converted, seem to go scot-free and enjoy life to the full?"

Our questioning is understandable; what is more, God has given us in the Bible the example of men like Job to show us that He understands our questioning. Nonetheless He assures us that, whatever pain and suffering He allows us to suffer, in the end we shall find that He is "full of compassion and mercy" (Jas. 5:11), and that if we dare trust Him and commit our suffering to Him, He will use that suffering to develop our character so that we become partakers of His holiness (Heb. 12:5-13). "Our light affliction which is for a moment [will] work for us an exceeding and abundant weight of glory" (2 Cor. 4:16-18).

On the other hand, the very fact that bitterness and doubt creep into our questioning shows that we have not yet come as near to the Father's heart as we could. And if, of course, the impossible were to happen, and we arrived in heaven still questioning the Father's love, uncertain about His faithfulness towards us, the very joys and splendors of heaven would turn sour; for the greater the joys, the greater our apprehension would be that one day those joys might be removed from us.

How, then, shall we be brought to the Father, to know the truth about Him, so that we are prepared to trust Him through thick and thin, assured that whatever happens His love is genuine and true? It will not be by merely reading verses in the Bible that say He loves us, though that will help enormously. It will have to be deeper than that. We shall need something to get inside and under all our neuroses and hang-ups, beneath our inferiority complexes and the basic sin of our fallen human state which is distrust of God. Says our Lord, "I am the Way to the Father, because I am the Truth about the Father; and I am not going to speak to you words only, I am going to send you another Advocate, another Counselor, the Spirit of truth." Not just words, then, but a Person. A Person whom we may know, and a Person who will not only be with us forever, but will be in us (vv. 16-17). And here is where the Lord's provision is so perfectly calculated to meet our need.

106

THE MINISTRY OF THE SPIRIT OF TRUTH

The Holy Spirit abiding in us is able to get underneath all our misconceptions and pour out, as Paul puts it in Romans 5:5, the love of God in our hearts. That is, not our love for God, (thus helping us to love God as we should, though doubtless the Holy Spirit does that for us as well), but God's love for us, as the context of Romans 5 shows. The Holy Spirit takes God's love for us, and pours it out into our hearts, as one might pour a glass of water out on the floor until the water trickles everywhere, into every nook and cranny. As we read the Word of God, inspired by the Holy Spirit of God, and it tells us of God's love for us, the Holy Spirit dwelling within us authenticates that Word, makes it credible and real, and thus, little by little, begins to disperse our misconceptions of God, and to undo the tangled knots of our doubts and fears; and so we come ever nearer to the Father.

Now we can begin to see what "coming to the Father" means. It would not be enough, even if it were possible, to come to the Father in some physical sense. After all, one can come to another human being and sit so closely that our bodies touch, and yet in heart we could be light years distant from one another. It is only when heart meets heart and spirit meets spirit that we really come to a person. And so it is between us and God. And the glory of it is that coming to the Father in this sense does not require that we come to the Father physically, and therefore it does not have to wait for our being taken home to heaven at death or at the Second Coming of Christ. In spirit we can come to the Father now. As Paul later puts it in Ephesians 2:18, "For through Christ we both (Jew and Gentile) have access in one spirit unto the Father." So our personalities, little by little, are transformed. In this way we become gradually more holy, more trustful, more devoted to the Lord, until, like Paul we can honestly say that, while sometimes we feel as if we were sheep daily delivered over to slaughter, yet we are fully persuaded that neither death, nor life, nor angels, nor principalities, nor things present, nor things to come, nor powers, nor height, nor depth, nor any other creature, shall be able to separate us from the love of God, which is in Christ Jesus our Lord (Rom. 8:38-39).

14

Christ—The Life Which We Share with the Father

"If ye love Me, ye will keep My commandments. And I will pray the Father, and He shall give you another Comforter, that He may be with you forever, even the Spirit of truth: whom the world cannot receive; for it beholdeth Him not, neither knoweth Him: ye know Him; for He abideth with you, and shall be in you. I will not leave you desolate: I come unto you. Yet a little while, and the world beholdeth Me no more; but ye behold Me: because I live, ye shall live also. In that day ye shall know that I am in my Father, and ye in Me, and I in you. He that hath My commandments, and keepeth them, he it is that loveth Me: and he that loveth Me shall be loved of My Father, and I will love Him, and will manifest Myself unto Him. Judas (not Iscariot) saith unto Him, Lord, what is come to pass that Thou wilt manifest Thyself unto us, and not unto the world? Jesus answered and said unto Him, If a man love Me, he will keep My word: and My Father will love him, and We will come unto him, and make Our abode with him. He that loveth Me not keepeth not My words: and the word which ye hear is not Mine, but the Father's who sent Me"

(Jn. 14:15-24).

The hour was getting late. Already in Christ's school of holiness the disciples had listened to amazing things which would take them years fully to digest and understand. Yet now the Lord Jesus began to teach them about yet another provision He was going to make for the maintenance and development of their holiness. He would not leave them as orphans. Not only would He one day come for them at His Second Coming and take them to the Father's house, but in the meanwhile He would from time to time come to them and manifest Himself to them. He would do it, however, in such a way that the world would not see Him.

But at this point Judas (not Judas Iscariot, who had gone out) found himself getting out of his depth. How, he asked himself, could it be that the Lord would manifest Himself to them without the world seeing it? Not being able to figure it out, he interrupted and put a question to Christ. "Lord," he asked, "What has happened that You will manifest Yourself to us, and not to the world?"

The first answer to his question is to be found in the Lord's words, "Because I live, you too will live." The Lord had already taught them many wonderful doctrines and, after His resurrection and ascension He would, by His Spirit, teach them more doctrines. But our Lord Himself is not a set of doctrines. He is a Person, a real, living Person; and the relationship between Him and us is the relationship of a shared life. Already, as the Creator who upholds all things by the word of His power, He maintains us in physical life. But physical life is not all there is to life, nor is it the most important element in life. Intellectual, aesthetic, and emotional life are also part of real life; and the highest level of life is the spiritual.

What Christ was telling His disciples was this: though He was leaving them physically, He would not leave them like orphans bereft of the parents who gave them life. He would still maintain them at the spiritual level continuing to share His life with them; and from time to time He would manifest Himself to them.

But it was just at this point that Judas' difficulty arose: how could the Lord manifest Himself to them and not to the world?

HUMBLE ANALOGIES

Having had more time than Judas to ponder the matter, we can, of course, think of analogies that would help us to understand how it could be done.

A man might show you a confidential letter he had received from a friend. You would understand the words; but not knowing any of the intimate secrets nor sharing any of the common interests possessed by the man and his friend, you would not be able to enter fully into the deeper significance of the letter.

Or take another analogy. Your pet dog can understand quite a bit about you. When he sees you eating some beef, he understands perfectly what is going on and the delightful sensations you are enjoying. For, though a dog, he has a stomach like human beings have, and he knows what hunger is, and the delights of satisfying that hunger with food. But show your dog a beautiful oil painting, and the dog will be completely bemused. He will not be able to make any sense of the thing whatsoever. He may try to smell the painting, or lick it, or even chew it, if you let him, for they are the only means he has of getting to know things. He does not possess a human spirit, such as you have; and therefore he will never understand your picture. That part of your life which you enjoy by means of your human spirit lies forever beyond the dog's limited experience of life. So then the artist by his painting reveals his thoughts and sense of beauty to you; but the dog, though he can see the painting, does not receive the artist's revelation.

Thus in giving us His Holy Spirit, Christ has opened our eyes to see a world of meaning, significance, and delight to which the unregenerate man and woman are completely dead. They do not possess the kind of life that is necessary for the enjoyment of these things. That is why you can read words out of Scripture and, for you, they are living and vibrant, and convey the very heart-throb of God; whereas an unregenerate person can read those same words and find them lifeless and dull. The reason is that, through His Word and through the life that He shares with you, the Lord is manifesting Himself to you. There is this practical fellowship of life between you and Him. You love the Lord and you keep His commandments. You feel the joy of pleasing Him, and He feels the joy of being pleased in you. And because you love Him, the Father will love you and the Lord will love you, and that mutual love will widen and deepen the channel of communication between you and Him (14:21); until both the Father and the Son will come and make Their dwelling place in your heart (14:23).

SPECIAL EXAMPLES

This, then, is the wonderful ministry that our Lord from time to time performs for us by His Spirit: He manifests Himself to us. Indeed, this ministry is so important that, after His resurrection and before He finally ascended, He gave His disciples some vivid and visible examples of this ministry. John tells us, for instance in chapter 21:1, "After these things, Jesus manifested Himself again to the disciples at the Sea of Tiberias." John says "again" because before this occasion the Lord has already manifested Himself at other times and in different ways to His people. On these occasions He appeared to His people visibly, so they could see Him with their eyes, and handle Him with their hands. We cannot expect Christ to appear to us thus visibly; but what He did for His people physically on those occasions He will still do for us at the spiritual level from time to time.

On the road to Emmaus, for instance, someone who appeared to be a stranger drew alongside two disciples as in their dejection they were walking back to Emmaus. Presently the Stranger began to expound the Old Testament to them, and as they walked on together, the Old Testament began to glow with life and glory until their hearts burned with awe and wonder within them. It was the Risen Lord who had come to them, and was now manifesting Himself to them through His Word (Lk. 24). Arriving at their home, they invited Him in to share their evening meal; and at the table they recognized Him as the Lord Jesus.

On another occasion He manifested Himself to Mary. She was standing, broken-hearted, at the Lord's empty tomb, when a man she thought was the gardener began to speak to her. It was, of course, the Lord. But this time He did not give her a biblical address or an exposition of the Old Testament prophets, as He had given to the two on the way to Emmaus, but He announced to her the new relationship that He had formed: "I ascend to My Father and your Father, to My God and your God." So real, so vibrant with the energies of eternal life did that relationship become to Mary from that moment onwards, that she abandoned the tomb for ever. She had discovered the reality of the Living Lord. She had discovered the truth of our Lord's statement, "Because I live, you too shall live"; and as a result she and all the other Christian women abandoned all idea of turning the tomb of Christ into a shrine, since people do not make a shrine to somebody who is living (Jn. 20).

On the occasion recorded by John in his twenty-first chapter, Simon and some other disciples had been out all night fishing and had caught nothing when, as dawn broke, they saw a Stranger standing on the shore. The Stranger called across the water and asked if they had caught anything. When they shouted back, "Nothing at all," He told them to let their nets down on the right side of the boat; when they did so, they took an enormous catch. Eventually, John realized who the Stranger was. "Peter," he said, "It is the Lord." And it was indeed. The Lord had come to them, not through reading the Bible, or through the tears of their sorrow as with Mary at the tomb, but in the course of their work; and through His guidance and the success that had attended that guidance, He manifested Himself to them.

He does the same for us still. We don't see Him, nor does it happen every day of the week, or every time we read the Scriptures or on every occasion that we do some work for Him; but from time to time in the midst of life's studies, griefs, and duties, true to His promise, He comes to us and manifests Himself in a way that is overwhelmingly real to our hearts. We sense the glow of His presence, the vibrancy of His life. We hear with the heart's inner ear the rustling of the Shepherd's robes beside us, and we say with deep conviction, "It is the Lord!"

AN ABIDING PLACE FOR THE
FATHER AND THE SON IN OUR HEARTS

Because He is the Life, and shares that divine life with us, He is for us the way to the Father. But He also shows us how, and on what conditions, the Father and the Son are prepared to come and make Their abiding place in our hearts. It stands to reason, of course, that anyone who professes to have the hope of being taken to the Father's house at the Second Coming of Christ will be keen to make the Father and the Son a dwelling place in his heart here and now.

What, then, are the conditions? "If anyone loves Me," says Christ, "he will keep My word, and My Father will love him, and We will come unto him, and make Our dwelling place with him. The person who does not love Me does not keep My

113

words: and the word which you hear is not Mine, but the Father's who sent Me." If we were expecting to welcome a merely human guest into our literal homes, mere courtesy would lead us to consult our guest's wishes, and to carry them out as best we can.

So then, if we are going to make the Father and the Son a dwelling place in our hearts, the conditions are that we first love Them, and loving Them, study Their Word to discover Their likes and dislikes; and then show our love by gladly and humbly seeking to please Them by doing what They like, and abstaining from what They dislike. So shall we experience ever more deeply Their love and fellowship. Of course, there is a side to God's love that is utterly unconditional. He loved us even while we were still sinners and still His enemies, and He will go on loving His people with that kind of unconditional love. But here we are thinking of our mutual enjoyment of one another's love, in intimate fellowship with the Father and His Son; and devoted attention and obedience to Their commandments are the only way towards that practical enjoyment of Their love.

We do well, therefore, to join the Apostle Paul in his prayer for us and all the people of God:

"For this cause I bow my knees unto the Father, from whom every family in heaven and on earth is named, that He would grant you, according to the riches of His glory, that ye may be strengthened with power through His Spirit in the inward man; that Christ may dwell in your hearts through faith; to the end that ye, being rooted and grounded in love, may be strong to apprehend with all the saints what is the breadth and length and height and depth, and to know the love of Christ which passeth knowledge, that ye may be filled unto all the fullness of God. Now unto Him that is able to do exceeding abundantly above all that we ask or think, according to the power that worketh in us, unto Him be the glory in the church and in Christ Jesus unto all generations for ever and ever. Amen" (Eph. 3:14-21).

There is no surer highway than this to the development of practical holiness.

15
Christ's Farewell Bequest

"These things have I spoken unto you, while yet abiding with you. But the Comforter, even the Holy Spirit, whom the Father will send in My name, He shall teach you all things, and bring to your remembrance all that I said unto you. Peace I leave with you; My peace I give unto you: not as the world giveth, give I unto you. Let not your heart be troubled, neither let it be fearful. Ye heard how I said to you, I go away, and I come unto you. If he loved Me, ye would have rejoiced, because I go unto the Father: for the Father is greater than I. And now I have told you before it come to pass, that, when it is come to pass, ye may believe. I will no more speak much with you, for the prince of the world cometh: and he hath nothing in Me; but that the world may know that I love the Father, and as the Father gave Me commandment, even so I do. Arise, let us go hence" (Jn. 14:25-31).

The first part of Christ's course of teaching on holiness was now almost over; and before His pupils left the Upper Room our Lord wisely and compassionately set Himself to encourage their faith and confidence.

Learning can be a difficult and discouraging task; and it would be no surprise if the disciples were beginning to feel they would never be able to remember the massive detail of the lessons they had been given, let alone understand and put into practice the difficult new concepts to which they had been introduced. It is a feeling that comes over us all from time to time; and it would be easy for us to get the impression that the learning necessary for developing holiness is a burdensome drudgery beyond the powers of ordinary people. It is not so, of course. Hard work it may be sometimes, demanding strength of purpose and perseverance. But our Lord stands ready to impart to us what He proceeded to plant in the hearts of His apostles: confidence that they would be able to master their lessons, underlying peace of heart amid life's battles, an unfailing source of joy, and the assurance of victory in putting their lessons into practice in a hostile world.

CONFIDENCE IN LEARNING

First came the assurance that they would not be left to struggle on their own to remember and understand what they had been taught. They would be sent a divine Counselor; and their success in learning would depend on the Counselor's ability to teach rather than on their ability to learn: "These things," said Christ, "I have spoken to you while still remaining with you. But the Counselor, the Holy Spirit, whom the Father will send in My name, will teach you all things and bring to your remembrance all that I have said to you."

This gracious promise applied, of course, in the first instance, to the apostles. It is the promise that underlies the validity of our New Testament. During His lifetime on earth, our Lord had taught His apostles multitudinous things. How, then, may we know for sure that, when we read our Gospels according to Matthew, Mark, Luke, and John, we have a valid and accurate record of what our Lord both did and taught? Even with the best will and brain in the world, how could they manage to remember all that Christ had taught them? The answer is that our Lord did not leave it to their unaided powers to perform this great task, and to provide the record that is fundamental to our Christian faith. He sent the Holy Spirit who, in His divine and superhuman way, would bring to the apostles' memories the things that they had heard Christ teach; and that is why we may be sure that when we read our New Testaments we have what Christ intended for us.

Moreover, He would help them to understand what they remembered. It is evident that what we have in the New

Testament is not just a plain, straight-forward record of what Christ said and did: it is a record-plus-interpretation. Now in our modern age, many people have found fault with the New Testament on these grounds. They say that if the Gospels are not simply a plain record of the life and teaching of Christ, but are a record-plus-interpretation, then we cannot be sure that the Gospels give us exactly what Christ said, or exactly what He meant. All we have, they say, is the early church's interpretation of what Christ said and meant.

But the argument is false; for what we have here in our Lord's promise (14:26) is the announcement that the Holy Spirit's authority lies behind both the records, and the interpretations, that we find in the Gospels. Moreover, the promise also contains the assurance that the Holy Spirit would teach the apostles all those things which our Lord was unable to teach His apostles while He was with them (16:12-13). Before His resurrection and ascension and the coming of the Holy Spirit, there were many things that they could not have even begun to understand. On those things, therefore, our Lord stayed silent at the time, intending to communicate them to His apostles after His resurrection and ascension—by the Holy Spirit. And these things, accordingly, we have now in the inspired epistles of the New Testament (see Acts 1:1-5; Eph. 3:2-21), delivered to us once and for all (Jude 3).

In this primary sense, then, the promise applied not to the hundreds of disciples that our Lord had made during His earthly ministry, nor to the post-apostolic Christian Church, none of whose writings are inspired in the way the New Testament epistles are, but to the unique foundation-members of the Church, the Lord's specially chosen apostles and prophets (Eph. 5:3).

That said, we may of course take the promise to ourselves in a secondary sense. The Holy Spirit has been sent specifically to help us to grasp Christ's teaching. We too find it difficult to understand what it means to have Christ dwelling in us, and the reality of it sometimes gets obscured in the hustle and bustle of life. But He remains with us to remind us of what we have learned, that holiness is not simply a question of our trying to struggle through somehow in our own strength: the Lord is with us! And not only with us, but in us, waiting to work out through us His mind and His reaction to the circumstances we are passing through. And just as a swimming instructor will teach a beginner to relax and trust the water to keep him up (which the water is well able to do), so the Holy Spirit will teach and train us to rely on Him for all the grace, power, and perseverance we need, both in learning the theory of holiness and in putting the theory into practice.

PEACE AMID LIFE'S BATTLES AND STORMS

Next came the bequest of His peace: "Peace I leave with you; My peace I give unto you. Not as the world gives, give I unto you. Let not your heart be troubled, neither let it be fearful" (14:27). Wonderful as this bequest is, we must not suppose it means more than it was intended to mean. Sometimes we hear this verse quoted by one Christian to another as though it meant that it would be wrong for any Christian at any time to feel upset or grieved or distressed; as if every Christian ought always to experience complete composure. The result is that when believers find themselves overwhelmed with disappointment or grief, they feel that they must be very unworthy Christians; and instead of finding comfort in our Lord's promise, their failure (as it seems) to realize its truth adds to their distress.

It is very important, therefore, to remember that the Saviour who spoke these words had, half an hour earlier, been very troubled in spirit as He announced to the disciples that one of them was going to betray Him (13:21). So, in one breath He would honestly admit that He was troubled in spirit, and yet in the next breath He talked of His peace; and obviously He saw no contradiction in that. Soon He was to leave the Upper Room and in the Garden of Gethsemane be deeply distressed and troubled, confessing, "My soul is overwhelmed with sorrow to the point of death" (Mk. 14:33-34). Yet, of course, we are not to think that the peace He talked of had now been suddenly washed away by the flood of His sorrow in the garden.

No, in the first place, in leaving them His peace He was, in Oriental fashion, bidding them farewell and, at the same time, assuring them of His love and loyalty and undying concern for them. In this way, when He was gone they could be absolutely sure that He had not deserted them but would still be faithful to them. Their confidence in His love and loyalty would bring them a deep-seated peace in their hearts so that, however the surface of their emotions might be ruffled by the wind and storm, their underlying peace would remain stable and secure. In that sense, He pointed out that He was unlike the world. The world is notorious for its fickleness and disloyalty. It will promise you its peace today, and then tomorrow forget you, or even prove treacherous to you, like Judas did to Christ.

The world has, in fact, no basic security, for by definition the world is a system of thought and a way of life that has lost real trust in God. Though it is God who has supplied them with all life's beautiful gifts, God in their mind is a threat, a source not of security but of insecurity. They are like the child who has stolen from the fridge the ice cream that its mother had prepared for its supper. The mother had intended to give the child the ice cream at a suitable time and, on going out, had told the child not to touch it before she came back; but while she was gone the child yielded to temptation and stole the ice cream, with the effect that now, instead of looking forward to Mother's return as a source of enjoyment, it senses Mother's return as a threat and the possibility of punishment. So it is that the world views God. Ever since Satan tempted Eve to take the fruit against God's prohibition, fallen man feels God as a threat and, therefore, tries to find what security he can in himself and in the little world around him. He tries to barricade his life to keep God from breaking in. But his world is a very fragile system. It is surrounded with vast natural forces that he cannot control; the piecrust of his little world can easily be broken through by illness or misfortune; and death ever stands at the door, threatening to enter. And since man cannot trust God, he finds that ultimately he cannot trust his fellow-man. He lives hovering on the edge of an abyss of insecurity. The world has no peace and ultimately cannot provide it. Only in God the Creator is there salvation and security and, therefore, only in God is there peace.

A NEVER-FAILING SOURCE OF JOY

And now our Lord pointed them to a reason for unlimited joy. His going away, when they rightly understood it, would prove to be a source, not of sorrow, but of rejoicing. "You heard," says Christ, "how I said to you, 'I go away and I come to you.' If you loved Me, you would have rejoiced because I go to the Father, for the Father is greater than I" (14:28).

We must ask, of course, in what sense His going could possibly prove a source of joy, and in what sense He meant it when He said, "The Father is greater than I." The two things are linked. As to His essential nature, our Lord was equal with the Father; but during His life on earth, as Paul pointed out in Philippians 2, our Lord was not on equal terms with the Father. He had voluntarily subjected Himself to the limitations of a human body, which could only be in one place at any given time. The Father is not thus limited. Moreover, Christ, as we have already said, could not be in His disciples while He was confined to the body of flesh and blood that He then had. The Father had no such limitation. The glory of the new situation would lie in two things. One, our Lord was going to the Father with all that that would mean in terms of the glorification of His human body and of His release from the limitations of earthly life. But He was not only going to the Father: He would from time to time come to them and, in His coming, He would no longer be tied to one place at a time, or to one person at a time. Like the Father, He would be able to be present with all His people in all places and at all times—in all His people everywhere and every moment and in every circumstance.

We may feel sometimes that it would be better for us if we could have the Lord physically with us, as He was with the apostles during His life on earth; but that feeling is mistaken. It is no insult to the apostles to remember that, while the Lord was physically with them on earth, their behavior sometimes left very much to be desired. Peter's grossest failure, for instance, occurred not after the Lord had left the apostles and gone back to heaven, but while the Lord was still with them on earth. We are now in fact in an infinitely better situation than the apostles were then. For the Lord, having gone to the Father, and having come to us by His Spirit, is nearer us than ever He could have been to the apostles before Calvary; and He is constantly with us in a way that it was impossible for Him to be when He was physically present on earth. And this is, by definition, a source of joy that can never be taken from us.

But all this, too, must have been very difficult for the apostles to take in. So much so that we might wonder why the Lord bothered to tell them even this at this stage. But there was wise purpose in His so doing: "I have told you this before it comes to pass" (14:29), He said, "so that when it comes to pass, you may believe." When, on the Day of Pentecost, they experienced the wonder of the coming and indwelling of the Holy Spirit, they would remember what the Lord Jesus had told them in the Upper Room, and their faith in Him would be strengthened. They would find themselves saying again and again, "He was right. What He said was true. It has turned out exactly as He promised." And we, for our part, may be confident that all the beautiful things we have learned in these chapters of John's Gospel were not invented by the Church *after* Christ's death; they were actually taught by Christ while He was here on earth.

AN ASSURANCE OF VICTORY

And now the final minutes of the first half of the course were ticking away, and very soon our Lord would tell His disciples to arise, leave the Upper Room and follow Him into the streets of Jerusalem. Our Lord was under no illusion about the conflict that was about to confront Him, but, having bequeathed His peace to His disciples, He now wanted to assure them, even before the conflict began, that He was utterly confident of victory. At the very beginning of His lessons on holiness (13:1-4) we were told of His supreme confidence in His ability to begin, and to perfect, His people's holiness in spite of Satan's opposition. Now at the halfway stage in the lessons, He speaks of that confidence again. "The prince of this world comes," He said; and the raging conflict that would then ensue would leave Him little time for further conversation with the apostles. But listen to the grounds for His certainty of victory. "The prince of this world is coming and he has nothing in Me; but that the world may know that I love the Father, and as the Father gave Me commandment, even so I do. Arise, let us go hence" (14:30-31).

We notice at once that the secret of His victory was His undeviating and utterly unbreakable love of the Father. Now it is the fact that we ordinary men and women often talk, and sometimes quite easily, of our love for God, though often our behavior contradicts our protestation of love. With the Saviour it was different. His love for His Father was always constant, full, and true. Yet throughout the whole of the Gospels our Lord is on record only once as saying, "I love the Father," and that once was on

121

this occasion. Significantly so. For now had come the moment when He must demonstrate to the world and before heaven, earth, and hell that His love for the Father was complete and unswerving.

Eve, in the Garden of Eden, surrounded by all the delights that God in His creatorial ingenuity and love had given her, was deceived into thinking that God was against her. She chose the forbidden fruit instead of God and His Word. She loved herself and the world more than she loved the Father. Now our Lord was to be met by Satan, the prince of this world, who would use all his venomous power to strip Him of everything He possessed, down to His last shred of clothing; and would add to Him all that He never deserved, the pain and the agony of Calvary which He might have avoided if only He had let go His love for the Father. But the prince of this world had nothing in Christ—no sin, no weakness that would yield either to his blandishments or to his hostilities. Christ would demonstrate to the whole universe what He thought of the Father. Given the choice between the kingdoms of the world and all its glories along with disloyalty to the Father, on the one hand, and on the other, loyalty to the Father along with all the agony that this world could inflict, He chose the latter. His love for the Father was unbreakable and unbroken.

This is holiness, and we suddenly become aware that our Lord who has hitherto been using object lessons and illustrations to teach us what holiness is, is Himself no mere theorist nor simply a divinely able teacher. He is presenting Himself as the supreme exhibition of true holiness. We saw earlier as we contemplated our Lord handing the sop to Judas, that true holiness is not to be found simply in the keeping of rules and regulations. True holiness is the heart's devotion to God. Here now that holiness is displayed in all its supreme glory and awesome wonder before our very eyes. Our Lord did not teach one thing and do another. He was what He taught. He did what He exhorted His disciples to do. One day our love, which still is so imperfect, will be perfected. But meanwhile, our hope of ever being perfectly holy ourselves is to be found in Him who loved us as the Father loved Him, who loved us while, unlike Him, we were imperfect and unlovable. Nor will He let us go until His love has made us all that He destined us to be.

As school first assembled, and just before the Lord began His lessons on holiness, John sketched in for us the background of the circumstances, and of our Lord's attitude to His disciples and to His teaching. "Having loved His own which were in the world," says John, "He loved them to the end" (13:1). And now that we begin to see what that holy love implied for Him, we can begin to understand more fully the fullness of His loyal farewell: "My peace I leave with you; My peace I give unto you. Let not your heart be troubled, neither let it be fearful." For one day His victory will be completely ours.

SCHOOL BREAK

16
School Break

School is now half-way through. In response to the Master's command, "Arise, let us go hence," the disciples have got up and moved towards the door. Some time will elapse as, one by one, they leave the room, file down the stone steps out into the night, and regroup themselves around the Lord on their way to Gethsemane, ready to receive the lessons that will form the second half of the course. Let's take advantage of the break to review the material we have so far covered, and to survey the material that lies ahead.

The first half of the course, we remember, contained three main parts: 1. the enacted parable of the foot-washing; 2. the exposure of Judas' treachery; and 3. the announcement of Christ's going, its purpose and implications. We shall find that the second half of the course likewise contains three parts: 1. the Parable of the Vine and the Branches; 2. the exposure of the world's hatred; and 3. the announcement of Christ's going, its necessity and implications. The two halves of the course, therefore, have the same formal structure:

CHAPTERS 13-14	CHAPTERS 15-16
I. The Enacted Parable of the Foot-Washing 13:1-20	I. The Parable of the Vine and the Branches 15:1-17
II. Christ's Exposure of Judas' Treachery 13:21-32	II. Christ's Exposure of the World's Hatred 15:18-27
III. Christ's Going 13:33-14:31	III. Christ's Going 16:1-33

and not only the same structure, but detailed similarity of theme all the way through, with many vivid contrasts as well.

PARALLELS BETWEEN THE TWO SECTIONS

Chapters 13-14	Chapters 15-16
I. THE PARABLE OF THE FOOT-WASHING A. *The Washing Itself* 13:1-11 He who has been bathed all over, does not need to wash, except his feet, but is completely clean. And you are clean, but not all...for He knew the one who should betray Him, therefore He said, "Not all of you are clean."	I. THE PARABLE OF THE VINE AND THE BRANCHES A. *"I am the True Vine and My Father is the Vine-dresser...abide in Me"* 15:1-8 Every branch that bears fruit He cleanses, that it may bear more fruit. Already you are clean through the word which I have spoken to you. Abide in Me...If anyone does not abide in Me, he is cast forth as a branch, and is withered; and they gather them and cast them into the fire.
B. *The Significance of the Footwashing* 13:12-20 1. I have given you an example that you also should do as I have done to you. 2. I am not speaking of you all: I know whom I have chosen.	B. *The Exhortation to Love* 15:9-17 1. This is My commandment that you love one another even as I have loved. 2. You did not choose Me, but I chose you, and appointed you...
II. CHRIST'S EXPOSURE OF JUDAS' TREACHERY A. *The Exposure* 13:21-30 One of you shall betray Me...Who is it?...He it is for whom I shall dip the sop and give it him. So...He gives it to Judas...He then having received the sop immediately went out...	II. CHRIST'S EXPOSURE OF THE WORLD'S HATRED A. *The Exposure* 15:18-25 If I had not come and spoken to them, they would not have had sin; but now they have no excuse for their sin...If I had not done among them the works that none other did, they

would not have had sin, but now they have both seen and hated both Me and My Father...They hated Me without a cause.

B. *The Divine Response* 15:26-27
But when the Comforter comes, whom I will send to you from the Father, even the Spirit of truth who proceeds from the Father, He shall bear witness of Me...

III. CHRIST'S GOING

A. *Its Necessity and Purpose* 16:1-15
1. These things I have spoken unto you that you should not be made to stumble...the hour comes that *whoever kills you shall think* that he offers service to God. But these things have I spoken to you, that when their hour has come you remember them, how that I told you...

2. These things I said not to you from the beginning, because I was with you. But now I go unto Him who sent Me; *and none of you asks Me, Where are you going?* But because I have spoken these things to you, sorrow has filled your heart (16:4-6).

B. *The Divine Response* 13:31-32
Now has the Son of Man been glorified and God has been glorified in Him. And God shall glorify Him in Himself and shall straightway glorify Him.

III. CHRIST'S GOING

A. *Its Necessity and Purpose* 13:33-14:17
1. Yet a little while I am with you...Wither I go you cannot come. Peter says...Lord, why cannot I follow you even now? *I will lay down my life for you.* Jesus answers...the cock shall not crow, till you have denied Me three times (13:33, 36-38).

2. *Simon Peter says to Him, Lord, where are You going?* Jesus answered, Where I go, you cannot follow Me now, but you shall follow afterwards...Let not your hearts be troubled. In My Father's house are many abiding places...I go to prepare a place for you and if I go...I will come again and receive you to Myself that where I am there you may be also (13:36; 14:1-3).

PARALLELS BETWEEN THE TWO SECTIONS

Chapters 13-14

3. I will pray the Father and He shall give you another Comforter, that He may be with you forever, even the Spirit of truth, whom the world cannot receive, for it beholds Him not, neither knows Him; you know Him for He abides with you and shall be in you (14:16-17).

B. *The Problem of the "little while" 14:18-24*
1. Yet a little while and the world beholds Me no more; but you behold Me; because I live, you shall live also...He who loves Me shall be loved by My Father, and I will love Him, and will manifest Myself unto him (14:19-21).

2. Judas (not Iscariot) says to Him, Lord, what has happened that You will manifest Yourself to us and not to the world? (14:22).

3. Jesus...answered...If a man loves Me, he will keep My word: and My Father will love him, and We will come to him and make Our dwelling-place with him (14:23).

Chapters 15-16

3. If I go not away, the Comforter will not come to you; but if I go, I will send Him to you. And when He comes, He will convict the world in respect of sin, of righteousness, and of judgment...He shall glorify Me (16:7-15).

B. *The Problem of the "little while" 16:16-24*
1. A little while and you behold Me no more; and again a little while and you shall see Me (16:16).

2. Some of His disciples said...What is this...A little while and you behold Me not; and again a little while, and you shall see Me?...We know not what He said (16:17-18).

3. Jesus said...You shall weep and lament, but the world shall rejoice...You therefore now have sorrow; but I will see you again, and your heart shall rejoice and your joy no one takes from you (16:19-22).

1. These things have I spoken to you while yet abiding with you. But the Comforter...shall teach you all things and bring to your remembrance all that I said to you (14:25-26).

2. You have heard how I said...I go away, and I come to you. If you loved Me, you would have rejoiced, because I go unto the Father: for the Father is greater than I. And now I have told you before it happens, so that when it happens, you may believe (14:28-29).

3. Peace I leave with you; My peace I give to you: not as the world gives, give I unto you. Let not your heart be troubled, neither let it be fearful (14:27).

1. These things have I spoken to you in proverbs: the hour comes when I shall no more speak to you in proverbs, but shall tell you plainly of the Father (16:25).

2. I came out from the Father and have come into the world: again, I leave the world and go unto the Father. His disciples say, Now You speak plainly...Jesus answered, Do you now believe? (16:28-31).

3. These things I have spoken to you, that in Me you may have peace. In the world you shall have tribulation; but be of good courage; I have overcome the world (16:33).

THE POINT OF THESE PARALLELS

Our first reaction to these numerous similarities between chapters 13 and 14 on the one hand and chapters 15 and 16 on the other ought surely to be one of relief. Obviously many of the basic principles that we have been taught in the first two chapters will be repeated in the second two. And since we have already tried to grapple with them, we shall find it easier to understand them when we meet them again.

On the other hand, while chapters 15 and 16 are very similar to chapters 13 and 14, they do not simply repeat them. In the human body the left hand is very similar to the right hand, but it is not simply another right hand. It is designed to complement the right hand, and therefore it is thus both its equal and opposite; and in certain major respects it is very different from the right hand. To be properly balanced and effective the body has two eyes, two ears, two arms, two legs. Moreover the fact that we have two eyes and not just one bestows on us an important functional advantage: it allows us to judge depth and distance more effectively. And two ears help us to judge more accurately the direction from which a sound comes.

Now the basic principles of holiness are the same all the way through: hence the similarities between the two parts of the course. On the other hand, the second part of the course is not simply a repetition of the first: it is its complement. There are two sides to holiness, in many respects the same, but in other respects very different. And both are necessary if our holiness is to be satisfactory, well-balanced, and complete. Hence there are necessarily two parts to the course; and hence also, the two parts of the course had to be taught in different surroundings: one inside the Upper Room, and the other outside of it.

Thirdly, the very similarities and differences between the two parts of the course will provoke profitable questions.

Why, for instance, is the topic of the believer's cleansing raised again in connection with the Parable of the Vine and the Branches, when it has already been dealt with—fully and adequately, one would have thought—in the enacted Parable of the Foot-Washing? Are the two cleansings the same? Does the cleansing in chapter 15 add anything to what chapter 13 taught?

Or again, the reason given in chapter 14 why our Lord must

go away is relatively easy to understand: He must go in order to prepare a place for us in the Father's house. But the reason given in chapter 16 why He must go away is different: He must go, for if He does not, the Comforter will not come. But why is that so?

And how, to ask one more sample question, can our Lord say at chapter 16:5, "But now I go unto Him that sent Me; and none of you asks Me, Where are you going?" when at 13:36 Peter has explicitly asked, "Lord, where are you going?"

But enough of this. If our rapid preview of chapters 15-16 has shown us that, as we learn their lessons, we must constantly be comparing and contrasting them with what we have learned in chapters 13-14, we are ready to rejoin the Lord and His apostles as He begins to teach them the second half of His course on holiness.

THE COURSE: PART TWO

A. *Holiness to Delight the Heart of God and Man*

Preview

In the first part of the course, we learned that the inner secret of true holiness is heart-devotion to the Divine Persons.

In this second part of the course, we shall be taught that true holiness will require believers to witness publicly to and for God in a hostile world that hates both the Father and the Son.

This witness is to be two-fold. It is, first, the witness of gracious, Christ-like behavior and life-style which demonstrates to the world at large what God is like, so that "men may see your good works and glorify your Father who is in heaven."

In the second place, it is the witness of the spoken word in personal conversation, in public preaching, and of the written word, using all appropriate media, to proclaim to people of every age, kind, race, and nationality the glorious message of Christ.

This is a huge responsibility for believers to bear. But in these chapters Christ will explain the provision He has made for His disciples and the resources He constantly makes available to them so that they can realistically and successfully discharge this double responsibility.

That provision, in a word, is this: the prime responsibility, the initiative, and the necessary resources for this world-wide witness all lie with the Father, the Son, and the Holy Spirit. Christ is the Vine through whom God's character, energies, and grace are expressed to the world. The function of believers is to be simply branches in the Vine, channels of resources that come altogether from God; and to be that under the care of the Father and the guidance of the Holy Spirit.

17
A Metaphor with a History

"I AM THE TRUE VINE" (JN. 15:1)

We now rejoin Christ and His apostles for the second half of
His course on holiness. There are, as we have earlier remarked,
two sides to holiness. The one side was taught to the apostles in
the intimacy of the Upper Room amid the soft, cosy glow of its
oil lamps and the hallowed atmosphere of the Passover meal.
There they learned the true and indispensable basis of holiness:
the unrepeatable washing of regeneration, and thereafter the
constant rinsing of the feet. There, too, it was vividly demonstrated before their eyes what true holiness consists in: devotion
to the Divine Persons. And then, as they learned that the Father
was dwelling in the Saviour, and thus present with them at the
table in the Upper Room, and was prepared to come and dwell
in their hearts, too, it must have seemed as though the very
glory of heaven surrounded them, shut in as they were with the
Lord they loved, secluded for the moment from the dark and
hostile world outside. They could willingly have stayed there
forever; for was this sacred communion with the Lord not only
the heart, but the sum total, of all true holiness?

No! It was only half the story. There was another, very different, side to holiness; and to learn it their minds and their bodies
had to be transported to another, very different, atmosphere.
"Arise," said Christ, "let us go hence" (15:31). We cannot be
completely sure whether at that very moment they rose up, left
the Upper Room, clambered down the stone staircase and out

into the streets of the city; or whether, after the command to 'arise and go hence,' they lingered still in the Upper Room until the remaining lessons had been completed, and then left; though the overwhelming probability is that upon the command they left immediately. But this, at least, we can say for certain: the command to arise and go hence would have taken their attention out from the coziness of the Upper Room to the realities of the world outside where the chilly night air was laced with the murderous intentions of the priests, and somewhere in the shadow there lurked the traitor, driven by the satanic powers of hell. Now they must learn that true holiness involves not only devotion to the Divine Persons, but witness to and for the Father and the Son. And they must grasp the all-important fact that this witness is to be conducted not simply in the warm, safe, seclusion of the Upper Room, where all hearts in unison beat out their loyalty to the Savior, but in the world outside, whose very streets breathed hostility to the Son of God.

Here, then, at the outset of the second half of the course, stands this simple, but searching, lesson for us too: There are two sides to holiness, and both are indispensable. One without the other is weak and inadequate. Public witness for the Lord that is not founded on private, personal devotion to Him would lack its necessary foundation. Private and personal devotion to the Lord that did not go on to express itself in public witness to the Lord would be maimed and unbalanced. Still today, in the course of our private devotions and in the fellowship of the church, we shall hear from time to time the challenging call of our Lord, "Arise, let us go hence."

ISRAEL: A VINE THAT RAN WILD

Hear, then, how our Lord began this second part of His course on holiness: "I am," said He, "the True Vine" (15:1).

To understand this obvious metaphor we must first spend a while delving into Old Testament history; for the metaphor is one which God Himself had used centuries before to explain His intentions in choosing the nation of Israel to be His special representative on earth. Here is a typical Old Testament passage:

"Let me sing for my well-beloved a song of my beloved touching his vineyard. My well-beloved had a vineyard in a very fruitful hill: and he made a trench about it, and gathered out the stones thereon, and

planted it with the choicest vine, and built a tower in the midst of it, and also hewed out a winepress therein: and he looked that it should bring forth grapes, and it brought forth wild grapes. And now, O inhabitants of Jerusalem and men of Judah, judge, I pray you, betwixt me and my vineyard. What could have been done more to my vineyard, that I have not done in it? wherefore, when I looked that it should bring forth grapes, brought it forth wild grapes? And now go to; I will tell you what I will do to my vineyard: I will take away the hedge thereof, and it shall be eaten up; I will break down the fence thereof, and it shall be trodden down: and I will lay it waste; it shall not be pruned nor hoed; but there shall come up briers and thorns: I will also command the clouds that they rain no rain upon it. For the vineyard of the Lord of hosts is the house of Israel, and the men of Judah His pleasant plant: and He looked for judgment, but behold oppression; for righteousness, but behold a cry" (Isa. 5:1-7).

This poetry talks of God tending Israel as a farmer would tend a vine in the expectation of producing grapes. The historical reality to which this poetry referred was as follows. God had freed Israel from slavery in Egypt, giving them personal experience of His liberating power. He had maintained them through their desert journey, raining down a daily supply of angels' food in the form of manna for their enjoyment. Graciously He had invited them to build a tabernacle, beautiful with many colors, and glowing with golden furniture, so that His glory might descend upon them and dwell among them. He had given them His holy law, informing their minds and guiding their behavior, so that the beauty of their conduct and the richness of their experience might stand in illuminating contrast to the Gentiles' grimy immoralities and crassly absurd and obscene idolatries. Then He installed Israel as a vine in the land of Canaan, protected them there with the wall of His presence and power, nourishing them constantly with His continuing blessings. And in return for all this investment in Israel, God looked for a crop of good grapes; that is, in their day-to-day treatment of one another, He expected them to show to others the same justice, mercy, and lovingkindness as He had showed to them. He had liberated them from slavery: they in turn were to show mercy to their workers, giving them one day in seven to rest free from work, and in general treating them and all others with justice and compassion. In this way, people in their business and social and political dealing with Israel could discover what Israel's God was like, could taste and see that the Lord is gracious, and be refreshed and gladdened as a thirsty man who comes upon a vine, gathers and tastes its luscious grapes, and gives thanks to the God whose creative mind invented the vine and its clusters.

In addition, God raised up special prophets in Israel so that people could discover what God was like not only by watching how Israelites behaved, but by listening to God speaking and revealing Himself through the words of His inspired messengers, or by reading those words recorded in what we now call the Old Testament.

How well did the scheme work? In some part, it must be said, it achieved enduring success. Still today we may come to that ancient vine and to the bunches of grapes that grew upon its more notable branches and taste in them the loveliness of God. We can watch the behavior of a humble woman like Hannah (1 Sam. 1:1-2). Or we can read King David's poetry: "Oh the blessedness of the man whose sin is forgiven, whose iniquity is covered, to whom the Lord will not impute unrighteousness" (Ps. 32:1-2). That lovely bunch of grapes grew out of David's personal experience of God's gracious forgiveness of his own bitter and disgraceful sin. That forgiveness not only restored to David the joy of God's salvation, but through David has ministered endless relief and deep satisfaction to millions who have subsequently read his psalm, heard in it the very word of the living God, and have come personally to experience what God's mercy is like.

How many thousands have, likewise, enjoyed the bunch of grapes which God grew on the vine of Israel through the ministry of His servant, the prophet Isaiah. Guilt-ridden hearts have discovered the words, "All we like sheep have gone astray; we have turned every one to his own way; and the Lord has laid on Him the iniquity of us all" (Is. 53:5-6), and through those words they have been pointed to Him who is the True Vine and have been able to "buy wine and milk without money and without price, and have been satisfied" (Isa. 55:1-2).

Tired servants of the Lord have, in their weariness, come upon yet another bunch of grapes growing on Isaiah's branch: "They who wait upon the Lord shall renew their strength; they shall mount up with wings as eagles; they shall run, and not be

140

weary; they shall walk, and not faint" (Isa. 40:31). They have sensed that these words were written by no mere theorist. Isaiah was a man called to a long and strenuous ministry for God, who, as the years went by, saw his congregations dwindle and depart ever further into apostasy (Isa. 6:9-13). He could therefore have become exceedingly discouraged, and it would have been understandable if he had abandoned his ministry altogether. But he was a branch whose resources stemmed from the living, inexhaustible, and unwearying God and, in spite of all his discouragements, he grew this delightful bunch of grapes that has refreshed and re-invigorated thousands of God's servants throughout the subsequent centuries.

There were many such branches, great and small, inspired prophets and ordinary Israelites, in that ancient vine. Indeed there were still some in our Lord's day, like the notable John the Baptist, and the less famous but equally valuable, Mary and Martha, Anna and Simeon, who continued to bring forth fruit for the satisfaction of God and the blessing of mankind.

But the sad fact is that Israel as a whole proved a disappointment: and it is not a form of anti-semitism to say so. God Himself had to complain in Isaiah's day: "Why, when I looked that it should bring forth grapes, did it produce wild grapes?... The vineyard of the Lord of hosts is the house of Israel, and the men of Judah His pleasant plant. And He looked for justice, but behold oppression; for righteousness, but behold the cry of the oppressed" (Isa. 5:4, 7). Their religious ritual and temple sacrifices had become a hollow sham. Their commerce was riddled with lying and cheating, with heartless exploitation and ruthless oppression of the poor. Their family and social life was rotten with unfaithfulness, immorality, and infanticide. Such misrepresentation of God's character on Israel's part in Isaiah's day eventually provoked God's indignant reaction: "I will tell you what I will do to My vineyard: I will take away its hedge, and it shall be eaten up; and break down its wall, and it shall be trodden down: and I will lay it waste: it shall not be pruned, nor digged; but there shall come up briers and thorns: I will also command the clouds that they rain no rain upon it" (Isa. 5:5-6).

THE TRUE VINE

But in all Israel's—and the world's—history things were never so bad as when Jesus left the Upper Room with His disciples to go to Gethsemane and the cross. High heaven was about to witness the most outrageous act of oppression that Israel had ever committed, to hear the bitterest cry that Israel had ever forced from an innocent sufferer. The Owner of the vineyard of Israel had sent His only Son to collect the fruit due to Him, and the tenants of the vineyard were about to take that only Son, thrust Him out of the vineyard and murder Him (Lk. 20:9-18).

What would the Owner's response to that be? Abandon the whole project of growing grapes? No, far from it! Rather to set about growing even more grapes and still sweeter grapes, not just in Israel but throughout the whole world; but to do so—and here comes the secret—by using a different vine and a different method of cultivation and production.

"Yes," says somebody, "that's right. God would now set Israel aside as His vine and put the Christian church in Israel's place as the new and better vine."

No, certainly not! If Israel, in spite of their long line of inspired prophets and godly saints, eventually failed, what realistic hope would the Christian church have of doing any better? Indeed, that unholy amalgam of religion and politics which men call Christendom has often been guilty of worse moral corruption, cruelty, and oppression than Israel ever was. No, Christ did not say, "Israel has failed, but you, my disciples, must try to do better." To imagine He did would be to run the risk of missing the glory of the gospel of holiness which our Lord was now about to announce. God's answer to Israel's failure was not the Christian church, but Christ. The Vine that was Israel had certainly failed; but, said Christ, "*I am* the True Vine."

THE MAGNIFICENCE OF GOD'S PROVISION

Let us pause, then, to consider the magnificence of this great provision for our holiness. God gave Israel a law with clear directives as to what conduct and testimony He expected from them. There was nothing intrinsically wrong with the law: it was holy, righteous, and good. The reason for its failure as a scheme for growing grapes was, as Paul puts it (Rom. 8:8), that "it was weak through the flesh." Israel, fallen and failing human beings like the rest of us, had not the moral and spiritual strength necessary to carry out the law to God's standards and requirements.

And Christians, in and of themselves, are no better or stronger than Israelites. Had God simply carried on with the same method, the result would have been as unsatisfactory as before.

No, God had a new method in mind, in fact since before the foundation of the world. It involved an altogether new and different kind of vine: the Son of God Himself. Rooted—if we may use such a metaphor—in the Godhead since He is Himself God, yet simultaneously truly human, He was and is and forever will be supremely able to express the character of God the Father in both deed and word, to God's unfailing delight and man's never fading blessing. He is, in his own words, the True Vine. Not that Israel was a false vine. Christ is the True Vine in the sense that He is the ideal, the ultimate, the perfect Vine, of which Israel was at best an inadequate prototype. (Cf. the use of the adjective 'true' in Heb. 8:2 and 9:11).

And Christ, the True Vine, was altogether new in another respect as well. Redeemed men and women, regenerated by the Holy Spirit, could now be incorporated into Him, like branches in a vine, so that His life, grace, goodness, and power could circulate through them and produce the fruit of the Holy Spirit in them—love, joy, peace, longsuffering, kindness, goodness, faithfulness, meekness and self-control.

This was new, marvelously and exhilaratingly new. Toweringly great as were the famous saints of the Old Testament, nowhere in all the many records of their spiritual experiences does any one of them speak of being incorporated into the Messiah. Understandably not. But nothing less than this is God's provision for us who live this side of the incarnation, death, burial, resurrection and ascension of the Lord Jesus and the coming of the Holy Spirit at Pentecost.

And so at the outset of this second part of the course a now familiar pattern begins to repeat itself. In chapter 13 the first lesson on holiness was not an exhortation, 'Try to be holy,' but the announcement of God's provision for making us holy: the once-and-for-all bathing-all-over, the washing of regeneration, after which the believer needs only to rinse his feet. Similarly here. Faced with our duty to bear witness for God in the world, we are not simply exhorted: Try to live lives of good, righteous conduct and graceful character that will delight God and truly represent Him in the world. Rather, the first thing that is impressed on us is this, that God Himself has provided a magnificent method of making Himself known to the world, and that method is Christ, the True and never-failing Vine, into whom God incorporates all His people so that Christ can express His own life, character, and power through them, as a vine expresses its life and power through its branches. But in this process it is self-evident that the Vine plays the most important and essential part. Once in the Vine, the branches need only to abide in the Vine, and grape-production is assured, but not by their self-effort, but by Christ's life, grace, and power working through them.

Once more, then, the basic and the most important element in our life of holiness is not what we do for God but what He does in and through us by Christ.

18

The Vinedresser and the Unfruitful Branch

"I am the true Vine, and My Father is the Husbandman. Every branch in Me that beareth not fruit, He taketh it away: and every branch that beareth fruit, He cleanseth it, that it may bear more fruit. Already ye are clean because of the word which I have spoken to you. Abide in Me, and I in you. As the branch cannot bear fruit of itself, except it abide in the vine; so neither can ye, except ye abide in Me" (Jn. 15:1-4).

In the literal world of viticulture the secret of producing good grapes is to start with the best vine you can get hold of; and then the vine itself will produce branches which in turn will draw on the vigor and resources of the vine and so themselves grow clusters of grapes. But that is not all that is needed. You have to have in addition an expert and diligent vinedresser who will constantly keep his eye on the branches and see to it that they do their part in the process properly and efficiently. In particular, he will from time to time cleanse, or prune, the branches; otherwise they will misdirect the energy and nutrients they receive from the vine and turn them into masses of useless foliage instead of grapes.

The same is true of the provision God has made for His people to produce the lovely fruit of the Spirit. There is no doubt whatsoever about the flawless excellence and inexhaustible resources of Christ, the True Vine. Nor is there any doubt about His ability and willingness to supply believers with all the grace, perseverance, and power they need to be fruitful in every good work and word. All they have to do as branches is to draw on the resources of the Vine. That may sound simple enough. But there lies a problem. Leave believers to themselves, rest the whole scheme on their unaided ability to draw on Christ's resources, and the result would be disappointing indeed. Believers are no more able by themselves to produce the fine fruit of the Spirit, than branches in a vine will automatically produce fine clusters of grapes without the constant attention of a vinedresser.

But God has foreseen the problem; and it is with great relief that we now hear the Lord Jesus say not only "I am the True Vine" but also "and My Father is the Vinedresser." We are not to be left alone to draw on the resources of Christ the best we can. We have our responsibilities, of course, and they are vigorous and far-reaching. But the prime responsibility is God's. His was the initiative that decided to express Himself, His character, His grace, His salvation through us. He it is who has placed us in Christ, "who by God has been made to us wisdom from God, even righteousness, sanctification and redemption" (1 Cor. 1:30). And He it is who constantly attends to each branch to see that it remains healthy, exploits its potential for growth and for increasing production of fruit. Why God should ever have decided to express Himself through us in the first place is perhaps an unanswerable question. But once He decided to do so, He certainly was not going to leave it to our sole and unaided responsibility to make a success of His purpose.

Yes, we do have our responsibility. Yes, we can—and alas we often do—impede His grace, and consciously or unconsciously thwart and delay the fulfillment of His purpose. But He never would have conceived the purpose in the first place or have designed the mechanisms for its fulfillment, if He had not been able triumphantly to have it declared in advance: "He who began a good work in you will perfect it unto the day of Jesus Christ" (Phil. 1:6).

THE VINEDRESSER'S ACTIVITIES AND
THE BRANCHES' RESPONSIBILITY

Four great sayings follow the announcement, "I am the True

Vine and My Father is the Vinedresser." They are:

1. 15:2 *The unfruitful branches:* "Every branch in Me that does not bear fruit He takes away."
2. 15:2 *The fruitful branches:* "Every branch that bears fruit, He cleanses it, that it may bear more fruit."
3. 15:3 *The means of cleansing:* "Already you are clean through the word which I have spoken unto you."
4. 15:4 *The branches' responsibility:* "Abide in Me and I in you. As the branch cannot bear fruit of itself, unless it abides in the vine, neither can you, unless you abide in Me."

We notice the proportions: three out of the four sayings state what the Father and the Son do in their care for the branches; one out of the four reminds the branches of their responsibility.

THE UNFRUITFUL BRANCH

It is surely a very striking thing that the first concern of the Vinedresser to be mentioned in this passage is His determination to get rid of all unfruitful branches. But on second thoughts it is understandable. The whole purpose in having a vine is to have branches that bear fruit. A vine-branch has no reason or existence other than to bear fruit. God made the point to Ezekiel long ago that the wood of a vine-branch is useless for any other purpose: you can't make anything out of it; you cannot even make a peg of it to hang things on (Ezek. 15:1-5). God is determined that every branch in His vine shall fulfill its intended function, or else....

But just at this point we must pause, for the meaning of the Greek word which is used here to describe what the Vinedresser does to unfruitful branches is disputed. Its basic meaning is 'to lift up;' but it has several other connotations according to context. It can mean simply 'to lift up' as for instance at 11:41, "Jesus lifted up His eyes"; or 'to take' as at Matthew 20:14, "Take what is yours." In other contexts it can mean 'to take up and carry' as, for instance at Matthew 11:29, "Take My yoke upon you"; or in still other contexts 'to lift up, take away and remove completely,' as for example at Luke 6:29, "The one who takes away your cloak" and (in the passive) at Mark 11:23, "Be removed and hurled into the sea."

Given these different possibilities, some expositors have suggested that what the Vinedresser does to the unfruitful branch is not to remove it from the vine, but to raise it up and support it. They think that our Lord is referring to a method of grape-production which, in the literal world of viticulture, is still practiced in the hills south of Jerusalem to this present day. The vines there run along the ground but, in order to protect the fruit from being bespattered with mud, vinekeepers will lift up the main branch and place under it a number of stones, so that the branch, being elevated on these stones, will attract more sun and, avoiding the mud and the dirt, will have air circulating all round it, and thus produce more and better fruit. So our Lord is saying, they think, that, if the vinekeeper sees a member of the Body of Christ not bearing any fruit at all, He will lift up that branch, taking it out of whatever muddy and difficult conditions it has got itself into, and so support it until it begins once again to bring forth fruit.

But it is unlikely that our Lord is referring to this process. In the first place, while the Greek word can mean 'lift up and carry,' it cannot so easily be taken to mean 'lift up and then put some support underneath.' Secondly, this action is said to be taken with the branch that bears no fruit; no mention is made of its being applied to the branch that does bear fruit. In south Judea all the vine-branches in a vineyard are supported on a pile of stones, not simply those that do not produce fruit.

So we come back to the rendering, "Every branch in Me that bears no fruit He [God] removes." But what in practical terms is this process?

Could it mean excommunication from the church? In 1 Corinthians 5:2 and 13, Paul rebukes the Corinthian Christians because they had not been concerned to see to it that one of their number who was unrepentantly guilty of a glaring social sin should be "removed from among you" (he uses the same Greek word as in Jn. 15:2). But on closer inspection, it becomes clear that it is not God but the Corinthians themselves that have to remove the guilty man from themselves: "Put away the wicked man from among yourselves" (1 Cor. 5:13; a stronger form of the same Greek word). Our verse would not appear to be referring to excommunication from the church.

Could the process, then, be that to which the Apostle Paul refers in 1 Corinthians 11:29-30, where God is said to discipline a careless and unrepentant believer by physical illness or even death? Again the answer would seem to be, no. For such a careless unrepentant person, though removed from this life by physical death, is obviously still a believer, for it is said that this person will not be condemned with the world. And it is difficult to think that a believer, however careless he or she may have become, could be described as a branch that produces no fruit at all. And yet this is what our Lord says of the unfruitful branch. His phrase, "bears no fruit," seems to be absolute, for the next verse says that every branch that produces any fruit at all is cleansed by the Vinedresser so that it shall produce more fruit. By contrast, the branch that is removed is a branch that produces no fruit whatsoever. It represents a person in whom no fruit of the Spirit has ever been seen.

What kind of a person is that, then? The New Testament writer, James, leaves us in no doubt. If anyone who claims to be a believer has no works at all to show as evidence that he is a believer, then his faith is dead. It is not true faith. His claim to be a believer is invalid (Jas. 2:14-26).

Elsewhere our Lord says the same thing. In the explanation of His famous Parable of the Sower (Lk. 8:13-15), He indicates that the unfailing mark of true believers is that they bring forth fruit with perseverance. Those who "believe for a while but in time of testing fall away" do so because they have no root. They never did have, and therefore, of course, could never have produced fruit. They were never true believers.

And there is further evidence in our own context in John that this was the type of person that our Lord was referring to when He said, "Every branch in Me that does not produce fruit, the vinedresser takes away." Go back for a moment to the first paragraph in chapter 13. Our Lord there remarked: "The person who has been bathed all over needs only to rinse his feet; otherwise he is completely clean. And you are clean, but not all." John explains the reason for the excepting clause: "For He knew the one who was to betray Him: and that is why He said, 'You are not all clean'" (13:10-11). Now look again at the first paragraph here in chapter 15. Having said, "Every branch that bears fruit He (the Vinedresser) cleanses...," He then comments once more, "Already you are clean" (15:2-5). But this time He does not add the limiting clause, "...you are clean, *but not all*"; and that for the obvious reason: by this time Judas Iscariot had gone out. Our Lord, therefore, could honestly say of all the remaining eleven, "You are already clean." His statement may strike us as exceedingly generous: Peter, as Christ had already pointed out, was about to deny Him, and the other ten, as Christ was soon to point out (16:32), were, in a moment of panic, to forsake Him. But there was an absolute difference between them and Judas. Little as their faith was, it was genuine: Judas was not a believer at all—never had been (Jn. 6:70-71). The eleven, Peter included, had brought forth some fruit, meagre though it was at times. And the Great Vinedresser who will never despise so much as one grape (see Heb. 6:10), had seen and recognized their fruit, and had patiently pruned and cleansed them so that they were ready now soon to produce much more fruit. Judas by contrast had never produced any fruit, for he was not a believer, not regenerate, not a child of God; and he was in process not of being cleansed but of being removed.

But, someone may say: 'In the parable the branch that bears no fruit is explicitly said to be in the Vine: "every branch *in Me* that bears no fruit." How could an unbeliever ever be said to be in the Vine, or, in Christ?' And the answer is: In the same sense that in 8:30-44, certain Jews are said to have believed on Christ. But when they were challenged to produce evidence that they were genuine disciples of Christ, they failed the test completely. Indeed, the only evidence they produced showed in the end that they were not believers at all, but were in fact children of the devil. Now the evidence that these 'believers' were called upon to produce to show that they were genuine disciples of Christ was this: "Jesus said to those Jews who had believed Him, 'If you remain in, continue in, abide in (the Greek word is the same as the one used throughout ch. 15 for abiding in the Vine) My word, then you are truly my disciples'" (Jn. 8:31). Scripture begins, then, by taking them at face value on the basis of their profession: they said they had believed, they are therefore referred to as believers. But then the test is applied to show whether their profession is genuine and they are found unwilling to abide in His word. So it was with Judas. Christ Himself had named him an apostle (Lk. 6:13). He had enjoyed an intimate and trusted place among the immediate companions of Christ. Any one would have said that he was 'a branch in Christ' as much as the others. But the test shows he was not.

And the lesson stands as a warning to us all. Salvation is by faith and not by works. But salvation gives the believer new spiritual life; and life will inevitably express itself. As we have said before, a baby does not get life by crying; but a baby that fails to cry at birth and never cries thereafter is probably still-born. A person who is genuinely in Christ will bear some fruit of the Spirit, however little. What the Vinedresser will not tolerate is a branch that bears no fruit at all. He has no room for merely nominal Christians.

19

The Vinedresser and the Fruitful Branch

"And every branch that bears fruit, He cleanses it, that it may bear more fruit. Already ye are clean because of the word which I have spoken unto you. Abide in Me, and I in you. As the branch cannot bear fruit of itself, except it abide in the vine; so neither can ye, except ye abide in Me" (Jn. 15:2-4).

The heavenly Vinedresser is easily pleased: He will generously recognize every piece of genuinely spiritual fruit, however small, that a believer produces. But He is not easily satisfied. If a branch in the Vine bears fruit, the Vinedresser will always proceed, says Christ, to cleanse it* in order to help the branch produce ever more fruit.

THE NATURE OF THE CLEANSING

But what in actual practice is this process which is here referred to as 'cleansing the vine-branch,' and by what means is it done?

The common answer has been that it refers to God's discipline of His people. When a vinedresser cleanses, or prunes, a vine he will take a sharp knife or a pair of secateurs and drastically cut

---

*That is, to 'prune' it; but for the sake of the deliberate parallel with the cleansing in 13:1-11, it is better to translate the Greek word literally.

away all excessive growth, so severely indeed that to an untrained eye he might appear to have devastated, or even destroyed, the vine. But in actual fact, far from destroying the vine, the drastic pruning re-directs the vine's energies so that, next season, instead of producing showy but fruitless foliage and wood, they turn themselves into larger, sweeter, and more numerous bunches of grapes. So our Heavenly Father allows pain, sorrow, persecution, suffering, and trials of every kind to come upon us so as to educate, train, if need be discipline and chastise us, so that we may be partakers of His holiness. God Himself admits that while the process is going on, it is far from joyous: it can be devastatingly grievous. But afterward, He points out, it yields peaceable fruit to those who are exercised by it, even the fruit of righteousness (Heb. 12:4-13).

CLEANSING BY THE WORD

Yet true as all this is, it is not only, perhaps not even primarily, by suffering and sorrow that a vine-branch is cleansed. "Already you are clean," says Christ, "by the word which I have spoken to you" (15:3). We look back again to chapter 13 and to our Lord's references to the once-for-all bathing-all-over. When we were studying it, we naturally thought about the washing of regeneration of which Paul speaks in Titus 3:5. But also we thought of Peter's description of regeneration and the means by which it is effected: "...having been begotten again not of corruptible seed, but of incorruptible, through the Word of God which lives for ever and ever...and this is the word of the gospel which was preached to you" (1 Pet. 1:23-25). And similarly our Lord's insistence in chapter 13 on the need for constant rinsing of the feet led us to think of His cleansing of the church by the washing of water through the Word (Eph. 5:25-26). Now here in chapter 15 the context is different: here we are thinking of the need by our behavior and spoken testimony rightly to represent God in the world. But the needed preparation is the same: we need constantly to be cleansed. And the means of that cleansing is the same: it is through the Word that Christ has spoken and still speaks to us.

There is no doubting that the eleven apostles truly believed that Jesus was the Christ right from the start. But at first—and for many months thereafter—they had very defective and distorted views as to what His purposes and methods as the Messiah were, indeed as to what exactly the office of Messiah entailed. John and James, for instance, would freely have called down fire from heaven on Samaritan villagers who were not prepared to give Christ a night's lodging in their homes (Lk. 9:51-55). The disciples were troubled when our Lord cancelled the food laws (Mt. 15:12). Peter, without thinking, took it for granted that our Lord was duty-bound, like everyone else, to pay a ransom for His soul in the form of the temple tax! (Mt. 17:24-27); and he often contradicted and corrected the Lord when it seemed to him that the Lord was mistaken. And none of the apostles could at first understand or bring themselves to agree with the Lord when He insisted that He must be rejected by the nation and crucified; they were in fact a long time coming to terms with it.

But come to terms with it they must if ever they were going rightly to represent God in the world; and hence our Lord's patient and constant instruction of them, His cleansing away of their false concepts and misunderstandings, their ignorance and worldly-mindedness. And it is a tribute to His gracious persistence that within a few yards of Gethsemane and Calvary He could say: "Now you are clean through the word which I have spoken to you."

Still today we need constantly to allow the Lord to cleanse us by His Word, to prune away our false ideas and to encourage the growth of a biblical mind, if we are going to behave in a way that pleases God and rightly represents Him to the world. How tragically Christendom misrepresented God in centuries gone by when it tortured and burned so-called heretics and raised crusades to go and slaughter Turks in order to recapture sacred sites and superstitious relics; and, what is truly lamentable, did it all in the name of Jesus, when the slightest knowledge of, and obedience to, the words of Jesus, would have outlawed all such conduct. Those sour grapes have left a nasty taste in the world's mouth ever since.

Today, perhaps, our danger lies at the other extreme. No amount of love, joy, peace, gentleness, and kindness can save the Church from seriously misrepresenting God and Christ in the world, if the Church under pressure from the world's thought-fashions neglects or abandons the Word of Christ, denies His virgin birth, and miracles, jettisons His deity and His exclusive claim to be the Saviour of the world, abandons the preaching of the cross and of Christ's atoning death, bodily resurrection, and second coming, and tries to make itself acceptable to the world by attempting to graft onto the True Vine whatever social, political, or religious philosophy happens to be currently fashionable in the world.

THE INDISPENSABLE CONDITION FOR FRUITFULNESS

"Abide in Me and I in you," says Christ. "As the branch cannot bear fruit of itself, unless it abides in the vine, so neither can you unless you abide in Me" (15:4). Certainly the Father is the vinedresser; but if we are going to benefit from His care and cleansing and so bear more fruit, we must stay put in Christ.

That might seem an easy thing to do. And from one point of view it is. After all, believers do not have to put themselves into Christ. God does that. And God in addition tends and prunes the vine-branches, and Christ it is who cleanses us through His Word.

But in actual experience Christians have often found it extraordinarily difficult to stay put in Christ. The temptation has been overwhelming to think that while Christ and His Word were sufficient for the apostles and early Christians in the first century, they could not possibly be sufficient for us in ours. Or to think that while Christ and His Word were sufficient to convert us individually and to bring us to God, they could not be sufficient for our further spiritual progress or as the center and substance of our witness to the world.

The temptation is in fact a very ancient one: witness the experience of the Christian church in Colosse in the first century. The word of truth of the gospel, says Paul (Col. 1:5-6), had come to them; and like it did wherever it went in the world, it bore fruit and grew in them as well, ever since they knew the grace of God in truth. But in spite of that, they were in grave spiritual danger. For there had also come to Colosse people who taught these new Christian converts that while Christ and His gospel were enough to begin their spiritual experience with, they would need other more advanced ideas and practices, if they were going to make substantial spiritual progress. And so they were advised to take up various man-made philosophizings, based not on God's revealed truth, but on mere human reasoning and conjecture as to what the spirit-world is like (2:8). They were also recommended to go in for meticulous observations of food laws, religious festivals, special seasons of the month, and Sabbath days (2:16). Others advocated various techniques for inducing visions and out-of-the-body experiences, holding out the promise that by these means it was possible to contact angels or even to have direct vision of God (2:18-19). And yet another popular recipe for advancing the spiritual life was asceticism, the attempt to subdue evil desires and promote godliness by inflicting severe and painful discipline and punishments on the body (2:10-23).

Bogus! says Paul, all of them, and positively dangerous, certain to lead to spiritual poverty if not disaster; and, saddest of all, utterly unnecessary; for "in Christ are all the treasures of wisdom and knowledge hidden...for in Him dwells all the fullness of the Godhead bodily, and in Him you are made full" (2:3, 9-10). There is no need to go outside of Christ. "As you have received Christ Jesus the Lord (i.e. at your conversion), walk *in Him*, rooted and built up *in Him*" (2:6). In other words, abide in Christ! Abide in the Vine! Stay put in Him! And not only so. The Lord's command is: "Abide in Me and I in you." It is the believer's responsibility to see to it that in this sense Christ abides in him or her. The command does not imply that Christ will at any time abandon a true believer. But what He looks for is not merely that we remain correct in our doctrines, but that we maintain a constant, intimate, practical fellowship with Him and He with us in our hearts. And to that end we would do well to follow Paul's advice to the Colossians: *"Let the word of Christ dwell in you richly in all wisdom; teaching and admonishing one another with psalms and hymns and spiritual songs, singing with grace in your hearts unto God"* (Col. 3:16).

20

The Branches' Relation to the Vine and the Vinedresser

"I am the Vine, ye are the branches: he that abideth in Me, and I in him, the same beareth much fruit: for apart from Me ye can do nothing. If a man abide not in Me, he is cast forth as a branch, and is withered; and they gather them, and cast them into the fire, and they are burned. If ye abide in Me, and My words abide in you, ask whatsoever ye will, and it shall be done unto you. Herein is My Father glorified, that ye bear much fruit; and so shall ye be My disciples" (Jn. 15:5-8).

Christ began this second part of His course on holiness by declaring, "I am the True Vine" (15:1). Now at 15:5, He repeats His declaration: "I am the Vine." But it is not mere repetition, as we shall soon perceive if we compare what followed the declaration on each occasion. At 15:1 He said, "I am the True Vine *and My Father is the vinedresser,*" thus laying emphasis on the relation of the Father to the branches, and His care for them. But here He says, "I am the Vine *and you are the branches,*" for now He is about to lay emphasis on the status of the branches in relation to the Vine. Believers are not the vine itself as Israel once was; and they do not have to try to be, thank God. Christ, the great I AM, is the Vine. Believers are, by God's grace, branches in the Vine, with all the wonderful potential which that implies; and again we thank God for that. But believers are only branches; they cannot afford to live, think, or act independently of the Vine itself.

And so once more the initial caption, "I am the Vine: you are the branches," is followed by four great sayings:

1. *An assurance that abiding in Christ will bring its reward:* "He who abides in Me and I in him, the same bears much fruit..." (15:5).

2. *A warning of the consequences of not abiding in Christ:* "If anyone does not abide in Me, he is cast forth as a branch and...burned" (15:6).

3. *An invitation to co-operate with the Vinedresser by asking for His attention:* "If you abide in Me and My words abide in you, ask whatever you will and it shall be done to you" (15:7).

4. *A reminder that the Father is glorified when the branches bear much fruit:* "Herein is My Father glorified that you bear much fruit; and so you will prove to be My disciples" (15:8).

The Branch that Abides and the Branch that Does Not

The assurance that, if we abide in Christ and He in us, we shall bear much fruit, is altogether unquestionable. Only consider who the Vine is, none less than the Almighty I AM Himself (ch. 8:24). But to the assurance Christ adds an explanation which is also a warning: He is not only utterly sufficient as the Vine, He is the only Vine there is. "Without Me (or apart from Me)," He says, "you can do nothing." Christ is not just one Saviour among many, one source of spiritual strength among a whole variety. The Godhead itself has only one Vine; by definition, then, apart from Him we can do nothing. Nor shall we ever reach a position when we have received from Him so much knowledge, grace, goodness, and power that for a while we can go on operating effectively by ourselves apart from Him, though sometimes we behave as if we could.

But next comes an even more solemn warning: "If anyone does not abide in Me, he is cast forth as a branch, and is withered; and they gather them and throw them into the fire and they are burned."

The first thing to notice about this sad state of affairs is that the person concerned takes the first step: he or she does not abide in Christ. And in saying this, we observe, Christ has for the moment dropped the metaphor, and is speaking literally and directly: if anyone, any person, does not abide *in Me*. He is not saying exactly the same as He said in verse 2. There it was a question of a branch in Christ that never produced any fruit and the Vinedresser stepped in and removed it. But here the person concerned takes the initiative himself; he does not abide in Christ; he removes himself. What kind of a person would do that?

For a first answer we recall once more chapter 13 and what it tells us of Judas: "He then having received the sop went out immediately; and it was night" (13:30). Now Judas' going out was, of course, literal and physical: he opened the door of the Upper Room and went out. And because it was night-time, the darkness he went out into was literal and physical darkness. But it was far more than that. In going out he was leaving Christ and his fellow apostles; and leaving them not just physically and temporarily. He was leaving them physically because in heart he had long since left them spiritually. The initiative had been his: he had decided to betray Christ. And even so, we remember, Christ did not throw Him out, but knowing all about him, still offered him the sop of His friendship. Had Judas repented, confessed and sought forgiveness, he could have remained. But he would not and did not repent. Instead he went out; and the darkness into which he went was not simply the darkness of the night hours: it was a spiritual darkness that would never know a dawn.

So then what happened to Judas, the man that had once been an apostle with the privilege of representing Christ to the world, but now had left Him and gone out? Why, even the priests, his pay-masters, had in the end no time for him (Mt. 27:3-10). He died a suicide's death, and the very estate which he had bought with his traitor's money became his grave-yard (Acts 1:15-26).

With this we turn back to our Lord's description of what will happen to the person who does not abide in Him (15:6). Having described his defection in straight-forward literal language—if anyone does not abide in Me—He returns to the metaphor of a vine and its branches to describe the consequences. What then, we may ask, happens to a literal vine-branch that does not stay in the vine, but removes itself? Why, the farmer will pick it up, and throw it outside the vineyard, where, because it is no longer connected with the vine, it will wither. And when it is all dried up, people will gather it along with other similarly withered branches, throw them all on the bonfire and burn them; for vine-branches that have severed themselves from the vine are value-less and good for nothing. And our Lord takes these literal processes and uses them metaphorically to describe the utter spiritual ruin that results from not abiding in Him.

An Instance Cited by John

Now the apostle John, who heard our Lord give this solemn warning, many years later used similar language to describe certain false teachers of his day (1 Jn. 2:18-22). First of all he called them antichrists: "Little children," he writes, "it is the last hour; and as you have heard that antichrist is coming (one day), even now there have arisen many antichrists." He then describes the serious nature of their false teaching: "Who is the liar but he who denies that Jesus is the Christ? This is the antichrist, even he who denies the Father and the Son." One could not possibly imagine any more fundamental heresy than this. And yet the startling thing is that these people, whoever they were, had once been members of a Christian church, and probably teachers as well. For John says of them: "They went out from us," which, of course, they could not have done if they had not first been members of a Christian church.

Does that mean, then, that they were once genuine believers, born of God, true children of the Father, and that subsequently they somehow ceased to be genuine believers and lose their sal-vation? No; for John himself tells us with all his apostolic authority: "They went out from us, but they were not of us; for if they had been of us, they would have continued ('remained,' or, 'abided'*) with us; but they went out, that they might be exposed how that they all are not of us." So they were not believers, and never had been, though of course, for perhaps a long while they had professed to be believers, and doubtless their fellow members in the church regarded them as believers

---

* The Greek word John uses is the same word our Lord uses for abid-ing in the vine and in Him.

and respected them as teachers. They appeared to be in Christ. And even after they left both the doctrine and the company of the apostles, they still maybe claimed to be Christians. But John's verdict is clear: they never were of us, they never were true believers. Had they been genuine believers, they would have remained with us. As it was, their going out exposed what had been true of them right from the start: "they were not of us."

From all this we conclude on the one hand, therefore, that true believers will never remove themselves from Christ, or separate themselves from the Vine. But on the other hand, the only visible evidence that people are true believers is that they abide in Christ. Since, however, false teachers can be very persuasive, it is all too possible for true believers to get temporarily caught up with false teaching and give the appearance of not being true believers. Which means that all of us must listen to John as he draws the lesson for his readers: "As for you, let that abide in you which you heard from the beginning (i.e. from the apostles). If that which you heard from the beginning abide in you, you also shall abide in the Son, and in the Father...And now little children, abide in Him; that when He is manifested, we may have boldness and not be ashamed before Him at His coming" (1 Jn. 2:24, 28).

AN INVITATION TO THE BRANCHES
TO CO-OPERATE IN THEIR CLEANSING

The third great saying in this series is this: "If you abide in Me and My words abide in you, ask whatever you will and it shall be done unto you" (15:7); and the best way of understanding this glorious invitation is to take it, in the first place at least, in close connection with the fourth great saying, which follows on its heels: "In this is My Father glorified that you bear much fruit and so prove to be My disciples" (15:8).

The fourth saying is easily understood. In the first place the mark of true disciples of Christ, is, as we have earlier seen from chapter 8:31, that they abide in Christ's Word and, because they abide in His Word, bear much fruit. Secondly, it is easy to see why the Father is glorified when Christ's disciples bear much fruit. After all, we were told at the very beginning that the Father is the vinedresser, who constantly tends and prunes the branches. As it is with a literal vine, so it is with the True Vine:

163

when the branches bear an abundant crop of fruit, it is not the branches that deserve the credit, but the vinedresser. And incidentally as far as it lies in our power, we should see to it that it is the Father and not ourselves who gets the credit for any spiritual fruit we bear: we are to let our light shine before men, so that they may see our good works and *glorify our Father* who is in heaven (Mt. 5:16).

But if the fourth saying makes obvious and excellent sense when taken strictly in its context, the safest way to interpret the third saying is to begin, at least, by taking it likewise strictly in its context.

The invitation to ask whatever we will and the promise that it shall be done to us is clearly not an open-ended invitation to ask for just any and everything we might happen to desire—a new car, a larger house, and so forth. The invitation is limited by two conditions: first, "If you abide in Me," that is remain in close and intimate fellowship and communion with the Lord. Secondly, "If My words abide in you." Both conditions must be met. If in our private devotions we enjoy intimate communion with the Lord, we shall become increasingly aware of His love for us; and His love will certainly give us confidence to bring Him our requests. But what shall we ask for? Here we shall need guidance. Devotion by itself, and determination to go for the very best, are not enough. John and James once came to the Saviour and asked Him to grant them to sit one on His right hand and the other on His left in His coming kingdom; and they assured Christ that they were prepared to suffer as much as He was, if only He would grant their request. But Christ had to tell them that they did not understand what they were asking, that it was not His to give, and that it was not necessarily in God's plan for them anyway (Mk. 10:35-40).

In order to ask aright, then, we must let His words abide in us, correcting our misconceived desires, opening up to us what God's purposes and objectives are for us and for others, so that we can shape our requests accordingly.

But granted that, the wonderful thing is that we are invited to co-operate with the Vinedresser in accomplishing His desires. After all, while we are, metaphorically speaking, vine branches, we are not literal, passive pieces of vine-wood. We are redeemed personalities. As we abide in Christ and His words, abiding in us, begin to renew our minds, we shall in the first place become aware of faults in our personalities, hard knots in the vine-branch, so to speak, that limit our fruitfulness and impede our growth. And when that happens we are invited to co-operate with the Vinedresser, and ask for these things to be removed, that more fruit shall result for His glory. We are not allowed to dictate to Him how He shall do it: we may well find that He chooses unexpected and sometimes painful methods. Nor are we allowed to dictate how long He shall take over it. We are not to suppose that habits and complexes ingrained over many years will necessarily be removed instantaneously. But we may ask, and go on asking, in the God-given assurance that our asking is not in vain. He will do for us what we ask; and when the resultant fruit brings Him the credit, we shall have the joy of knowing that we co-operated with Him in achieving His glory; and the added joy of realizing that our fruit-bearing demonstrates that we are genuine disciples of Christ.

Of course, if Christ's words abide in us, we shall not only ask for things to be done to and for ourselves; we shall ask for the benefit and blessing of others, perhaps even more than for ourselves. But that is a subject for another chapter.

21

The Functioning of the Vine: A Pattern for the Branches in the Manner of Christ's Love

"Even as the Father hath loved Me, I also have loved you: abide ye in My love. If ye keep My commandments, ye shall abide in My love; even as I have kept My Father's commandments, and abide in His love. These things have I spoken unto you, that My joy may be in you, and that your joy may be fulfilled. This is My commandment, that ye love one another, even as I have loved you" (Jn. 15:9-12).

So far in His parable of the Vine and the branches, our Lord has dealt with the Vinedresser's care of the branches, and then with the status of the branches in relation to the Vine. Now in the second half of the parable He is about to describe the functioning of the Vine itself, and then to point out that the functioning of the Vine necessarily lays down the pattern for the functioning of the branches.

The function of a literal vine is easily described. Rooted in the soil itself in a way that the branches are not, the vine draws up through itself all the nutriments that a vine needs in order to produce fruit, and then passes them on to the branches. The branches for their part take those nutriments and, in their turn, pass them on to the public in the form of grapes. Neither the vine itself nor the branches may act as a dead end, receiving the nutriments but not passing them on; for if this happens at any point, the result will be no fruit at all.

Watch then how our Lord acts as the perfect Vine, receiving the love of God and then passing it on undiminished to His disciples: "Even as the Father has loved Me, I also have loved you" (15:9). Watch again how our Lord acts as the perfect Vine, passing on to His disciple without reserve everything He has heard from the Father: "All things that I heard from My Father I have made known to you" (15:15). God's heart and God's mind, His love and His Word, both fully and faithfully transmitted: so does the function and practice of the perfect Vine set the pattern which the branches are expected to follow, and must follow if there is to be fruit.

With the Vine this was no mere theoretical talk. We look back once more to chapter 13. There, having loved His own who were in the world, He loved them to the end, stripped Himself and humbly washed their feet, before resuming His seat and saying: "If I, then, the Lord and Teacher have washed your feet, you also ought to wash one another's feet. For I have given you an example that you also should do as I have done to you" (13:14-15).

But Christ's practical expressions of love to us are not meant to be an end in themselves. If they were, they would be in danger of spoiling us. We have all come across spoiled children. Their parents constantly shower them with gifts of every kind; and their giving sets the children a clear, practical example of sacrificial love. But somehow, while the parents' gifts get to the children, their sacrificial love does not get into the children and through them to the children next door or even to their own brothers and sisters. Indeed the more gifts these spoiled children receive, the harder and more selfish they seem to become.

It could happen to us at the spiritual level; and therefore our Lord has taken steps to see that it shall not. The first step is our incorporation into Christ as branches in a vine, so that the very life and love of God may flow from His heart into ours; as Paul put it in his delightful way: "God's love for us has been poured out in our hearts through the Holy Spirit who was given to us" (Rom. 5:5). In other words, not only do we have the practical, external expressions of Christ's love for us as examples which it is our duty to follow: we have the daily living supply of the life and love of Christ channeled into our hearts to be our motivation and strength to put His example into practice.

And the second step is the way the Vine actually functions in relation to the branches. But to see that, let us now notice that this second half of the parable falls into two parts as the first half did. Each half once more begins with a caption or statement of basic thesis:

PART 1   15:9   *The manner of Christ's love for His disciples:* "Even as the Father has loved Me, I also have loved you."

PART 2   15:13   *The extent of Christ's love for His friends:* "Greater love has no one than this, that he lay down his life for his friends."

And each caption or statement of basic thesis is followed by four great sayings which draw out its implications. The first set runs as follows:

CAPTION: "Even as the Father has loved Me, I also have loved you."

SAYINGS: 1.   *The way to enjoy Christ's love:* "abide in My love" (15:9).

2.   *The necessary practical condition for abiding in His love:* "If you keep My commandments, you shall abide in My love…" (15:10).

3.   *The purpose of this exhortation:* "…that My joy may be in you, and that your joy may be full" (15:11).

4.   *The commandment above all others that must be fulfilled in order to abide in Christ's love:* "…that you love one another as I have loved you" (15:12).

THE PRACTICAL ENJOYMENT OF CHRIST'S LOVE

Our study of these verses, then, must begin where Christ Himself begins them, otherwise we might be in danger of misconstruing their exhortations. Christ begins not with a conditional promise: 'I will love you if…' but with the statement of a glorious unconditional fact: "I have loved you, I have set My love on you," and have done so "in exactly the same way as My Father has loved Me."

There was no exaggeration in the statement. Christ was not

romantically recalling the past three years and, in the glow of memory, painting them in warmer colors than realism would have permitted. Yes, James and John had been selfishly ambitious for the top two places in Christ's kingdom, and the other apostles were indignant at them, doubtless for trying to preempt the place which they, each one of them, secretly felt should be theirs (Mk. 10:35-41). Yes, even the sacred atmosphere of the Upper Room had been temporarily polluted as the eleven, with seemingly incorrigible selfishness, bickered among themselves over who of them should be regarded as the greatest (Lk. 22:24). But Christ's love, once set on them, persisted undiminished, as chapter 13 once more reminds us: "Having loved His own who were in the world, He loved them to the end," completely, perfectly. Nor would the ensuing years, nor yet the immeasurable eternity to come, ever witness any diminution of that love.

But while Christ's love for His apostles, indeed for all His people, remains constant, their and our practical enjoyment of it is quite another thing. Suppose parents in their love for their children give one of them a large bar of chocolate with instructions to share it with his brothers and sisters; and suppose this child refuses to share it with the others, and when his parents remonstrate with him, flings a tantrum and runs off. The parent will go on loving their selfish child as before; but it is certain that the child himself will not be enjoying the sense of his parents' love as long as he runs away and refuses to share the chocolate.

And so it is with us. Christ has set His love on us and that will never cease or diminish; but what He is telling us to do here is to abide in that love, that is, to see to it that we remain in the practical enjoyment of it.

And how is that to be done? Once more Christ provides the pattern for our functioning. His Father's love for Him was, of course, constant; but in addition there never was one moment—except it was at Calvary when He was forsaken by God on account of our sins—that His practical enjoyment of His Father's love was impeded. For without variation or reserve He kept His Father's commandments and so never once lost the sense of His Father's love. If we then would know the practical enjoyment of Christ's love, we must in our turn keep His commandments.

Then why don't we always do so? Very often for the same reason that the little child ran off with the chocolate. His parents' command that he share the chocolate with others seemed to him an intolerable threat to his enjoyment. He must protect his own interests, as we adults say. With so much chocolate at stake, he felt he could not afford to be so wildly generous as his parents suggested. And we can understand it in a child, who has not yet learned the joy of giving that his parents knew, how that it is more blessed to give—even chocolate!—than to receive. Indeed the immediate woeful prospect of seeing the major part of the chocolate disappearing down the throats of his brothers and sisters completely hides from him the fact that there is more chocolate where this one slab came from, and that obedience is bound to be rewarded both with more chocolate and with the more lasting joy of a deeper understanding of his parents' love, as well as the discovery of the joy of giving.

And so it has often been with us. Asked to forgive an erring but repentant brother, we feel we cannot afford to. Asked by Christ to sacrifice our present joys, our time, energy, money, comfort, for the sake of others, we feel the demand is unreasonably costly, and, like Jonah, we take ship to go in the opposite direction, to protect our own enjoyments (Jonah 1).

THE VINES' GENIUS FOR JOY

For this very reason, Christ who knew His apostles' hearts, and ours too, added an explanation at this point: "These things I have spoken to you that My joy may be in you, and that your joy may be fulfilled." In other words, He assured them that His commandments were not aimed at diminishing their joy but increasing it. It is after all the pride and joy of a vine to produce grapes that by their fruit and wine bring joy to others. If dumb nature could speak, a vine-stock would never complain that it was always having to pass on its rich nutriments to the branches to produce grapes for other people's consumption. Vines, if they could feel, would hugely enjoy their God-given function of producing joy for others, as Jotham's parable long since observed (Jud. 9:12-13).

Christ, the True Vine, certainly did, and does still. After a long, dusty, and tiring journey to bring spiritual satisfaction to one lonely woman, He explained to His disciples that doing God's will in this way and bringing His work to completion was food

171

and drink to Him (4:31-34). He rejoiced in the Holy Spirit, says Luke (10:21), and thanked His Father, the Lord of heaven and earth, that God had used Him to reveal His treasures to babes. And He sang a hymn even as He left the Upper Room for the sacrifice of Himself at Calvary (Mt. 26:30).

His instructions to us, therefore, that the only way of remaining in the practical enjoyment of His love is to keep His commandments, is designed so that His joy as the self-giving Vine should flow unimpeded to, and through, us to others, and that we in turn should find our own joy brought to its peak as we thus fulfill our God-given function as branches in the Vine.

The commandment therefore above all others that He gives us, as He brings this small section of His teaching to a close, is that we love one another after the same pattern of love that He has shown to us (15:12).

22

The Functioning of the Vine: A Pattern for the Branches in the Extent of Christ's Love

In our last lesson Christ taught us that to become beautiful and graceful people like Himself and to produce for other people's enjoyment the lovely fruit of the Spirit, we must love others in the same manner as He has loved us. But how far must we go? This next lesson will answer that question; and it does so by once more laying down as a caption a statement of basic principle and then adding four great sayings which draw out its implications:

CAPTION: "Greater love has no one than this that he lay down his life for his friends."

SAYINGS: 1.   *How we become friends to Christ:* "You are my friends if…" (15:14).

2.   *What Christ's treatment of us as His friends involves:* "No longer do I call you servants; for the servant does not know…" (15:15).

3.   *The implication of the fact that Christ chose us not we Him:* "You did not choose Me, but I chose you and appointed you that you should go and bear fruit…" (15:16).

4. *The point and purpose of the preceding command-ments:* "that you love one another" (15:17).

Obviously the first thing to do is to make sure we have under-stood the point of the statement of basic principle. Some have thought that our Lord was pointing out how superior His love was to the very best love that mere men are capable of: Greater love has no *man* than this that a man lay down His life for His *friends;* whereas *Christ* loved and gave His life for His *enemies.* Now it is true that Christ died for us while we were still His ene-mies (Rom. 5:6-10), but that was not the point of our Lord's statement here. For here Christ was talking to those who were already His friends as the next verse makes clear; and obviously He was not telling them that while He loved them to some extent, He loved His enemies even more.

No, the context is that our Lord had just commanded His dis-ciples that they must love one another as He had loved them (15:12); and therefore He must now explain what the extent of their love for one another would have to be, if they were going to love each other after the pattern of His love for them. Love can go no further than to lay down its life for others; and this, and nothing less than this, was the extent to which their love must be prepared to go.

That being so, we must obviously take care to understand what is implied by the phrase 'to lay down one's life for one's friends.' It can, of course, mean literally 'to die for one's friends.' Christ literally laid down His life for us on the cross; and there may come times when we are called upon literally to lay down our lives for the sake of our fellow-believers. Or if not that, to *be prepared* to lay down our lives for them. "Greet Priscilla and Aquila," writes Paul (Rom. 16:3-4); and that shows that Priscilla and Aquila were still alive when he wrote. But he adds that at some unspecified time in the past "they laid down their necks for my life; and not only I but all the churches of the Gentiles thank them."

Normally, however, we are not called to heroic action of that kind but to something that may in fact be far more difficult: to the laying down of our lives, that is our time, our energies, our patience, our care, and attention in the interests of others, in the everyday affairs of life in the home, in business and in the church. That may be far less romantic, but it doubtless forms the regular agenda of ordinary Christian life.

John points out in his first epistle that, since Christ laid down His life for us, we ought to lay down our lives for the brethren; but he goes on to make a very practical observation. What would be the use of our declaring our readiness to lay down our lives literally for our fellow-believers, if at the same time we were not prepared to share with our fellow-believers who are in need the ordinary means of life from day to day: "Anyone who has this world's goods, and sees his brother in need, and shuts up his compassion from him, how does the life of God abide in him?" (1 Jn. 3:17). John's phraseology is true to life. Every true believer, seeing another's need, will automatically feel compassion welling up within him, born not merely of sheer human goodness, but from the indwelling Saviour Himself. But it is all too possible for a believer, having become tainted by selfishness or by the standards of the world, to suppress these feelings of compassion, until there is very little outward evidence that the love of God dwells in him at all.

A TWO-WAY FRIENDSHIP

We, then, are to lay down our lives for our friends. But friendship is not just one-way traffic. If we, as members of God's family, act as friends to our Christian brothers and sisters, they in their turn are just as responsible to act as friends to us. If those whom we treat as our friends never act like friends to us, how are they worthy of the name of friend?

But once begin to think like that and our Lord's next saying will bring us up sharp: "You are My friends, if you do the things which I command you" (15:14). The conditional conjunction, "if," is inescapable: "...*if* you do My commands."

Perhaps at this point someone will want to object: How can it be said that Christ's love for us is conditional on our keeping His commandments? Did He not love us originally while we were still sinners? And does He not remain our Friend even when in our weakness we fail to keep His commandments?

Certainly He does. He who was described by His critics, malevolently but quite correctly, as a friend of quisling tax-collectors and prostitutes, will never cease to be a loyal friend to those who trust Him, even when, like Peter, they fail and fall.

But the objection rests on a misunderstanding: Christ does not say, "I am your friend if, and only if, you do the thing which I command you." What He says is: "You are My friends, if you do the thing which I command you." True friendship even between the Lord and us, let us never forget it, is a two-way process. It would be a shocking thing if we relied on our Lord always to act as a friend to us, but ourselves made little deliberate attempt to act as friends to Him by doing what He commands us to do.

THE STATUS OF CHRIST'S SERVANTS

Consider how magnificently He treats us. He had every right to treat us as slaves, simply commanding us to do things without giving any reasons or taking us into His confidence. But He has not done so. Although it is an honor for us to be allowed, along with the apostles, to call ourselves 'slaves of Jesus Christ' (cf. Phil. 1:1), that is not what *He* calls *us* nor how He treats us: "No longer do I call you slaves; for a slave does not know what his master does. But I have called you friends; for all things that I heard from My Father I have made known to you" (15:15).

He does not seek to get His desired results by acting the slave-master and driving us to carry out His commands in blind, uninformed, unthinking obedience. He is the Vine, and without Him, we the branches, as we were earlier reminded, can do nothing. Yet, by God's grace, we the branches are an integral and—let it be said with bated breath—a necessary part of God's process of making Himself known; and Christ recognizes and treats us as such. With the perfect self-giving of the True Vine that He is, He has shared with us, the branches, all that the Father has told Him.

It would, then, be a shameful thing, if we did not joyfully respond to His friendship, by being in word and act a friend to Him and laying down our very lives for Him so as to do what He commands us to do. Indeed if we had any true sense of the relationship which Christ has set up between Himself and us, or any realistic conception of its potential, we should constantly be taking the initiative and positively pestering Christ to choose us to do this or that task for Him. But He has long since, all unasked, taken the initiative Himself, and chosen us both for salvation (2 Thess. 2:13) and for His service (1 Pet. 2:9). We need only ask Him for what particular task He has chosen us.

THE IMPLICATIONS OF CHRIST'S INITIATIVE

"You did not choose Me," said Christ, "but I chose you and appointed you that you should go and bear fruit, and that your fruit should abide: that whatever you shall ask of the Father in My name, He may give it to you" (15:16).

There is perhaps more than one way in which we can read the lessons of these words, depending on how we construe the thought-flow of the preceding verses. But whichever way we interpret them, we must begin by remembering that they were primarily spoken to the Eleven, and referred to Christ's choice of them to be His official apostles. Once more we look back to chapter 13, for Christ, we remember, had already referred to His choice of them earlier in the evening (13:18-20). There it had become necessary for Him to inform them that He was aware that one of those He had chosen was a traitor, and that His choice of the traitor had not been made either in ignorance or in error. He had always been aware of what the Scripture had predicted about Judas. From the start He had known the kind of man Judas was, and had foreseen what he would do. He had never expected that Judas would "go and bring forth fruit and that his fruit should remain"; and He certainly had never given Judas permission to use His name in prayer to God (if Judas ever prayed). Now His announcement to the Eleven that He had chosen them and appointed them to bear lasting fruit would by contrast fill their hearts with confidence.

It was not that in a moment of enthusiasm, temporarily excited by seeing one of His miracles, they had suggested to Him that He take them on as His representatives, and He, under the pressure of their insistent pleas, had consented. That would have been no recipe for the patient production of lasting fruit. No, it was Christ who had taken the initiative and chosen them, in full knowledge of what kind of men they were, of their temperaments, strengths, and weaknesses, and indeed of their future mistakes and shortcomings. And yet He had chosen them for this awesomely wonderful purpose of being functional extensions of Himself, as branches are to a vine. And so unreservedly was He giving Himself to them, and identifying Himself with them that they were to be permitted to use all the merit and authority of His name when appealing to the Father to act in the interests of the work that Christ had given them to do. The self-giving of the Vine to the branches was utterly without reserve: the branches would be expected to yield themselves to the Vine with similar self-abandon.

The confidence, then, engendered in the apostles' hearts by this announcement of Christ's choice would be a large ingredient in their vigorous production of fruit, as would be His permission, indeed His encouragement, to use His name and authority in their requests to the Father. But not only so; in days to come amid opposition, frustration, and failure, the memory of His initiative and choice would itself bring reviving of spirit and produce that perseverance without which lasting fruit-production is not possible. The apostle Paul has expressed it well: "I thank Christ Jesus our Lord, who has given me strength, that He had considered me faithful, appointing me to His service. Even though I was once a blasphemer and a persecutor and a violent man, I was shown mercy because I acted in ignorance and unbelief. The grace of our Lord was poured out on me abundantly along with the faith and love that are in Christ Jesus...But for that very reason I was shown mercy so that in me, the worst of sinners, Christ might display His unlimited patience as an example for those who would believe on Him and receive eternal life" (1 Tim. 1:12-16).

Encouraging as it was, however, our Lord's announcement that He had chosen His apostles and not they Him, could also be read as implying a warning, particularly if we remember the earlier exhortation that as branches in the Vine they were expected to lay down their lives for their friends. An independent trader could choose a farmer to act as his supplier of grapes. Having received the grapes, he would then be free to sell them to everybody or only to a select few; to sell them for a profit or give them away; or neither to sell them nor to give them away, but to keep them simply for his own enjoyment. But if a grape-farmer chooses a man as his servant and appoints him to distribute his grapes free of cost to all those designated by the farmer himself, the servant is not free to do what he likes with the grapes, and certainly not to keep them for himself. He must fulfill the directive of the farmer who chose and appointed him. "When I preach the gospel," said Paul, "I cannot boast, for I am compelled to preach. Woe to me if I do not preach the gospel!...I am simply discharging the trust committed to me" (1 Cor. 9:16-17).

The Lord's choice of His apostles, then, would certainly fill them with encouragement; but likewise it would leave them with no real option other than to discharge their God-given function as branches in the Vine: to lay down their lives as channels to bring the love and loveliness of God to their fellow-men. And the point was pressed home by the last great saying in the series: "These things I command you that you may love one another" (15:17).

We for our part may feel that, compared with the apostles, we are scarce worthy to be regarded as substantial branches in the Vine; but what was originally said to these branches applies, we may be sure, in due proportion to every twig and tendril in the Vine. Every believer can say: "Christ laid down His life for me personally." Every believer is called upon to be a friend to Christ by doing His commandments; and Christ treats every believer as a friend, confiding in him all that He has heard from the Father. Every believer has been deliberately and personally chosen by Christ to bear fruit that shall last. Every cluster of Christian virtues and graces that have been developed in a believer's character; every person brought to faith in Christ as a result of witnessing the quality of that believer's life; every piece of fruit will last eternally. The joy of it shall never die away.

And notice the generous way in which the Lord phrases Himself: "I chose you...that you...should bear fruit and that *your* fruit should abide." Your fruit! Do we, then, produce it? In one sense, no. Without Him we could do nothing. He had to supply the wherewithal. He had to maintain us. It was the Father who was the Husbandman. Yet, when the result is accomplished, He genuinely calls it our fruit. For this process is not one that swamps our personalities. We are not just impersonal branches, pipes, channels, through which some Almighty Being pours out His blessings. We are personalities that, though joined to Christ, retain their personality. And indeed, being joined to Christ develops our personalities. God who designed us and knows our potential, develops us to the full. Though Christ was its source, the resultant fruit is genuinely described as *our* fruit. We shall see it and enjoy the sight of it eternally.

And every believer is permitted, indeed encouraged, to use Christ's name and authority in his requests to the Father. Just think what this means. It is as though a wealthy man were to set up a poor friend of his in business and, knowing that the poor man would never have enough resources of his own to maintain the business in a healthy and prosperous state, gave the poor man permission to use his name when the poor man went to the bank. The effect would be that when the poor man went to the bank and quoted the name of his rich friend, the bank would give him all the resources he needed. Now just fancy that! We who were once rebels, who still often sin, though now redeemed, may enter the very bank of heaven and, using the name of the Son of God Himself, ask the Father for the resources we need, and the Father, honoring the name of His Son, will give us what we ask for. How could Christ possibly act as a greater friend towards us? Shame on us indeed, if we do not in response act as friends towards Him. And so as He ends, He sums up again the chief commandment He lays upon us, if we wish to act as friends to Him: "These things I command you, that you love one another" (15:17).

THE COURSE: PART TWO

B. The Exposure of the World's Hatred

Preview

In our last session we learned that an essential part of true holiness is to witness to and for God in the world, first by a life that produces the attractive fruits of the Spirit, so that people in contact with us may taste and see that the Lord we represent is good; and secondly by the word of our spoken testimony both in private and in public.

Now in this session our Lord will prepare us for our task by pointing out that the world in which, and to which, we are to witness is marked by an underlying hatred both of God and of Christ.

That hatred put Jesus Himself to a cross; but God's answer is not to abandon, still less to destroy the world, but to send us into it to bear our witness to what God is really like so that some at least may have their eyes opened and be reconciled to God.

We cannot necessarily expect any better treatment than Jesus Himself received. But this session will end with Christ's announcement of the magnificent provision He has made for us. We shall not be required to carry the heavy burden of the prime responsibility for witness to Christ in the world. That prime responsibility will be borne by the Holy Spirit whom Jesus has sent from the Father. Ours is simply the highly honored, but subsidiary, role of being His helpers and instruments in His divine witness to Christ.

23

Understanding the World's Hatred

"If the world hateth you, ye know that it hath hated Me before it hated you. If ye were of the world, the world would love its own: but because ye are not of the world, but I chose you out of the world, therefore the world hateth you. Remember the word that I said unto you, A servant is not greater than his lord. If they persecuted Me, they will also persecute you; if they kept My word, they will keep yours also. But all these things will they do unto you for My Name's sake, because they know not Him that sent Me" (Jn. 15:18-21).*

Why would anybody hate Jesus Christ? The Prince of Life, the King of Righteousness and Peace, the Friend of sinners, the Bringer of God's forgiveness, the Author of the Sermon on the Mount—why would anyone hate Him so much as to crucify Him? That people should hate tyrants, like Hitler, is understandable. But Jesus Christ?

The idea that one day the responsible leaders of the nation would contrive to have Him crucified seemed to Peter and his fellow-disciples, when they first heard it from Jesus Himself, grotesquely mistaken. "Get that out of your head, Lord," said

---

* For a preliminary definition of the term 'world' see pp. 60-61, and then p. 229.

Peter; "nothing like that will ever happen to You" (Mt. 16:22).

But it did, of course; and the world that crucified Jesus would not necessarily treat His disciples any better when He was gone. If, therefore, they were going to be required to go out into the world and witness to and for Christ, they would have to be prepared to face the world's hatred. And that would mean being helped to understand its true cause; for with understanding would come compassion, like that of their Master who prayed for those who drove the nails through His hands and feet, "Father, forgive them, for they know not what they do." And with compassion would come an urgent desire to witness to the truth about God and His Son, so as to dispel that fatal ignorance, if possible; and a willingness to endure whatever hatred they must in the process.

Four things, to begin with, the disciples would need to bear in mind about the world's hatred for them, when they encountered it:

1. *It had a precedent:* "the world...hated Me before it hated you" (15:18).
2. *What it is about Christ's followers that provokes the world's hatred:* "...because you are not of the world, but I chose you out of the world, therefore the world hates you" (15:19).
3. *Christians cannot expect better treatment than Christ:* "...if they persecuted Me, they will also persecute you; if they kept My word, they will keep yours also" (15:20).
4. *The deep-seated underlying cause of the world's hatred:* "but all these things will they do to you for My Name's sake, because they know not Him that sent Me" (15:21).

THE PRECEDENT

The gospel of our Lord Jesus Christ is so delightful, offering as it does full and complete forgiveness, the free gift of eternal life, peace with God, the daily companionship of Christ, assurance of heaven at last, and many more joys and blessings besides, that often a new believer will hurry to tell his friends about it. He imagines that the only reason they have not believed in Jesus till now is that they have never really known what salvation is like. And he thinks that since his friends are reasonable people, they will only have to be told about it, and they will gladly receive it.

When in fact, as often happens, he is met with stony indifference, or ridicule or even animosity, he is quite bewildered. He cannot understand why he is not accepted; he can even begin to wonder whether what he has is the right thing. Had Jesus not forewarned His apostles, it might well have been a very unsettling thing for them too when they found the spiritual leaders of their nation, the chief priests and the Council, united in bitter hostility to them and to their gospel.

In such circumstances it is only natural if a new Christian asks himself: Is there something wrong with me? There could be, of course. Sometimes a new Christian's enthusiasm can lead him to be less than tactful, or even rude and disrespectful in his witness to others. And sometimes the poor quality of the behavior of older believers seriously undermines the credibility of the gospel they preach. The non-Christian's resentment of Christians can sometimes be the Christian's fault. And that unholy mixture of politics and religion that men call Christendom has often been guilty of such unchristian cruelty and wickedness that people have understandably and rightly hated it.

But when due allowance has been made for all that, there remains a resentment that has an altogether different cause. We can see it is so, as soon as we remember that long before the world hated Christians, it hated Jesus Christ Himself—and Him more than them. And there was nothing wrong with Jesus: no unbalanced fanaticism, no loveless religiosity, no insensitivity to people's feelings. Yet they hated Him virulently. Were we not desensitized by the all-pervasiveness of the world's wickedness, we should surely consider it a very strange phenomenon indeed, that the Fairest Man that ever lived was crucified by His fellow-men. After that, it is not necessarily His followers' fault, if the world resents them too.

What it is about Christ's Followers that Provokes the World's Hatred

The world's resentment of Christ's followers stems from a deep-seated clash of ultimate loyalties. "If you were of the world," says Christ, "the world would love its own; but...you are not of the world." The world senses it and resents it. To make matters worse, Christ's followers were originally like everybody else "of the world": they shared the world's fundamental attitudes, presuppositions, values, ambitions, goals. But that has now changed. Christ has chosen them out of the world. They have transferred their fundamental allegiance to a different kingdom against which the world, as a basic principle of its existence, is in rebellion. The world, therefore, is ill at ease with Christ's followers. Sometimes vaguely and unconsciously, at other times with vivid awareness, the world feels that a true Christian is a kind of deserter who has gone over to the other side, over to the One whom the world in its heart feels to be the Ultimate Threat.

Some Necessary Explanations and Definitions

But at this point we ought to pause and enquire what exactly Christ means when He talks of 'the world.' Obviously He is using the term in a specialized sense; for when He says, "the world loves its own," He does not mean that all non-Christian people and nations love each other! They clearly don't! Look at all the civil and ethnic wars that still rage in many parts of the world.

And when He says "because I have chosen you out of the world, therefore the world hates you," He does not mean that every non-Christian person hates every Christian. That is not true, and Christ knew it: He had no persecution mania; He did not imagine hatred where there was none. Mothers, we are told, trusted Him enough to bring their little children to Him, and He took them in His arms and blessed them (Mk. 10:13-16). He had compassion on the masses of people: He felt for them as for sheep that had no shepherd, fed them, healed their sick, so that they glorified God for Him (Mt. 9:35-36; 15:30-32). Merciful towards the fallen and sinful, He accepted their invitations to dinner and received them to His own table, so much so that His very religious contemporaries accused Him of being a friend of tax-gatherers and sinners (Lk. 15:1; 19:7). As late as the last week before His crucifixion, we are told that the crowds of ordinary people in Jerusalem (as distinct from the authorities) listened to Him with delight; and though they were eventually manipulated by the authorities to shout for His death, at Pentecost and afterwards thousands of them gave Him their allegiance, faith, and love, and followed Him (Mk. 12:37; 15:11; Acts 2:41; 4:4). So

186

when Christ said to His apostles: "Don't be surprised if the world hates you," He certainly did not mean that every non-Christian person would hate every Christian.

That said, we only have to look at the world at large to see that the world is everywhere permeated with evil; and the Bible attributes it all basically to mankind's alienation from God. It would be helpful, therefore, at this point to recall what we learned from our Lord's exposure of Judas about the world's alienation from God. It started in the Garden of Eden where Satan who has become the Prince of this World (Jn. 12:31; 14:30; 16:11), persuaded Adam and Eve that God was against them, and that the way to enjoy life was to rebel against God and His Word and seize and enjoy all life's good things in independence of God. They fell for Satan's lie, and the resultant guilt feelings and bad conscience made them feel that God must certainly now be against them. They ran away, trying to hide from God, who for them had now become the Great Threat (see Gen. 3).

People still try to run away and hide from God, though of course they do it in much more sophisticated ways. Many take refuge in science, which they like to believe has proved that there is no God outside our universe, or if there is, He can neither enter, nor interfere with things inside, the universe. Science, of course, has proved no such thing.

Many seem to think that if they just ignore God, He will somehow go away. One very self-deceptive technique of the human heart is to adopt religion, hoping thereby to appease God, buy off His displeasure, and perhaps earn a place in His heaven. But that attitude subtly perpetuates the basic, false stance of independence from God.

Suppose a neighbor has an allotment and has grown a lot of potatoes. Suppose also that I have had a bitter row with him. He might in spite of it sell me potatoes if I pay him enough for them. But if I am bankrupt and helplessly dependent on him to give me the potatoes I desperately need, then I cannot maintain my independence. I must cast myself on his mercy and be reconciled to him before I can expect him to give me anything.

So it is between man and God. God calls on men to give up their false, independent stance, acknowledge their moral and spiritual bankruptcy, cast themselves on His mercy, be reconciled to Him, and receive forgiveness and eternal life from Him as a gift. But as long as people out of pride or ignorance try to maintain their independence of God, the alienation continues, and God appears to them as a threat. They don't like Him, let alone love Him. And if they meet a true Christian who insists on talking, when appropriate, about Jesus, and seems evidently in love with God and Christ, and urges their claims upon the world, they don't particularly like him either, for he makes them feel ill at ease. Developed to its extreme, this dislike will result in governments that seek to eliminate the very idea of God from society altogether by force of the law.

CHRISTIANS CAN EXPECT THE
SAME TREATMENT AS CHRIST

"Remember the word that I spoke unto you," said Christ: "A servant is not greater than his lord. If they persecuted Me, they will also persecute you." Christ was certainly honest with His disciples. He never pretended that discipleship would be cost-free. He called for loyalty at the cost, if need be, of life itself; and thousands of believers have paid that price for His sake.

On the other hand, Christ added—and here we see His balance of thought—"If they kept My word, they will keep yours also." And of course there had been many during our Lord's earthly ministry who had believed His word, whose faith had saved them, and they had gone in peace. So likewise after Pentecost there would be ever increasing multitudes who would believe the word of Christ's disciples—and believe it indeed because it was in fact the word of Christ.

True holiness, therefore, requires that we take sober, realistic account of the world's hostility; but it does not require us to be paranoid pessimists. Uncountable millions shall yet believe the gospel.

THE DEEP-SEATED UNDERLYING
CAUSE OF THE WORLD'S HATRED

And now finally Christ puts His finger on the deep underlying cause of the world's hostility; and if we allow ourselves to reflect upon it, it will surely move us to compassion.

"The world will hate and persecute you," says Christ, "for My Name's sake." That much became obvious immediately after Pentecost. The Jewish Council soon ordered the Apostles "not to speak at all nor teach in the name of Jesus"; and when they persisted, the Council reminded them, "We strictly charged you not to teach in this Name," and reinforced the reminder with a thrashing.

The Apostle Paul, explaining before King Agrippa why before his conversion he had persecuted the Christians so severely, remarked, "I was convinced that I ought to do all that was possible to oppose the name of Jesus of Nazareth." And still today, when Christians repeat Christ's claim, "I am the Way, the Truth and the Life: no one comes to the Father but by Me" (Jn. 14:6), and when they insist, as the Apostles did, that "Salvation is found in no one else, for there is no other name under heaven given to men by which we must be saved," then the exclusive claims of Christ provoke the displeasure not only of atheists but of religious people as well (see Acts 4:18; 5:28; 26:9; 4:12).

But Christ's diagnosis went deeper: "They will do all these things to you for My Name's sake, *because they know not Him that sent Me.*" And that was true, as we have said, not only of pagans and atheists, but of many religious people as well. Saul of Tarsus, who became the Apostle Paul, is once more a case in point. Like many of his fellow Jews, he was exceedingly religious and thought he knew much better than the pagans around him what God was really like. But when God came down to earth in the Person of Jesus, Saul of Tarsus not only failed to recognize God: he actually persecuted Him; and confessed later on that he did it in sheer ignorance (1 Tim. 1:13).

Could anything be more poignant? It moved the strong Son of God to tears. As He approached Jerusalem and saw the city, He wept over it and said, "If you, even you, had only known on this day what would bring you peace—but now it is hidden from your eyes...you did not recognize the time of God's coming to you" (Lk. 19:41, 44).

And still today, when we as Christ's disciples go out to offer to the world our most wonderful Saviour, and we meet the same ignorant hostility, it should fill our eyes too with tears of compassion.

24

God's Magnificent Response to the World's Hostility

"If I had not come and spoken unto them, they had not had sin: but now they have no excuse for their sin. He that hateth Me hateth My Father also. If I had not done among them the works which none other did, they had not had sin: but now have they both seen and hated both Me and My Father. But this cometh to pass, that the word may be fulfilled that is written in their law, They hated Me without a cause. But when the Comforter is come, whom I will send unto you from the Father, even the Spirit of truth, which proceedeth from the Father, He shall bear witness of Me: And ye also bear witness, because ye have been with Me from the beginning"

(Jn. 15:22-27).

We are now to learn of God's response to the world's hatred, rejection, and crucifixion of His Son. But to see that response in all its magnificent glory, we shall first have to allow the Lord Jesus to give us His assessment of His contemporaries' guilt.

In our last lesson we learned that the world's rejection of Jesus sprang from their ignorance of God who sent Him. But there are two kinds of ignorance: one is blameworthy and the other is not. For example, in the Middle Ages people living in Europe and Asia were completely unaware of the existence of Australia. They could not help being ignorant. No one had seen it; no one from Australia had come to tell them about it. They could not rightly be blamed for not knowing about, or believing in, the existence of Australia. It would, of course, have been a very different thing if someone living in St. Petersburg during the 1800s had refused to believe in the existence of France. Ignorance of that, in the face of all the available evidence, would have been wilful and blameworthy.

Then what about Christ's contemporaries in Israel? According to Christ, as He told us in our last lesson, their rejection of Him stemmed from the fact that they did not know the Father who sent Him. But the question is: Could they have known the Father if they had wished to? And the answer is: Yes, most certainly they could. They need not have remained in ignorance; their ignorance was therefore blameworthy.

So now our Lord makes three solemn statements on the blameworthiness of His contemporaries' hatred both of Himself and of the Father. And then in a fourth statement He announces what God's magnificent response will be to that culpable ignorance, hatred, and hostility: He will not wipe them off the face of the earth; He will send them yet another divine Person, the Holy Spirit of God, to witness to them about Christ and lead even them, if possible, to repentance, faith, reconciliation with God, and forgiveness.

1. *The world's rejection of Christ's words:* "If I had not come and spoken to them, they would not have had sin; but now they have no excuse for their sin. He who hates Me hates My Father also" (15:22-23).
2. *The world's rejection of Christ's works:* "If I had not done among them the works which none other did, they would not have had sin; but now they have both seen and hated both Me and My Father" (15:24).
3. *The Old Testament's advance warning:* several psalms had forewarned the nation of Israel that when Messiah came they would hate Him (15:25).
4. *God's response to the world's hatred:* the sending of the Spirit of Truth to bear witness to Christ (15:26-27).

Since numbers 1 and 2 are closely related, let us consider them together.

CULPABLE IGNORANCE

First, a technicality. In verses 22 and 24 Christ twice uses the (Greek) phrase: "they would not have had sin." He does not mean, of course, that if He had not come and spoken and performed miracles His contemporaries would have been completely virtuous and sinless. In that sense they were as generally sinful as anyone else. The phrase "to have sin" means to be blameworthy, culpable. If a man with no sense of smell entered a room full of gas fumes, and not realizing that fact, struck a match and blew the room up, you could not rightly blame him: he would not "have sin." If on the other hand, knowing the room to be full of gas fumes, he deliberately threw a lighted match into it, then he would "have sin."

Secondly, a basic principle of immense importance. In these verses Jesus tells us that at the Final Judgment—and He is going to be the Judge (Jn. 5:22-23)—people will be held responsible for what they have done with the light, the evidence, the information, about God and Christ, which they actually had, or could have had, if they had sought it. They will not be responsible for the light which they did not have and could not possibly have had. All men have some light; for God has filled His universe and our earth with pointers to Himself, intending that men should follow up these pointers and seek Him. Some do, but many don't bother to, or even deliberately ignore them (Acts 14:13-17; 17:26-28; Rom. 1:18-32; 2:14-16). They will be held accountable for it.

But those who have never heard of Jesus, cannot, and will not, be blamed for not having believed on Jesus (though they will be for many other things). On the other hand, Christ's contemporaries in Israel had heard His self-evidently God-given words, that told out the very heart, justice, and love of God. They had seen His unique miracles which had confronted them with undeniable signs of His divine power, and had simultaneously provided practical illustrations of His ability to meet man's need at the highest spiritual level.

They had, then, seen Christ, and in seeing Him they had seen a perfect exhibition of the Father. But, with their eyes open, they had resented and rejected both. Of course, many of them would have maintained it was only Jesus they were rejecting: they still believed in God. But that was impossible. Jesus was God Incarnate. He who hates Me, says Jesus, hates My Father also.

AN OLD TESTAMENT WARNING

As a result of Christ's coming, preaching, and miracles, they, the nation of Israel had no excuse for their ignorance of God and rejection of Christ. And there was another reason that left them without excuse. Their first and greatest king, David, was not only a poet but a prophet who, in a number of psalms, warned the successive generations of Israel that when his great Son, the Messiah, came the nation would hate Him for no fault of His own (see Ps. 35:19; 69:4; 109:5). When, therefore, Jesus' contemporaries found themselves hating Him and rejecting His claim to be the Messiah, it ought to have given them second thoughts and pulled them up in their tracks. But, well versed in the Old Testament though they were, the nation's leaders were so hostile to Jesus and so determined to prove He was not the Messiah that they forgot about these Old Testament predictions, and crucified Him (so, incidentally proving He was the Messiah. See Acts 13:27-30.) So they added to the culpability of their rejection of Jesus.

GOD'S RESPONSE TO THE WORLD'S HATRED

What then would God do in response to all this wilful, culpable, hatred of Himself and of His Son? Forthwith abandon them to the dire consequences of their inexcusable hostility?

No! Indeed not! That's not God! Not willing that any should perish, but that all should be saved and come to the knowledge of the truth, God would make yet another effort to save His now openly declared enemies. He would send the Spirit of Truth to witness to them that Jesus was His Son, and their God-appointed Saviour, willing still to save them if only they would repent.

Now what the Holy Spirit could do to win their hearts more than Jesus had hitherto done, will be taught us in the next session. But meanwhile, we must notice two highly significant things.

First, "When the Counselor has come," said Christ, "...He shall bear witness of Me. And you also shall bear witness, because you have been with Me from the beginning." This promise referred primarily to the Apostles as we see from the fact that their unique authority to be the official witnesses to Christ lay in this, that "they had been with Him from the beginning." Subsequently, according to Acts 1:21-22, the Apostles showed themselves keenly aware of their unique authority as apostles; for when they set about choosing another Apostle to take the place of Judas Iscariot, they laid it down as an absolutely necessary qualification that He must be one who had "companied with us all the time that the Lord Jesus went in and went out among us, beginning from the baptism of John, unto the day that He (Jesus) was received up from us...(and was) a witness with us of His resurrection." No individual, and no Council, in the post-apostolic centuries has ever had the same foundational and binding authority as the original Apostles.

But that having been said, in its secondary sense the promise applies to all Christ's disciples in all ages. To all of them is given the stupendous honor of being witnesses to Christ.

And the second thing we should notice at this point is that here once more there recurs that delightful pattern that has marked every lesson our Lord has taught on holiness so far.

In chapter 13 our Lord did not begin by saying, "This is a filthy world; you try to do your best to cleanse yourselves;" but first He announced the great provision that He was making for their cleansing in the bathing all over of regeneration and the constant rinsing of the feet.

Similarly, at the beginning of chapter 14, He did not say, "Try to follow Me closely, so that wherever I am you will be"—though of course the disciple has the responsibility to follow the Lord as closely as he can. Rather, the Lord began by announcing the provision He was making for the disciples, "I go away to prepare a place for you. And if I go away, I will come again, and receive you to Myself; that where I am, there you may be also" (14:3).

And then again, as we have recently observed in chapter 15, He did not begin by saying, "Israel as a whole has failed in the role as the vine which God planted in the earth. Now you try to do better." No, first of all He announced the glorious provision that God has made for us that we may bear fruit for His pleasure: "I am," said Christ, "the True Vine, and My Father is the Husbandman."

So here, at the beginning of this next lesson, He does not say "The world is hostile to God, but you are to go out and try to witness for Me and for My Father." He first of all announces the great provision that He has made for witnessing to Himself in this world. That provision is nothing less than the coming of the Holy Spirit. "When the Counselor comes," says Christ, "He shall bear witness of Me." Every believer, of course, has responsibility, according to his or her gift, to witness for the Lord, just as the apostles did: "You also shall bear witness of Me." But we would get things utterly out of proportion if we thought that the chief responsibility for witnessing was ours. The prime responsibility for witnessing to Christ in the world rests, not with us as individuals, nor with the Church as a whole, but with the Holy Spirit. He it is who carries the heavy end of the load, who bears the chief burden. Even the apostles were but junior servants, and how much more junior are we? It is as we grasp this glorious fact that we shall be delivered from undue stress and strain in the course of service for the Lord, and shall constantly find our strength renewed as we learn to rest on the almighty Spirit of God.

Indeed, it is an encouraging and invigorating thing to look back from time to time and see how effective the Holy Spirit has been in His witness to the world. In spite of mountainous seas of opposition that have continued to run all down the centuries, the gospel today is being preached around the world more than it has ever been preached in the past twenty centuries. Indeed, millions more people are currently hearing the gospel than ever was dreamed of even a century ago; and walls which hostile governments built round their countries, in their attempt to stamp out the Christian faith and prevent this gospel reaching their citizens, have come tumbling down. We may then have every confidence in the power and wisdom, the tactic, the strategy, and the effectiveness of the Holy Spirit's masterminding of the campaign of witness for Christ in the world. And in that confidence we may pursue our own witness for the Lord.

C. The Secret of Holiness' Effective Witness, Irremovable Joy, Indomitable Courage, and Ultimate Victory

Preview

In our last school session, we learned that the main responsibility for witness to Christ in the world would lie with the Holy Spirit. All believers, however, would have their part in this witness since it was to the believers that the Holy Spirit would be sent and largely through them that He would conduct His witness.

In this session, we shall be taught that the key to the effectiveness of that witness is Christ's 'going away'—that is His death, resurrection, and ascension—as the Holy Spirit draws out the implication of His "going," first for the world, and then for the Church.

Then we shall be invited to consider our Lord's post-resurrection appearances to His disciples which became for them—and through them to us—a source of irremovable joy.

As school comes to an end, we shall hear Christ examine His pupils to see if they have really grasped the fundamental fact on which all He has taught them depends; and then He will finally assure them, in spite of all their weaknesses, of ultimate triumph as He shares His victory with them.

25

The Holy Spirit's Witness: Convicting the World

"These things have I spoken unto you, that ye should not be made to stumble. They shall put you out of the synagogues: yea, the hour cometh, that whosoever killeth you shall think that he offereth service unto God. And these things will they do, because they have not known the Father, nor Me. But these things have I spoken unto you, that when their hour is come, ye may remember them, how that I told you. And these things I said not unto you from the beginning, because I was with you. But now I go unto Him that sent Me; and none of you asketh me, Whither goest Thou? But because I have spoken these things unto you, sorrow hath filled your heart. Nevertheless I tell you the truth; it is expedient for you that I go away: for if I go not away, the Comforter will not come unto you; but if I go, I will send Him unto you. And He, when He is come, will convict the world in respect of sin, and of righteousness, and of judgment: Of sin, because they believe not on Me; of righteousness, because I go to the Father, and ye behold Me no more; of judgment, because the prince of this world hath been judged"

(Jn. 16:1-11).

PERVERTED RELIGION

The last session of the school opened somberly enough as our Lord warned His apostles of the hostility they would meet from the world once they began their witness to Him. But, if it opened in gloom, it ended with a glorious burst of sunshine: the

199

promise that Christ would send to them the Holy Spirit of Truth from the Father to bear the prime weight and responsibility of conducting the world-wide witness to Christ.

Now as we begin this final session of the school, a somber note is struck once more as Christ returns to the topic of the world's hostility. But this time He concentrates on one particular direction from which the hostility will come: the apostles' own Jewish national religion. This is made clear by the terms used to describe the persecution: "They will put you out of the synagogues...whoever kills you will think that he offers service to God." As an example of this we can cite once more Saul of Tarsus (Acts 7:50-60; 9:1-9); and we cannot doubt his sincerity: he really thought he was pleasing God by persecuting the Christians. What a sad and evil thing religion can become; and not only primitive pagan religions with their superstitions and cruelties, but even classical monotheist religions. It was a heartbreaking tragedy that, in the time of Jesus, the leaders of Israel's God-given religion had, in their personal ignorance of God, so perverted their religion as to use it to justify the murder of God's Son. Christendom's record, be it said at once, is far worse. Professing to follow Jesus, Christendom has often ignored His prohibition on the use of violence, and persecuted, executed, and slaughtered many more thousands than Israel ever did. It is not merely in the brothel, or the drunkard's den, or the atheist's seminary, and such places, that men and women show their alienation from their Creator. Religion itself can be a subtle form of rebellion against God. Certainly religion, as such, cannot save. It stands under the judgment of God as part of the world. Only the Living God and His Son Jesus Christ can save.

But why should Christ choose to revert to this gloomy topic at this particular moment? Let Him explain (16:4). First, in order to forewarn them, so that when the persecution arose, they might remember He had said it would, and their confidence in Him would be strengthened and not shaken. Secondly, He had no need to tell them before this, because He was with them, sharing with them any hostility that had come their way. But now He was going; and unless He told them in advance of the persecution that would break out after His departure, they might think that He had gone and left them just when they needed Him most, because He had not anticipated the trouble.

But then, if He knew that persecution would break out after He went, why did He persist in going? It must all have seemed so strange and unnerving to the Apostles to hear Him speak like this as they walked slowly along the dark, hostile streets and paths of Jerusalem towards the shadows of Gethsemane's garden.

WHY CHRIST HAD TO GO

Why, then, did Christ have to go? If witness to the world was the main task that lay ahead, how would it not be far better for Him to stay and conduct that witness Himself? How could it make sense for Him to tell His disciples, "It is expedient for you that I go away," and then to add, "If I do not go away, the Counselor will not come to you" (16:7)?

We have discussed these matters before in another context, for they came up in Part One B of the school-course (see ch. 9, p. 76). But we must make sure we understand what our Lord meant by 'going away.' We must not be like the disciples. They were so sorrow-filled at the announcement that none of them had thought to ask Him in more detail where He was going to (16:5-6). True, Peter had earlier asked Him (13:36-37), where He was going; but his further remark, "Why can I not follow You even now?...I will lay down my life for You," seems to show that for him 'going' meant simply 'going to His death.' Now our Lord was certainly about to die; but dying was not the goal of His going. He was 'going to the Father' (16:10), and that would involve not only His dying, but His bodily resurrection, ascension, and exaltation.

And now, perhaps, we can begin to see the relevance of Christ's going to the problem that has just been mentioned in our present context: the hostility towards Jesus and His disciples on the part of their Jewish contemporaries. If the Holy Spirit was coming to witness to people like that, how would He do it? What would He say? Jesus, in His life on earth, had preached many sermons and done extraordinary miracles. In spite of it, they remained unbelievers. They would have said, if asked, that they were believers in God: it was only Jesus that they did not believe in. In a sense, of course, it is true that they were believers in God: they believed God existed, was All-holy and All-mighty. They were proud that they knew that there is only one True

God: paganism's polytheism was to them an absurdity and an abomination. They believed also that God had chosen their nation Israel for a special role in history, and had revealed Himself to them through the Old Testament prophets.

But in another sense, indeed in the most important sense of all, they were not believers in God! They were in fact rank unbelievers. For Jesus Christ was God in human form, the God who had made Himself known to them as the I AM (Ex. 3; see further pp. 223-224, 238). In not recognizing Him, it was God they did not recognize: "they have not known the Father, nor Me," said Christ (16:3). And not believing in Jesus, they showed themselves to be unbelievers in God.

A GOD-GIVEN EXAMPLE

As an example, we can take yet again the apostle whose conversion experience is explicitly said in Scripture to be an example "of those who should hereafter believe on Him (Jesus Christ) unto eternal life" (1 Tim. 1:16). In his pre-conversion days, Saul of Tarsus would have believed in God, would have been zealous to keep God's law, and punctilious in his religious observance, all in the hope of meriting acceptance with God. But in the most important sense of all he was not a believer. His persecution of God-Incarnate in Jesus, showed it. And after his conversion he confessed it: "I obtained mercy because I did it (persecuting Jesus and His followers) in...*unbelief*" (1 Tim. 1:13). Moreover in later years, discussing God's strategy for the conversion of all Israel, he points out that before God can have mercy and save them, He will have to bring them to the point of discovering and confessing that hitherto they have been unbelievers (Rom. 11:30-32).* The lesson should not be lost on us Gentiles. It is possible to be a sincere believer in God in one sense, and yet in the sense of 'being justified by faith' not to be a believer at all.

But to get back to our context. We may put to ourselves two questions:

1.   If, after a lifetime's preaching and miracles, Jesus had not

---

* The Greek verb used in these verses is often translated "to be disobedient." In the New Testament it everywhere, without exception, means 'to disobey the gospel,' i.e., 'deliberately to refuse to believe in God, Christ, and the gospel.' See, for example, Acts 14:2.

convinced the Jews that He was the Son of God, what more could the Holy Spirit say or do to convince them that He was?

2. It was a prerequisite for their being saved that they should be brought to realize and confess that their unbelief in Jesus was unbelief in God, and that it was heinously sinful. They must also acknowledge that they were therefore sinners, as bad as any pagans, and had now no hope of meriting salvation by their efforts to keep God's law, but must be saved solely by faith in God and His mercy. What, then, could the Holy Spirit do to bring them to such radical repentance and faith?

The answer to these questions is this: the Holy Spirit would be able to proclaim—and by His presence and power demonstrate—that the very Jesus whom they had crucified, God had raised from the dead and that Jesus had now ascended into heaven and had gone back to the Father from whom He had come.

Now we can see one of the main reasons why the Holy Spirit would not come unless Jesus went. If Jesus had not 'gone,' that is, if He had not been crucified, buried, raised from the dead, gone back to the Father and glorified, the Holy Spirit would have lacked the necessary message to preach!

Let's get this clear in our heads: the Holy Spirit did not achieve the conversion of thousands of Jews from Pentecost onwards by reminding them of Jesus' Sermon on the Mount, and urging them to reconsider it and try to put it into practice. Nor will the world today be converted through the preaching of Christian ethics, important as they are in their proper place. The message which the Holy Spirit preached was Christ Himself: His Person, His redeeming work, His death, resurrection, ascension, and eventual return! "The gospel by which you are saved" writes Paul (1 Cor. 15:1-3) "is that Christ died for our sins according to the Scriptures, and that He was buried, and that He has been raised on the third day according to the Scriptures; and that He will come again" (15:50-58).

THE CASE WHICH THE HOLY SPIRIT ARGUES BEFORE THE WORLD

The Holy Spirit, said Christ, would convict the world of three things: of sin, of righteousness, and of judgment. But He is careful to explain in what sense He meant these three terms. So let us study them in order. The Holy Spirit will convict the world:

1. *"Of sin*...because they believe not on Me."

Notice at once that the sin in question is not sin in general, lying, stealing, adultery and so forth, but the particular sin of not believing in Jesus. And if we ask how He will convict them that this refusal to believe was sinful, the answer is given in the second item:

2. *"Of righteousness,* because I go to the Father and you behold me no more."

'Righteousness' must be understood in its basic legal sense. By raising Jesus from the dead and exalting Him to His own right hand, God has vindicated Jesus, has declared Him to be right, and by that same token has reversed the world's verdict and shown the world to be wrong and sinful in refusing to believe in Jesus.

3. *"Of judgment,* because the Prince of this world has been judged."

In the first place all Satan's schemes—to have Jesus betrayed, officially condemned by the religious and then by the political authorities, utterly discredited, crucified and destroyed—have been brought to nothing and reversed by Jesus' resurrection.

Secondly, the Prince of this world has been morally defeated. One Man has finally stood firm in His loyalty to God in spite of every Satanic temptation and has been crucified for it: and His faith and loyalty to God have been fully and publicly vindicated. God has raised Him from the dead and placed Him at the pinnacle of universal power.

Thirdly, in the great spiritual contest between Satan and God, Satan has been shown to be a slanderous liar. Ever since Eden Satan had argued that God was against man. But the cross of Christ has shown the opposite. For, on God's side, the death of Christ was God's provision for man's redemption, forgiveness, and reconciliation. In giving His own Son, God has commended His love towards mankind in that Christ has died for them even while they were still sinners, ungodly, and enemies of God (Rom. 5:6-11). The most violent rebel can be forgiven and reconciled; the filthiest sinner can be justified and cleansed and all free and for nothing by God's grace. None need perish. If any do, none, not even Satan himself, will be able to argue that it was God's fault. Satan's age-long lie has been shown to be what it is.

And fourthly, Satan's moral and spiritual defeat has sounded his death knell; which in turn warns those who persist in taking his side, that they must one day share his doom.

THE SEQUEL

The disciples may not have understood all this very clearly, if at all, at the time. But when we open the Acts of the Apostles and observe how they witnessed on the Day of Pentecost and thereafter, it is evident that the Holy Spirit had come and was doing precisely what Christ had said He would do. The apostles and preachers did not concern themselves with denouncing individual sins, nor with encouraging people to develop worthy virtues. That is not because the early Christians were indifferent to ethical issues and human values: the letters which the apostles wrote to their early converts are full of such moral instruction.

But in their witness to the world, they—or rather the Holy Spirit through them—were preoccupied with one particular sin of overwhelming significance. The resurrection of Christ had demonstrated Him to be the Son of God with power; and the inevitable implication was appalling: Israel had crucified their God-sent Messiah; human beings had killed the Source of their life (3:15); mankind had murdered its Maker. The crucifixion of Christ, as the early Christians saw it (basing themselves on the Bible), was sheer human rage against God: a concerted effort by both Jews and Gentiles to cast off God's restraint and claims upon them (4:23-31). This is no exaggeration. The cross of Christ diagnoses the basic trouble of the whole world at all times. It is not man's hostility to man: that is only a secondary symptom. It is man's hostility to God. The crucifixion of God's Son was but the cone of a volcano through which, at a certain time and place in history, there erupted that deep-lying resentment and rebellion against God which, ever since man first sinned, have smoldered in everybody's heart, religious or irreligious, ancient or modern.

But if this is how, according to the Holy Spirit, the cross of Christ diagnosed and exposed man's sin, the matter was not allowed to rest there. Simultaneously the Holy Spirit proclaimed to all who would hear, that the death of Christ, His resurrection, and His exaltation to the throne of God were the very basis on which God could now offer forgiveness of sins and the gift of His Holy Spirit to all who repented and believed. And this is still the message that we, as the Holy Spirit's junior partners, may and must proclaim as maturing holiness leads us to witness to the world.

26

The Holy Spirit's Witness: Glorifying Christ

> *"I have yet many things to say unto you, but ye cannot bear them now. Howbeit when He, the Spirit of truth, is come, He shall guide you into all the truth: for He shall not speak from Himself but what things soever He shall hear, these shall He speak: and He shall declare unto you the things that are to come. He shall glorify Me: for He shall take of Mine, and shall declare it unto you. All things whatsoever the Father hath are Mine: therefore said I, that He taketh of Mine, and shall declare it unto you"* (Jn. 16:12-15).

By now the little party of eleven apostles, clustered closely round the Lord Jesus to catch His every word, must have been getting near the Garden of Gethsemane. Soon all instruction must cease for the time being. Many things that the Lord had to say to them would have to be left unsaid. It was not simply lack of time that would prevent Him from saying them: it was that the apostles could not have borne them, even if He had said them. Months before, they had come to believe and confess that Jesus was the Christ, the Son of the Living God (Mt. 16:16). But how, before they had seen and felt His glorified, resurrection body and experienced His ascension, could they have formed any adequate concept of these further things: of the fact, for instance, that this One whom they would presently see sweat in agony in the garden, and crucified on a cross and buried in a tomb, was the One through whom the universe was made? He would not, therefore, tell them these further things now; but He would tell them later on. And this is how He would do it.

"I have yet many things to say to you, but you cannot bear them now. But when He, the Spirit of truth comes, He shall guide you into all the truth."

Here, then, is the witness of the Holy Spirit not only to the world, but to the apostles and through them to us; and there were three major things about this witness that the Lord Jesus impressed on the apostles.

The Source of the Truth into Which the Holy Spirit Would Guide the Apostles

Notice that having said that the Spirit "will guide you into all the truth," the Lord Jesus immediately added an explanation as to how the Holy Spirit would be able to do this when the Lord Jesus Himself did not do it during His lifetime on earth. The explanation made clear three important things about the source of the truth that the Holy Spirit would communicate to Christ's disciples:

A. *The Holy Spirit is not Himself an independent source of truth*

"He shall not speak from Himself," says Christ.*

B. *The Holy Spirit does not replace the Lord Jesus as the Teacher of Christ's people*

Yes, of course, the Holy Spirit's gracious, divine ministry includes that of teaching the people of God. Our Lord had earlier said explicitly (14:20): "But the Counselor, the Holy Spirit, whom the Father will send in My Name, He shall teach you all things"; and, of course, the Lord Jesus is not denying here what He said there. But what He is informing us about here is the *source* of the Holy Spirit's teaching: "He shall not speak from Himself, but what things soever He hears, these shall He speak."

---

* Some translations render the Greek: "He shall not speak 'of Himself,' and this has in turn been taken by some to mean 'about Himself.' But that is a mistranslation. The New Testament epistles, inspired by the Holy Spirit, speak much about the Holy Spirit.

So the teaching which the Holy Spirit imparts to the people of God He has first heard from Someone else. From whom? From the Lord Jesus, who in turn received and receives all His words from the Father (see again 14:10: "The words that I say unto you, I speak not from Myself, but the Father abiding in Me").

Let's take an actual example of this which we find in the New Testament itself. The Book of the Revelation describes itself as "The Revelation of Jesus Christ, which God gave Him to show to His servants, even the things which must shortly come to pass." Then it tells us who actually communicated this revelation to Christ's servants and how it was done. Christ Himself communicated it by sending an angel, or messenger, to His servant John: "and He (that is, Christ) sent and signified it by His angel to His servant John" (1:1). For that purpose, John tells us, the Risen Christ appeared to him in a vision in all His majestic glory and personally dictated to him seven letters to be sent, one each, to seven churches in Asia Minor.

Each letter begins with a personal address from the Lord Jesus to the church in question, in which He calls attention to one or more of the features that He displayed in the vision. For example: the first letter begins (2:1), "These things says He who holds the seven stars in His right hand, He who walks in the middle of the seven golden lampstands." This is exactly how John saw Him in the vision, and it leaves no doubt that it is the Lord Jesus who is dictating the letter. But at the end of the letter, the Lord Jesus says: "He who has an ear let him hear what the Spirit is saying to the churches" (2:7). From this we gather that it is the Spirit who is saying what the Lord Jesus is saying to the churches. And then the Lord Jesus ends the letter by saying, "To him who overcomes I (Jesus) will give to eat of the tree of life which is in the paradise of God" (2:7).

From all of this it is clear, then, that the Lord Jesus reveals to His own what God gives Him to reveal; and the Spirit communicates what He hears the Lord Jesus say. The risen Lord Jesus remains the Teacher of His people; Teacher likewise though the Holy Spirit is, He does not replace the Lord Jesus as the Teacher of His people.

C. *The scope of the Holy Spirit's teaching to the apostles*

On this topic the Lord Jesus indicated that the Spirit of Truth would guide the apostles into all the truth, and that He would declare to them the things that are to come (16:13).

To see the proper significance of this wonderful promise we must be good historians and notice to whom the Lord Jesus was speaking when He made the promise: "the Holy Spirit will guide *you* into all the truth." He was talking to the apostles, not to all the subsequent generations of believers. And He was talking about the revelation to His apostles and prophets—who formed the foundation of the church—of truth that no one had ever heard of before because it had not been revealed before. As the Apostle Paul later put it: "By revelation there was made known to me the mystery...which to other generations was not made known unto men as it has now been revealed to His holy apostles and prophets in the Spirit..." (Eph. 3:3, 5). Christ was not talking about that other gracious ministry of the Holy Spirit by which He helps us today, for instance, subjectively to understand more and more the meaning of what the Lord Jesus revealed to His apostles after Pentecost.

Similarly, when He earlier said: "I have yet many things to say to you, but you cannot bear them now," He was not talking to us and telling us that there are many things in the truth which He revealed to His apostles and prophets which we as yet cannot grasp, but which He will explain to us later on; though that may well be true. He was telling His apostles that, though He had already revealed much truth to them, there were still truths which He could not reveal to them at the moment, because they were not yet able to bear them. But after the resurrection, ascension, and the coming of the Holy Spirit at Pentecost they were able to bear these further revelations, and did actually receive them to the full. They were guided into all the truth. And by the time Jude, one of our Lord's half-brothers, wrote his epistle, he could describe the faith as having been "once and for all delivered to the saints" (Jude 3). It would take centuries to understand it fully and to draw out all its implications; but the faith itself would never need addition or modification.

Likewise our Lord's promise that the Holy Spirit would declare to the apostles "the things that were to come," is very carefully worded: not merely 'some coming events' but "*the* things that are to come." That is nothing less than all that God would be prepared to reveal of His divine program for the world. Understanding that program, given to us in the New Testament, has been the work of centuries; and none could rightly claim that he has completely understood it yet. But the program itself was delivered once and for all by the New Testament apostles and prophets; it left no room or need for later additions.

THE PURPOSE AND CONTENT OF THE HOLY SPIRIT'S WITNESS

"He shall glorify Me," said Christ; and this has been the supreme and delightful object of the Holy Spirit right from the very first moment that He came on the Day of Pentecost. Filled with the Holy Spirit, Peter pointed out to the crowd on that occasion not only that the ascension of Jesus had been followed by the pouring out of the Holy Spirit, but that it was the risen and ascended Jesus who Himself had poured out the Holy Spirit: "Being therefore by the right hand of God exalted, and having received from the Father the promise of the Holy Spirit, He (Jesus) has poured forth this which you see and hear" (Acts 2:33). But then the Holy Spirit is not some impersonal power. He is a member of the great Tri-unity that is God. If Jesus Christ, then, has poured out the Holy Spirit, who must Jesus Christ be? Only One who was Himself God could pour out the Spirit of God. And so the Holy Spirit Himself through Peter draws out for the crowd the implication of this amazing phenomenon: "Let all the house of Israel *therefore* know assuredly that God has made this Jesus, whom you crucified, both Lord (in the fullest sense of the term) and Christ" (Acts 2:36). So did the Holy Spirit from the very first glorify the Lord Jesus.

"Moreover," said the Lord Jesus, "He shall glorify Me by taking of what is Mine and declaring it to you." And if we ask, "How much does this phrase, 'What is Mine' comprehend?" the answer Jesus gives is stupendous: "all things whatever the Father has are Mine; that is why I said 'He takes of Mine and shall declare it unto you.'"

Our first reaction to this should be to pause right here and now at this very moment and worship the Lord Jesus in our hearts.

Our second reaction should then be to remember all through life that we shall never know more about God than the Lord Jesus reveals to us through the Spirit. "All things," said Christ on another occasion, "have been committed to Me by My Father...and no one knows the Father except the Son and those to whom the Son chooses to reveal Him" (Mt. 11:27). How could it be otherwise if, as we have just heard the Lord Jesus say, "All things whatever the Father has are Mine"?

This then is, always has been, and always will be, what the Holy Spirit teaches Christ's people. All theories of holiness that claim that by the use of certain disciplines and techniques people can come to a fuller knowledge and vision of God, and a fuller union with God, than Jesus Christ could give us, are thereby shown not to come from the Holy Spirit's teaching. They are false. Let us resolve to shun them entirely.

AN EXAMPLE OF THE HOLY SPIRIT'S MINISTRY OF GLORIFYING CHRIST

Now as we come to the end of this particular lesson, what could be more fitting than to read slowly, attentively, and thoughtfully one instance of the Holy Spirit inspiring an apostle to reveal to us the glories of the Lord Jesus: His relationship with the Father, His relation to creation, and to the reconciliation of the universe, His relationship with the Church, His work on the cross for us in the past, His dwelling in us in the present, and His future manifestation in glory along with His redeemed at His return. And having read these things, let us worship Him once more.

"Giving thanks unto the Father who made us meet to be partakers of the inheritance of the saints in light; who delivered us out of the power of darkness, and translated us into the kingdom of the Son of His love; in whom we have our redemption, the forgiveness of our sins: who is the image of the invisible God, the firstborn of all creation; for in Him were all things created, in the heavens and upon the earth, things visible and things invisible, whether thrones or dominions or principalities or powers; all things have been created through Him, and unto Him; and He is before all things, and in Him all things consist. And He is the head of the body, the church: who is the beginning, the firstborn from the dead; that in all things He might have the pre-eminence. For it was the good pleasure of the Father that in Him should all the fullness dwell; and through Him to reconcile all things unto Himself, having made peace through the blood of His cross; through Him, I say,

whether things upon the earth, or things in the heavens.

And you, being in time past alienated and enemies in your mind in your evil works, yet now hath He reconciled. In the body of His flesh through death, to present you holy and without blemish and unreproveable before Him: ff so be that ye continue in the faith, grounded and steadfast, and not moved away from the hope of the gospel which ye heard, which was preached in all creation under heaven; whereof I Paul was made a minister.

Now I rejoice in my sufferings for your sake, and fill up on my part that which is lacking of the afflictions of Christ in my flesh for His body's sake, which is the church; whereof I was made a minister, according to the dispensation of God which was given me to you-ward, to fulfill the word of God, even the mystery which hath been hid from all ages and generations: but now hath it been manifested to His saints, to whom God was pleased to make known what is the riches of the glory of this mystery among the Gentiles, which is Christ in you, the hope of glory: whom we proclaim, admonishing every man and teaching every man in all wisdom, that we may present every man perfect in Christ; whereunto I labor also, striving according to His working, which worketh in me mightily.

For I would have you know how greatly I strive for you, and for them at Laodicea, and for as many as have not seen my face in the flesh; that their hearts may be comforted, they being knit together in love, and unto all riches of the full assurance of understanding, that they may know the mystery of God, even Christ, in whom are all the treasures of wisdom and knowledge hidden.

This I say, that no one may delude you with persuasiveness of speech. For though I am absent in the flesh, yet am I with you in the spirit, joying and beholding your order, and the steadfastness of your faith in Christ. As therefore ye received Christ Jesus the Lord, so walk in Him, rooted and builded up in Him, and stablished in your faith, even as ye were taught, abounding in thanksgiving. Take heed lest there shall be anyone that maketh spoil of you through his philosophy and vain deceit, after the tradition of men, after the rudiments of the world, and not after Christ: for in Him dwelleth all the fullness of the Godhead bodily, And in Him ye are made full, who is the head of all principality and power: in whom ye were also circumcised with a circumcision not made with hands, in the putting off of the body of the flesh, in the circumcision of Christ; having been buried with Him in baptism, wherein ye were also raised with Him through faith in the working of God, who raised Him from the dead.

And you, being dead through your trespasses and the uncircumcision of your flesh, you, I say, did He quicken together with Him, having forgiven us all our trespasses; having blotted out the bond written in ordinances that was against us, which was contrary to us: and He hath taken it out of the way, nailing it to the cross;...If then ye were raised together with Christ, seek the things that are above, where Christ is, seated on the right hand of God. Set your mind on the things that are above, not on the things that are upon the earth. For ye died, and your life is hid with Christ in God. When Christ, who is our life, shall be manifested, then shall ye also with Him be manifested in glory" (Col. 1:12-2:15; 3:1-4).

27

Christ's Post-Resurrection Appearances: A Source of Irremovable Joy

"A little while, and ye behold Me no more; and again a little while, and ye shall see Me. Some of His disciples therefore said one to another, What is this that He saith unto us, A little while, and ye behold Me not; and again a little while, and ye shall see Me: and, Because I go to the Father? They said therefore, What is this that He saith, A little while? We know not what He saith. Jesus perceived that they were desirous to ask Him, and He said unto them, Do ye inquire among yourselves concerning this, that I said, A little while, and ye behold Me not, and again a little while, and ye shall see Me? Verily, verily, I say unto you, that ye shall weep and lament, but the world shall rejoice: ye shall be sorrowful, but your sorrow shall be turned into joy. A woman when she is in travail hath sorrow, because her hour is come: but when she is delivered of the child, she remembereth no more the anguish, for the joy that a man is born into the world. And ye therefore now have sorrow: but I will see you again, and your heart shall rejoice, and your joy no one taketh away from you. And in that day ye shall ask Me nothing. Verily, verily, I say unto you, If ye shall ask anything of the Father, He will give it you

in My name. Hitherto have ye asked nothing in My name:
ask, and ye shall receive, that your joy may be fulfilled"
(Jn. 16:16-24).

By this time the disciples must have been getting tired, so tired indeed that when they reached the Garden of Gethsemane, they fell asleep when they should have shared Christ's vigil. They had been taught so much in the past few hours, a great deal of it completely new, and some of it very difficult to grasp. One of Christ's statements, in particular, they found very puzzling, and they began to discuss it among themselves, under their breath, so to speak.

The statement was this:

"A little while and you behold Me no more; and again a little while, and you shall see Me."

Two things about it troubled them. First, they found these two short intervals, these two "little whiles," quite incomprehensible. How would He disappear from their sight after a short interval and then after another short interval re-appear to view? And how did the explanation that Christ had given, "Because I go to the Father," help to solve the problem? Perhaps that last phrase meant that very soon He was going to die? That would then account for the first "Yet a little while and you behold Me no more." On the other hand, when people died and their spirits returned to God who gave them, you did not see them again after a short while. What could it all mean? Was He going to come back from the dead? They had seen the widow of Nain's son brought back from the dead (Lk. 7:11-17). Three of them had witnessed Jairus' daughter released from the sleep of death (Lk. 8:49-56). And all of them had witnessed Lazarus being called back to life (Jn. 11). But in all three cases, the people who had been called back to life had then continued living here on earth: obviously they had not "gone to the Father."

It was all very puzzling, and it was not only because they were tired that they could not work it out. To start with, the resurrection of Lazarus, like those of the other two, was not a full resurrection in the same way as Christ's would be. It was what might be better called a revivification. Lazarus was called back to the same kind of physical life in the same kind of physical body as he had had before. His revivification was a sign pointing to the great resurrection, but it was not an instance of that resurrection. Lazarus would eventually die again, and when he did so, his body would be laid in the grave, while he himself would depart to be with Christ in Paradise. There he would have to await the resurrection of the body, so that he might be "clothed upon with his house from heaven" (2 Cor. 5:1-6).

But with Christ things would be very different. He was certainly leaving earth to go to the Father, but not in the form of a disembodied spirit whose body still lay in the tomb. He would rise from the dead with a body still fully human, able to interact with this world, yet already belonging to the world beyond; visible and tangible by His disciples, but already changed and able to ascend into the very presence of God and subsist there eternally. The disciples would therefore actually see Him, touch Him, talk with Him, eat with Him after His resurrection and before He ascended. But His body would have properties that it did not have before. It would be able to appear instantaneously, apparently out of nowhere, and just as instantaneously disappear. And when He eventually ascended, He would not leave that body behind; it would be forever part of Him. At His ascension, He would go to the Father as a complete human being, body, soul, and spirit.

THE UNAVOIDABLE REALITY OF PAIN AND SORROW

The resurrection of Christ, then, would be something absolutely new; nothing like it would ever have been seen before. No wonder the disciples were puzzled by our Lord's remarks, if those remarks needed a resurrection of that kind fully to explain them.

Then, we may well ask, Why did not our Lord put an immediate end to their perplexity by explaining to them in detail the nature of His resurrection-body?

One reason may have been the difficulty of explaining such things in words to them at that late hour. And why attempt to do so, when in three days' time they would learn about it the easier way by actually seeing and touching His resurrection body?

But more probably there was a deeper reason. Their immediate and urgent need was to be prepared for the very intense sorrow and pain that within a few hours they must face. The agonies that Christ Himself would undergo—Gethsemane, the arrest, the trials, the scourging, crucifixion, dereliction and death—all these He had to suffer in a body of flesh and blood like our present bodies. The fact that He would rise again with a glorified body—and knew it—did not diminish His actual sufferings in His body of flesh and blood. His experience would not be that of an angel impervious to physical suffering inflicted by human beings. And, when the apostles saw Him suffer and die, it would be seriously misleading if talk of His resurrection body, only half-understood, had made them think that His sufferings were in any degree unreal or unfelt.

And what is more, the disciples themselves must be allowed to face and feel the full reality of the world's hatred, both to Christ and to them, exhibited in His crucifixion. They must face the worst that the world could do, not only its physical cruelty, but its malicious sense of joy and triumph. The reality of Christ's eventual resurrection would not make their present suffering any less real either. It would rather prepare them for their suffering later on when in the future they were forced to suffer persecution, imprisonment, torture, and death for the sake of their testimony for Christ. The certainty of their own resurrection would not make that suffering less real. To use our Lord's analogy: the prospect of the birth of a child does not make a woman's labor pangs less real.

IRREMOVABLE JOY

On the other hand. when the risen Christ came to them, and they saw Him, and felt Him, and talked with Him, and ate with Him, they found that He was not a disembodied spirit; death had not destroyed His body; no part of Him was dead at all—He was totally alive as a complete human being. Death had not been survived: it had been undone; the body that before His death had been an integral part of His human personality had not been left behind, but resurrected; not superseded, but glorified. When they discovered this, then they would not only rejoice: theirs would be a joy that the world by definition could never take from them. The risen Christ was forever beyond the world's power to harm Him. And more than that! for even a dead body is beyond the power of the persecutor to torture any more. But Christ was alive, not with a maimed body and a diminished personality, but with a human personality totally glorified in all its parts.

This demonstration would serve them well when they, in their turn, came to suffer for Christ; for, to return to Christ's analogy once more, there is nothing like witnessing the joy on the face of a mother after the birth of her baby, to sustain a young mother-to-be in her own labor. Having witnessed Christ's death and then His resurrection, they could never be robbed of their joy again.

And that is why, having experienced this vast event them-selves, the apostles became aware that one of their distinctive qualifications and responsibilities was to be a witness for the resurrection of Christ. When they sought someone to be an apostle in the place of Judas, he must, they said, be a witness not only of Christ's life and ministry on earth, but also of His resur-rection (Acts 1:22). And, presenting his credentials as an apostle, Peter later remarked to the Gentile, Cornelius, "We ate and drank with Christ after He rose from the dead" (Acts 10:41).

We of this century have never seen the risen Lord or touched His resurrection body. But as we bear our testimony to Christ in our generation, let us remember that an indispensable part of our gospel is that "He appeared to Cephas; then to the Twelve; then...to above five hundred brethren at once...then...to James; then to all the apostles; and then...to me (Paul) also" (1 Cor. 15:5-9). And we too have been "begotten again unto a living hope by the resurrection of Christ...wherein we rejoice with joy unspeakable and full of glory" (1 Pet. 1:3, 8). It is this that will give us the courage and strength to endure, whatever hostility the world throws at us.

Joy Filled Full

It is difficult at first sight to imagine what joy there could be beyond seeing the risen Lord; but before this lesson ended the Lord assured the disciples that there would be such joy.

First, He pointed out that in that day they would not need to ask Him questions. This promise must of course be read in its context. They would—and did, so Luke tells us (Acts 1:6)—ask Him for information about various things. But when it came to His resurrection and ascension, the reference to which they found so puzzling at the moment, they would not need to ask

Him for any explanation. The direct experience of these things would be enough. And in an extended sense, this is true of all believers even though they have not physically seen the risen Lord. They do not have to ask agonizing questions about the ascension, or demand explanations as to how the Lord Jesus can still have a human body and be in the presence of God and yet be with and in every one of His people here on earth. A believer, because he knows God as a child knows its father, knows without question that these things are true. We, as scientists, ask questions about birds: how do they manage to fly; how do they know to migrate at the right time, in the right direction to the right places even when they have never done it before? But birds don't need to ask such questions. Their "knowledge" of these things is part of their very life as birds. And so it is with believers: since they share the life of the risen Saviour, they instinctively know the witness of the apostles to be true, the resurrection and ascension of Christ to be facts.

ASKING IN THE NAME OF THE LORD JESUS

But experience of the risen Christ and of His 'going to the Father' would make a profound difference to their praying. They had been used to praying to God; but never before had they asked for anything from God in the name of Jesus, any more than they would have asked God for anything in the name of some now dead saint like Moses, or Jeremiah, or of one of their saintly contemporaries. But when they saw the risen Christ ascend, and under the Holy Spirit's instruction came to understand what it meant for Him, who had come forth from the Father, to return to the Father, they would find that if they asked the Father for things which Jesus had taught them to ask for and which they could thus ask for in His name, the Father would grant their requests. And their joy in consequence would be filled full. Experience would thus show that the Jesus who had lived and walked and talked with them on earth was now not only at the pinnacle and throne of the universe, but at the heart of the Godhead.

28

Christ's Farewell Exhortation and Assurance of Victory

"These things have I spoken unto you in proverbs: the hour cometh, when I shall no more speak unto you in proverbs, but shall tell you plainly of the Father. In that day ye shall ask in My name: and I say not unto you, that I will pray the Father for you; for the Father Himself loveth you, because ye have loved Me, and have believed that I came forth from the Father. I came out from the Father, and am come into the world: again, I leave the world, and go unto the Father. His disciples say, Lo, now speakest Thou plainly, and speakest no proverb. Now know we that Thou knowest all things, and needest not that any man should ask Thee; by this we believe that Thou camest forth from God. Jesus answered them, Do ye now believe? Behold, the hour cometh, yea, is come, that ye shall be scattered, every man to his own, and shall leave Me alone: and yet I am not alone, because the Father is with Me. These things have I spoken unto you, that in Me ye may have peace. In the world ye have tribulation: but be of good cheer; I have overcome the world" (Jn. 16:25-33).

As in any good and efficient school, so in the school of Christ: the final session was devoted to summarizing the essential point which the disciples must grasp and remember. Much of the surrounding detail could be left for the Holy Spirit to bring back to

221

their memories later on, but two basic and essential points from all that Christ had taught them must now be summarized and riveted on their memories and understandings.

THE ESSENTIAL TEACHING ABOUT THE FATHER

"These things have I spoken to you," said Christ—but the word He used next has been variously translated. Some have rendered it 'in proverbs,' and others 'in parables.' But in this context it means rather 'enigmatically,' that is, 'in cryptic language.' "These things," then, "I have spoken to you in cryptic language," said Christ; "but the hour comes when I shall no longer speak to you in cryptic language, but shall tell you plainly of the Father."

THE ENIGMATIC REVELATION

Looking back over the records of His public ministry in the four Gospels, we can see that there had always been a certain enigma in the way He had spoken of Himself, of His "coming down from heaven," of His relationship with the Father, and especially of His death and going away; and we can but admire the divine wisdom and grace that moved Him to reveal His relationship with the Father in this gradual and cryptic way. He had not called on Peter the very first time He met him, nor on Andrew, nor on any of the Eleven, to accept and believe that He, the Carpenter of Nazareth, was the One by whom the universe was created. What could they possibly have made of such a statement at that time?

No, He had let them listen to the testimony of His Forerunner, John the Baptist, then watch the humility, yet the nobility, of His own deportment. They were struck by the self-evident wisdom and authority of His teaching; they felt the strange, irresistible power of His call that made them leave their fishing-nets and follow Him. Then they discovered, sometimes by uncomfortable personal experience, that He knew what was in man and did not need anyone to tell Him. There were moments when in His presence they felt an awesome holiness; and sin, hidden so deep in their hearts that they had not realized it was there, was exposed in all its uncleanness. Yet they were simultaneously astonished at His claim to have authority to forgive sins—and His evident ability to use that authority effectively—that had people gasping, "Who is this who forgives sins? Who can forgive sins but God alone?"

Of course, He had also done astounding miracles of superhuman power, which showed, He said, that He had been sent by the Father. But then Moses had done great miracles, and so had Elijah and Elisha, which showed that they too had been sent by God. But none of those three had ever claimed to be one with the Father. Of course they hadn't; they were the strictest of monotheistic Israelites. Yet the words that Jesus had spoken in explanation of His miracles had gone far beyond anything that any ancient prophet had said. When at Moses' word there came down manna from heaven to feed the Israelites in the desert, Moses did not turn round and say, "See! I am the Manna of Life." But when Christ miraculously multiplied a few loaves and fishes and fed a vast crowd of people, He startled them afterwards by stating, "I am the Bread of Life which came down from heaven;" and for many people He was self-evidently so, for they found He was able to satisfy their soul's hunger as nothing else had done.

"I am the Light of the World; I am the Good Shepherd; I am the Resurrection and the Life:" so had He gradually built up in their minds their early understandings of who He was; until on one occasion He had actually taken to Himself the awesome, personal Name of God, and said, "If you believe not that I Am, you shall die in your sins" (Jn. 8:24). Some of the Jews, catching the implication of His words, said it was blasphemy and picked up stones to stone Him. But others, the disciples included, could not bring themselves to believe that One they knew to be so holy, who had done such miracles as were incontrovertibly the work of God, would or could have spoken blasphemously. And all this while as they had been observing Jesus, the Father was working in their hearts, unknown to them, till when Jesus challenged them to say who they thought He was, Peter replied for them all: "Thou art the Christ, the Son of the Living God." And Christ had commented: "Flesh and blood has not revealed this to you, but My Father who is in heaven" (Mt. 16:17).

Yes, they had come a long way on the road of discovery as to who Jesus was. And yet the enigma remained. True, on the Mount of Transfiguration they had seen the Cloud, the emblem of God's presence, and heard the Voice out of the Cloud say of

Jesus, "This is My beloved Son." But the vision passed; and they were left with the ever increasing question: What amazing relationship did this word 'Son' imply? And how would all this be reconciled with His ever more frequent statements that He must die, go away, go back to the One who sent Him, go to the Father?

When, therefore, in the Upper Room, Jesus had called on them to place in Him that same unlimited faith as they had hitherto placed in God, Philip, we remember, had requested that now, at last, He should show them the Father. But Christ simply said, "He who has seen Me has seen the Father. Don't you believe that I am in the Father and the Father in Me?" The enigma remained. There came no exhibition of the majesty of God, not even such as Israel was allowed to see burning like fire and lightning on Sinai. And for a very good reason: they would have recoiled in terror from such an exhibition.

If then, right from the beginning, Jesus had both announced and exhibited the divine majesty of His essential relationship with the Father, one of the major purposes of the Incarnation would have been frustrated. They might still have fallen flat on their faces and acknowledged Him as the Creator in whom, by whom, and for whom, the universe was created. But God was seeking a relationship with men infinitely higher than that of a Creator with His creatures. He wanted to raise His creatures, by a spiritual 'birth from above' to a relationship of children, and then grown-up sons, with the Father. And that spiritual birth would depend on their forming a one-to-one personal relationship with His Son. That in turn would depend on their being attracted to Him, and unafraid of Him, with growing faith, and an ever-deepening understanding, with enough revealed of Himself at any one time to draw out their faith and love still more, yet never so much that it overwhelmed their human personalities and made it impossible for them to act as friends toward Him.

Many nations have in their folklore the story of a royal prince who unaccountably falls in love with a poor girl in the town. Determining to win her as his bride, he leaves the palace, puts on ordinary clothes, approaches her as an ordinary man, though somewhat above her level and handsome not only in looks but more importantly in his demeanor and behavior. Yet generally he hides his glory so that she should not be afraid of him, nor, at the other extreme, love him simply for the sake of his wealth and position and not for his own sake. And then when he has won her heart and she has demonstrated her loyalty to him, gradually he reveals to her, so the story goes, ever more of his wealth and majesty until the stunning glory of the public wedding and the eventual coronation.

Such—not in folklore, but in historical reality—is the story of the Incarnation of God's Son, when He came to earth truly Man, yet God of very God, to seek us for Himself. And what can we say but to exclaim, Oh blessed enigma! Great is the mystery of godliness: God was manifest in the flesh (1 Tim. 3:16).

THE PLAIN REVELATION OF THE FATHER

But this enigmatic way of speaking, geared to their present limited powers of understanding, was not going to last forever. "The hour comes," said Christ, "when I shall no longer speak to you in obscure and cryptic phrases, but shall tell you openly and plainly of the Father." And that hour came with His death, resurrection, and ascension.

His resurrection demonstrated, more eloquently than words could, that He was "the Son of God with power" (Rom. 1:4).

His resurrection also demonstrated that the cross was neither an accident nor a disaster, and it was certainly not inconsistent with the Being and character of God. It was, in fact, the clearest expression of the heart of God in all earth's history. The Center Point of time and eternity, planned by God before the foundation of the world by His determinate counsel and foreknowledge (1 Pet. 1:20; Acts 2:23), foretold in the prophecies of the Old Testament (Lk. 24:25-27) and carried out at God's appointed hour, it was the mightiest, profoundest, and utterly unambiguous telling out of the Father's heart that man could ever hope for, or God Himself devise.

God possesses almighty power; but the Bible nowhere says that God is power—it says that God is love. If that, then, is what the Father is really like, where could we perceive it better than in the cross of Christ? "Herein was the love of God manifested in us, that God has sent His only begotten Son into the world that we might live through Him. Herein is love, not that we loved God, but that He loved us, and sent His Son to be the propitiation for our sins.... The Father has sent the Son to be the Saviour of the world" (1 Jn. 4:9-10, 14).

But Christ would not even so be content. What if He told out the Father's character to the full at Calvary, but we, for our part, were unable to take it in? And so to complete His plain and open revelation of the Father He would, after His ascension, send the Holy Spirit to every one of His people to pour out the love of God in their hearts to secure their subjective grasp and enjoyment of that love.

THE CHIEF POINT TO BE GRASPED

However much or little, then, the apostles had understood of all that Christ had taught them up to this point, the chief point that they needed to grasp was this: "The Father Himself loves you" (16:27). It is still the chief thing that every one of Christ's disciples needs to grasp, be he or she a new convert or an aged saint. For as we wrestle with life's problems, as we try to shoulder our Christian responsibilities, or even as we try to work out the doctrinal and theological implications of our faith, it is easy to let fade from our minds the sense of the Father's direct, personal, love of each one of us. Lose that sense of His love, and we could turn our very prayer-life into a burden, weighed down by doubt and fear.

Our Lord, for instance, had told them in the previous lesson that after His resurrection and ascension they would be able to make requests of the Father in His name; and that the Father would honor His name and give them what they asked for. But He foresaw that without further instruction they might misread even this gracious promise. They might think that the reason why they had to pray in the Name of the Lord Jesus was that the Father Himself was not really interested in them, and would be unlikely to grant their requests unless cajoled and persuaded to do so by the Lord Jesus.

Of course, that was not so at all. The Father Himself loves you," says Christ. When you make your requests of Him in My

* The Greek word for 'ask' (aiteō) in the first part of verse 26 means 'to ask for something,' 'to make a request.' The Greek word for 'pray' or 'ask' in the second half of that verse (erōtaō) means here 'to enquire of someone about something or about someone.'

name, I shall never need to come and enquire of Him, "Why have you not attended to the requests My disciples have made? Why have you not granted them?"* "The Father Himself loves you," says Christ, "and can be trusted to grant your requests that are consistent with My name."

It is true, of course, that Christ does now act as our Intercessor before God, and in that capacity He does pray for us. We shall have an example of it as soon as this lesson is over. But He does not have to intercede for us because God, left to Himself, would be against us. His appointment as our Intercessor is itself an expression of God's love for us and of His determination to do us good (Heb. 5:1-10; 7:20-25).

And finally, let us notice that when Christ assured His apostles that the Father Himself loved them, He was not thinking of that general love which God has for all His creatures, but of that special love and affection that the Father has for those who love His Son and have believed that Jesus came forth from the Father (16:27). To love sinners while they were still sinners cost God the pains of Calvary, which He willingly endured. To those who persist in spurning that love, who trample underfoot the Son of God and consider His blood worthless, God's response must be everlasting indignation (Heb. 10:28-29). But when people respond to God's love by accepting and loving His Son as the love-gift of the Father's heart, then it draws forth a response of love and affection for the Father that is beyond all bounds.

THE ESSENTIAL TEACHING ABOUT CHRIST HIMSELF

And now the time had come to test whether the disciples had truly grasped what was the most important thing of all that He had taught them about Himself. The validity of all He had ever said depended on this great fundamental fact:

"I came out from the Father and have come into the world. Again, I leave the world, and go unto the Father" (16:28).

There spoke One who, with the Father and the Holy Spirit, was part of the Tri-unity that is God. No Old Testament prophet, not even the greatest of them, had ever said anything like this. Elijah had referred to God as "the Lord, the God of Israel, before whom I stand" (1 Ki. 17:1). The angel Gabriel announced, "I am Gabriel who stands in the presence of God" (Lk. 1:19). But neither prophet nor angel could say, "I came out from the Father:

again I leave the world and go to the Father."

This, then, the apostles, and all the Christians that came after them, would need to understand, believe and hold to firmly as they went out to witness to Christ in face of the colossal pressures of the world. To see why that was so, let us use a piece of Old Testament history as an illustration.

The Book of Genesis (ch. 15) tells us that God called the patriarch Abraham and appointed him to be the Original Ancestor of a new nation that God would raise up to carry a special role in history. God then outlined to Abraham what the course of this nation would be. At a certain time in history, the nation, now known as Israelites, would be led to emigrate from Canaan to Egypt. But eventually the Egyptians would oppose them; and God would then intervene to set them free and bring them out of Egypt to their Promised Land of Canaan. And so it turned out (see Ex. 1-12).

But the point we need to notice is this. When God sent Moses as His people's deliverer into Egypt to demand of Pharaoh, the king of Egypt, that he let God's people go, Moses presented that demand on the following grounds: "Long ago," he said, "before this people came into Egypt, God had dealings with their ancestors, made a covenant with them, and revealed His purposes to them. The people would at a certain point in history enter Egypt and live there. But the stay was never intended to be permanent. God had a future for them outside of Egypt in the land that God had promised to their ancestors to give them. Now, therefore, the time has come for their release from Egypt: Pharaoh must let them go."

And Pharaoh's reaction? Why, he laughed in Moses' face. To start with, he did not recognize Moses' God. He dismissed as empty legend the whole idea that the nation had had a past in which God had revealed His purposes for them to their ancestors. He denied also the whole idea that the nation had a future outside of Egypt; and as for their belief that there existed a Promised Land to which God was going to bring them one day—it was nothing more than a fairy tale, which his officers in the labor-camps would soon knock out of their heads. As far as the Israelites were concerned, Egypt was the only world there was; and life for them would never be anything else than work, eating, sleeping, and eventually death.

And so, in order to deliver the Israelites, God had, of course, to destroy Pharaoh. But even before He did that, He had to get the Israelites to believe that Moses had indeed been sent into Egypt by God and that there was in all sober reality a Promised Land outside of Egypt to which Moses, if they believed him, would bring them.

This ancient story becomes a parable for us. Satan, the Prince of this World, has persuaded millions of people that this world is the only world there is. He has persuaded them that there was never any divine purpose behind the creation of the universe, since there was, and is, no God. And he has convinced them to believe that there is no heaven beyond this life. All talk of the Paradise of God, according to him, is a fairy tale; and he has persuaded millions, who do not know enough about the philosophy of science to see through his lie, that belief in God and heaven is somehow unscientific. In this way Satan has, for them, turned this world into a prison-house and life within it into literally hopeless existence.

To deliver mankind from this poverty-stricken bondage, God has sent His Son Jesus Christ into the world. But if ever we are going to be delivered, there is one thing above all others that we must come to see and believe. And that is not simply Christ's ethical teachings. It is this: "I came out from the Father," says Christ, "and have come into the world." So then, this world is not the only world there is! Nor is this world self-made. Behind and before it stands the Father. "Again," says Christ, "I leave the world and go to the Father." So then, this world is not the end: there is life beyond it. Since this is true, Satan's lie is exposed; and for those who believe Christ, Satan's power to turn this world into a prison house is broken.

CHRIST'S CHALLENGE TO HIS DISCIPLES

But did Christ's disciples believe this? They said they did. Indeed they claimed that now at last Christ had spoken plainly. They could see that He knew everything, and that no one need ask Him for further clarification: "by this we believe," they assured Him, "that You came forth from God."

Doubtless they meant every word. But it is one thing to say you have understood your lessons perfectly: it is another thing when faced with an examination to demonstrate that you have.

In His mercy, therefore, Christ gently questioned their excessive self-assurance: "Do you now believe?" Within a few hours an examination of the utmost severity would confront them. Their faith would waver, their grasp of the truth would prove to be not as firm as they had thought: they would desert Christ and run away to protect their lives and interests in this world.

THE ASSURANCE OF VICTORY

Would all then be lost? No, indeed. Standing alone with none but the Father with Him, Christ would face all that the world and its Prince could bring against Him, torture and death included. And He would triumph. "Be of good courage," He said, even as His disciples were about to lose their nerve and for the moment run away defeated. "In the world you shall have tribulation; but in Me you may have peace. I have overcome the world." He would lay low the Satanic jailer. He would burst the bars of His prison-world. His death and resurrection would fling its doors wide open; and as He strode out victorious and ascended to the Father, He would share His victory with all His people. In Christ they too would be more than conquerors through Him that loved them (Rom. 8:37). "For I am persuaded that neither death nor life, nor angels nor principalities nor powers, nor things present, nor things to come, nor height, nor depth, nor any other creature shall be able to separate us from the love of God that is in Christ Jesus our Lord."

If we in our generation would rise up and witness to the reality of Christ before our contemporaries, we too must learn the secret of overcoming the world. And here it is in the words of one of Christ's apostles: "For whatever is begotten of God overcomes the world. And this is the victory that overcomes the world, even our faith. Who is he that overcomes the world, but he who believes that Jesus is the Son of God" (1 Jn. 5:4-5).

THE COURSE: PART THREE

A. The Teacher Prays

29

The Son Reports to the Father

And now Christ's formal teaching on holiness was over for the time being. His disciples would of course learn profound and deeply moving lessons as they watched Him face the conflict of Gethsemane and the appalling sufferings of the cross. But comparatively few words would now pass between Him and them until He came to them in the ecstatic joy and wonder of the Resurrection-day.

But while formal teaching must cease for the time being, the Teacher's work was not yet finished. Up to this point He had been talking to His disciples about the Father; now He must talk to the Father about His disciples. He will report how well He has taught them and how well they have received and believed what they have been taught.

There are always two sides to any teacher-student relationship in school. On the student's side there is the question of their willingness to learn, their diligence in study, and their ability to take in and assimilate what they are taught. And at this level we have already heard the Lord Jesus, somewhat earlier in the evening, remark that He was limited in what He could tell them at the time because of their inability to cope with anything more (16:12).

But success in learning does not all depend on the students; for on the other side there is the question of the teacher: can he communicate his subject efficiently? Is he able to explain the profoundest things clearly and simply so that even a student with limited powers can grasp them?

And this question assumes supreme importance when the subject to be taught is the knowledge of God on which our eternal salvation depends. For if our salvation ultimately depended on our intelligence and ability to learn, who could possibly be saved? No, in this matter all depends on the ability of the One whom God sent to be our Teacher. He knew His subject perfectly. And He knew His students perfectly, knew the way the human mind worked, for He had made them; and, what is more, He had become human Himself. With Him as Teacher, none who wished to know God would fail to know Him.

THE SON REPORTS TO THE FATHER
ON HIS PERFORMANCE OF HIS MISSION

"These things spake Jesus; and lifting up His eyes to heaven, He said, Father, the hour is come; glorify Thy Son, that the Son may glorify Thee: even as Thou gavest Him authority over all flesh, that whatsoever Thou hast given Him, to them He should give eternal life. And this is life eternal, that they should know Thee the only true God, and Him whom Thou didst send, even Jesus Christ. I glorified Thee on the earth, having accomplished the work which Thou hast given Me to do. And now, O Father, glorify Thou Me with Thine own self with the glory which I had with Thee before the world was" (Jn. 17:1-5).

HOW WELL HE HAS EXPOUNDED HIS SUBJECT

First let us notice how He defines the subject He has been teaching: "You gave Him (Your Son) authority over all flesh, that whatever You have given Him to them He should give eternal life. And this is eternal life, that they should know You and Jesus Christ whom You have sent."

From this we learn a number of fundamentally important things:

1. Holiness, which we have been studying all through this book, is not a subject like chemistry or physics. In physics, for instance, it is enough if a student learns Einstein's famous formula: he does not need to know anything about Einstein, still less to get to know Einstein personally and form a relationship with him. But to be truly holy means getting to know not a sub-

ject but a person, and that Person is God, and getting to know Him, not in the sense of merely learning a lot about Him (important as that is) but getting to know Him person to Person.

2. Then we should notice that there is a big difference between getting to know a thing, and getting to know a person. Take an atom, for instance. If you want to learn all there is to be known about an atom, you can put it in a cyclotron, bombard it with high-powered particles, and eventually the atom will yield up all its secrets. It can't help doing so: it is only a thing.

But you can't get to know a person that way. You could put my brain in a brain scanner, measure its electrical wave patterns and discharges, analyze the chemistry of the brain cells, compute the blood pressure, and submit the brain to every test known to science—and you would still not know me. For I am not a thing but a person; and unless I allow you to get to know me by communicating by mind and heart to you, you will never know me. You may get to know a lot about me, but not me myself.

In that same way, only more so, no one gets to know God unless God allows that person to get to know Him, by communicating Himself to him.

3. But to allow a human being to get to know Him in this direct and personal way, God has to impart to them not merely information, but His own very life. For eternal life of which the Bible speaks is not simply another way of referring to survival after death, or even of "going to heaven when you die" (though, of course, both these things are involved). Eternal life consists in knowing the only true God and Jesus Christ who was sent into our world by God—knowing them person to Person in a living relationship. And that is why, incidentally, the Bible speaks of every believer already having eternal life and enjoying it while still here on this earth long before they go off to heaven. For, as we hear Christ saying in His prayer, the Father gave Him authority to give this eternal life to as many as God gave Him.

4. But holiness means not only getting to know God, but believing Him, loving Him, being loyally devoted to Him. To the Son of God, then, was given this high task: He must visit our world, and, in face of all the slanders about God which Satan had infiltrated in men's heart, reveal God to men as He really is, in all His love and purity, His majesty, grace, and beauty. In a

word, it was the Son's mission so to glorify God among men, that He would change the way men thought of God, to turn them from being haters of God to lovers of God, from being indifferent to God to being passionately devoted to Him as the All-Wonderful, All-Glorious, All-Worshipful Father.

If this, then, was the subject which the Teacher had to expound, how well did He expound it? Perfectly and to the full! Listen again as He reports to the Father: "I have glorified Thee on the earth, having finished the work which Thou hast given Me to do." As He said this, He was doubtless looking back over the whole of His life hitherto. But He was also looking forward. For, as He Himself remarked to His Father, "The hour had come," the hour that had been planned before the foundation of the world, the hour when, by His mighty work on the cross, He would show to the world His love for God and what He thought of God; and simultaneously reveal what the God of all holiness thought of the world's sin, and how the God of all love loved them in spite of it. The cross of Christ would say it all. Never to all eternity would anyone ever discover something about the heart and character of God that was not revealed at Calvary.

So the hour had come, and Christ stood ready, as soon as His prayer was finished, to cross the brook Kidron, and set foot in Gethsemane, there to begin the overture of the mighty work of the cross. And so confident was He of completing that work to the eternal and infinite glory of God, that He referred to it already in the past tense: "I have glorified Thee on the earth in finishing the work that Thou gavest Me to do."

Yet to complete that exhibition of the character of God, one further and final step would have to be taken, and that by God Himself. "I have glorified Thee on the earth," said Christ; "and now, O Father, glorify Thou Me with Thine own self with the glory which I had with Thee before the world was." That is, the Father must respond to the Son's supreme devotion by raising Him from the dead and exalting Him to the place of glory He enjoyed along with the Father before creation. For if—to think the unthinkable—God had failed to authenticate the sacrifice of His Son by raising Him from the dead, and had left His death to be slanderously misinterpreted by His perverted critics, or pilloried by atheists as an example of how all belief in, and devotion to, God is a superstition that ends in the dust of an eternal grave—then heaven itself would have turned black, and the very character of God would have been destroyed forever.

But there was never any danger of that. With supreme confidence in the Father He knew, loved, and expounded to men, the Son of God called on His Father to complete the revelation of His name by raising His Son from the dead and glorifying Him with the erstwhile glory of His eternal Sonship. And that glorification of Christ alongside the Father would not only restore the Son to His pre-creation honor: it would tell the world that in seeing Jesus they had seen the Father.

THE TEACHER REPORTS HOW WELL HIS DISCIPLES HAVE LEARNED THEIR LESSONS

"I manifested Thy name unto the men whom Thou gavest Me out of the world; Thine they were, and Thou gavest them to Me; and they have kept Thy word. Now they know that all things whatsoever Thou hast given Me are from Thee: for the words which Thou gavest Me I have given unto them; and they received them, and knew of a truth that I came forth from Thee, and they believed that Thou didst send Me" (Jn. 17:6-8).

The report reads very well:

1. "They have kept Thy word";
2. "Now they know that all things whatever Thou hast given Me are from Thee";
3. "They have received the words Thou gavest Me to give to them";
4. "They have known of a truth that I came forth from Thee";
5. "They have believed that Thou didst send Me."

Full marks then? But the credit for this triumphant result belongs not to the disciples but rather to the Teacher. For consider how, and by what means, He drew out their faith and elicited their love and devotion to God.

A. First of all, He manifested God's Name to them:

This may well remind us once more of the way God delivered the Israelites from Egypt. The situation was, you remember, that that generation of Israelites had never known anything other than the most bitter slavery under the seemingly unbreakable power of the Pharaoh of Egypt. Escape or rebellion were both self-evidently impossible, when Moses came with the message that God had sent him to deliver them. How could he possibly expect the Israelites to believe either him or his talk about God?

But Moses had anticipated the problem, and when God commissioned him, he asked: "When I come to the children of Israel and say to them, The God of your fathers has sent me to you, and they say to me, What is His name?, what shall I say to them?" "I AM THAT I AM," God replied, "Thus shalt thou say unto the Israelites, I AM has sent me to you." Moreover God said: "Thus shalt thou say to the Israelites, 'The Lord, the God of your fathers, the God of Abraham, the God of Isaac, and the God of Jacob, has sent me to you: this is My name forever, and this is My memorial to all generations'" (Ex. 3:13-15).

And so Moses went to the Israelites and proclaimed the Name of God, I AM THAT I AM, the Self-Existent, and Eternal One, who, when He enters into relationship with any one of His creatures, be it Abraham or Isaac or whoever, remains utterly and undeviatingly constant and unchangingly and eternally loyal to that person; He will faithfully fulfill all His promises, and in His power and compassion will certainly save them.

Listening to the proclamation of that name, the Israelites found their hearts moved, their spirits stirred. God had remembered them because He was the kind of God He was. He would not take up any of His creatures, profess to love them, make promises to them, and then, growing tired of them, abandon and forget them as a child discards a toy in which it has lost interest. Moreover, this eternal, unchanging God was not remote or unfeeling; He had seen their pains and sorrows, heard their groanings, and had come down to deliver them (Ex. 3:6-8).

So Israel believed both Moses and the God whose name he expounded. For faith is not working oneself up into a feeling of confident conviction: faith is our response to the revealed character of God. It is a faintly similar situation when a man comes to love and trust a woman enough to marry her. He does not have to work himself up into some feeling of confidence. He sees her beauty and is attracted; observes her grace and kindness and loyalty and finds his heart drawn out to her so much that he is prepared by an act of the will to commit himself to her in a life-long relationship.

What Moses did for the Israelites, Christ did for His disciples, and for all mankind. He made known God's name, expounded God's character in word and action; and supremely by His death on the cross showed us God's infinite love and loyalty to us, His creatures. God's very own Son would suffer and die rather than that any perish.

B. Secondly, the Lord Jesus not only expounded God's name, and not only conveyed God's word, that is, God's message (17:6), but the very words in which He did so were words given to Him by the Father:

And so it was that the disciples did not have to get behind the actual words which Jesus used in order to come at the message that God had for them. The very words in which He conveyed the message were the words of God. And the disciples perceived it was so, and came to realize that everything Christ had was given Him by the Father. Hence arose their absolutely certain knowledge that the Lord Jesus came forth from God; and they believed that God had sent Him.

And still today that is how faith comes. "Faith comes by hearing," says the Bible (Rom. 10:17), "and hearing by the word of God." God is His own evidence: His words carry their own divine power to convince people of their truth, and so to draw out their faith and trust. The reason why many people do not believe is that they never listen to God's words, never read the Bible. They will listen to many people's arguments for and against the existence of God, for and against religion; and these arguments may, or may not, be helpful. But if we are going to trust a person, we must listen to that person's words. And if we are going to trust God, we must listen personally and directly to God's words. It was God's words that Jesus spoke. We do not need to be enormously clever, or brilliantly intellectual, or trained theologians: we can hear, or read, Christ's words and take them at their face value. When He says, "Verily, verily, I say unto you, He that heareth My word, and believeth Him that sent Me, hath eternal life, and cometh not into judgment, but hath passed out of death into life" (Jn. 5:24)—these are God's words addressed to us personally. We can believe and receive them simply and straight-forwardly and in so doing receive eternal life. For as the Gospel elsewhere puts it: "He who has received (Jesus') witness, has set his seal to this, that *God* is true; for He whom God has sent speaks the words of God" (Jn. 3:33-34).

30

The Son Prays for the Preservation of His Disciples' Faith

"I pray for them: I pray not for the world, but for those whom Thou hast given Me; for they are Thine: and all things that are Mine are Thine, and Thine are Mine: and I am glorified in them. And I am no more in the world, and these are in the world, and I come to Thee. Holy Father, keep them in Thy name which Thou hast given Me, that they may be one, even as We are. While I was with them, I kept them in Thy name which Thou hast given Me: and I guarded them, and not one of them perished, but the son of perdition; that the scripture might be fulfilled. But now I come to Thee; and these things I speak in the world, that they may have My joy fulfilled in themselves" (Jn. 17:9-13).

So there they stood, the eleven disciples, awed into silence as they listened to the Son of God praying to the Father for them. They had believed on Him, and believing in Him had believed in the Father. But the practical question that arose was this: they were believers now, but would they remain believers forever? Would their faith hold firm in the face of the storm that was about to break around them? And throughout all life's changes right to the end? Or could it be that persecution, or illness, or bereavement, or disaster, or sorrow might come upon them so severely that it would break their faith, sever them from Christ, and land them in perdition forever? This is a question that sooner or later every believer must face; and therefore it is of the utmost importance that we listen now to what our Lord had to say about it.

THE ISSUE AT STAKE

Our Lord had, of course, foreseen the problem, and was aware of exactly in what sense their faith would need to be guarded and maintained. They had been believers in God's existence even before they had encountered Jesus. Jesus never had to convert them to faith in God's existence. But Jesus had summoned them to believe in Himself with a faith equal to that which they placed in God. In one and the same breath He had said: "You believe in God: believe also in Me."

Many a Jew at the time had considered it the height of blasphemy for Jesus to demand that people should put equal faith in Him as they did in God. But the disciples had done so, and it was not blasphemous: they had, said Christ, been given to Him by the Father. "Thine they were (as believers in God) and Thou hast given them to Me" (17:6), so as to become believers in Christ, to belong to Him in the same absolute sense as they belonged to God. "I am praying," said Christ, "for those whom Thou hast given Me; for they are Thine." Believing in Christ did not take them from God, or diminish their absolute loyalty to God; and for Christ to be glorified in His disciples did not detract from the glory of the Father. For "all things that are Mine," said Christ, "are Thine, and Thine are Mine." Christ was, and is, the Son of the Father. One with the Father.

But after He had gone, His disciples had to go out and face their fellow-nationals who claimed to believe in God, and were, many of them, zealously religious; but they regarded Jesus as a blasphemer, and were prepared to persecute any who believed on Him. The danger was, therefore, that under persecution the disciples might be tempted to think that they could give up faith in the deity of Jesus, and yet still retain faith in God.

That, of course, is impossible. John, the Apostle, had subsequently to warn his fellow believers: "Whoever denies the Son,

242

the same has not the Father" (1 Jn. 2:23). Nonetheless, it has all down the centuries been a temptation to many people to think that they can still be believers in God, and even still call themselves Christians, even if they regard Jesus merely as man "uniquely in touch with God," or "the greatest of religious leaders" or something similar, but are not prepared to confess that Jesus is one with the Father, and that the Word of God who was eternally with God, and was God, became flesh in Jesus and dwelt among us. Indeed in the West this temptation has not only been rampant in theological circles during the last hundred years, but widely succumbed to.

THE TRUTH ABOUT APOSTATES

It raises the gravest of questions. People who in this sense abandon faith in the deity of the Lord Jesus, and do so deliberately and permanently—were they ever true believers in Christ to start with? The Bible's answer is, No!

Hear it first, once more (see pp. 162-163 for an earlier discussion) from the Apostle John (1 Jn. 2:18-29). He speaks of people who once associated with the apostles and with Christians in general, but who later denied that Jesus was the Son of God. And he bluntly says, "They went out from us (doctrinally, if not physically), *but they were not of us.* For if they had been of us, they would have continued with us; but they went out that they might be made manifest how that they all are not of us."

And then John proceeds to make a clear-cut distinction between these who "went out," and true believers. Of the latter he says, "And you have an anointing from the Holy One, and you know all things. I have not written to you because you do not know the truth, but because you know it, and because no lie is of the truth. Who is the liar but he who denies that Jesus is the Christ…He who denies the Son, the same has not the Father."

A true believer knows instinctively that Jesus is the Son of God; for he knows that his forgiveness, reconciliation, and peace with God, indeed his whole salvation, depends on the fact that the Son of God loved him and gave Himself up to the curse of God's law in his place, and died a substitutionary death for him. But no merely human being, however holy, could offer himself as a substitutionary sacrifice to God on behalf of another human being, let alone for the sins of the whole world. A true believer understands this instinctively and knows that any doctrine that denies the deity of the Lord Jesus is a lie.

Our Lord's Implied Verdict

Returning to our Lord's prayer, we learn the same lesson from Him as we have just learned from the Apostle John. He begins by explicitly excluding the world from the scope of His prayer: "I am not praying for the world..." He did not mean that, unlike His Father, He did not love the world and long for their salvation (see 3:16). Nor did He mean that, unlike the Apostle Paul, He was not prepared to pray for the salvation of the world (see Rom. 10:1; 1 Tim. 2:1-2). But in this part of His prayer He was about to pray for the preservation of the faith of His own in Himself. And there would have been no point or sense in praying for the preservation of the world's faith, for in this sense the world hadn't (and still hasn't) got any faith. The world encompasses by definition those who do not believe in the Son of God, and therefore do not believe in the Father either. Such people, even if they profess to be Christians, and maybe teach theology, are just as much "of the world" as any non-Christian. Judas Iscariot did not cease to be "of the world," because for some time he served as an apostle. He remained what he always was: "the son of perdition" (17:12).

Our Lord's Request

Our Lord was here praying, then, for those who were true believers, and what He prayed was this: "Holy Father, keep them in Thy name which Thou hast given Me, that they may be one, even as We are" (17:11).*

To help ourselves understand the phrase, "Thy name which Thou hast given Me," we can once more refer to the story of the Exodus. Said God as He led the Israelites out of Egypt to begin their journey to their promised land, "Behold, I send an angel before thee, to keep thee by the way and to bring thee into the place which I have prepared. Take heed of Him and hearken to His voice...*for My name is in Him.*" That is to say, the angel that

---

* Some translations read: "...keep through Thy own name those whom Thou hast given Me"; but this rendering is based on manuscripts that at this point are inferior.

led them was entrusted with the authority of God. To disobey Him was to disobey God.

Now in a far fuller sense, the Father had given His name to the Son; and the disciples needed to be kept guarded in the power of that name. They needed to be kept believing that the Lord Jesus carried the very name of God, since He was one with the Father. It would not be enough that they should continue to behave morally; nor enough that they should believe, like the crowds in Israel did at the time, that Jesus was a great prophet, or even Elijah returned from the world beyond (see Mt. 16:13-17). They must be able to answer at all times when challenged by Jesus' question, "Who do you say that I am?" "Thou art the Christ, the Son of the Living God; Thou and the Father are one."

And since the Father and the Son are in fact one, it was important that all true believers should be one in their faith and in their testimony about the Lord Jesus. Not only the effectiveness of their testimony in the world, but their whole salvation would depend on their remaining true to the faith and true to the Lord Jesus in this.

THE EFFECTIVENESS OF OUR LORD'S PRAYER

With so much at stake, then, we cannot help asking how effective our Lord's prayer was likely to be.

Fortunately for us, we know how effective His own guarding of His eleven true disciples had been, for He Himself comments: "While I was with them, I kept them in the name which Thou hast given Me; and I guarded them and not one of them is lost, none has perished (except Judas)."

Not one lost! That was a magnificent claim; but it was not an exaggeration, nor a rare and exceptional statement that could not be taken too literally because of its unusualness. Our Lord had said the same thing earlier just as emphatically: *"All that which the Father giveth Me shall come unto Me; and Him that cometh to Me I will in no wise cast out. For I am come down from heaven, not to do Mine own will, but the will of Him that sent Me. And this is the will of Him that sent Me, that of all that which He hath given Me I should lose nothing, but should raise it up at the last day. For this is the will of My Father, that everyone that beholdeth the Son, and believeth on Him, should have eternal life; and I will raise him up at the last day"* (Jn. 6:37-40).

So then, the disciples were safe while Christ was with them; safe, not because of their own strength to maintain their own faith, but safe because He kept them and preserved their faith. But what about the future, now that He was leaving them and was no more in the world? Who, or what, would keep them now? The answer is that Christ now asks the Father to take on the task of keeping them: "While I was with them, I kept them: now, Father, You keep them."

The only question each true believer nowadays needs to ask, therefore, is this: "Will the Father be less diligent, less effective in keeping me and preserving my faith, than the Lord Jesus was in keeping the faith of His eleven apostles? The answer is self-evident: "Of course, not!" But for the sake of double certainty, let us listen again to what our Lord said about it on a previous occasion: *"My sheep hear My voice, and I know them, and they follow Me: and I give unto them eternal life; and they shall never perish, and no one shall snatch them out of My hand. My Father, which hath given them unto Me, is greater than all; and no one is able to snatch them out of the Father's hand. I and the Father are one"* (Jn. 10:27-30).

At this, every true believer will experience a surge of profound joy, which is exactly what our Lord intended. He had gathered His disciples round Him as He prayed that they might hear exactly what He prayed for them, and be certain that it would be answered: "These things I speak in the world," said He, "that they might have My joy fulfilled in themselves."

A Case in Point

"But what about Peter?" someone may ask. "Does not the very next chapter of the Gospel tell us that, in spite of our Lord's prayer, Peter denied him?"

Yes, alas it does. And that certainly reminds us that it is all too possible for a believer under pressure to act inconsistently and to compromise his faith.

But Peter was no Judas. Peter was a true believer. And when the Lord Jesus prayed that the Father would keep Peter, the Lord Jesus had foreseen, and indeed predicted, that Peter would temporarily deny him (13:37-38). He prayed for him nonetheless. And His prayer was answered. Read the last chapter of the Gospel and find out how. Peter was not lost. He was fully restored, his faith refined, and himself kept loyal to the Lord throughout the rest of his life until he glorified God in a martyr's death.

So did our Lord's proud claim stand unbroken, and will stand firm for every true believer to the end of time: "Of all the Father has given Me, I have lost not one."

31

The Son Prays for His Disciples' Sanctification and Mission in the World

"I have given them Thy word; and the world hated them, because they are not of the world, even as I am not of the world. I pray not that Thou shouldest take them from the world, but that Thou shouldest keep them from the evil one. They are not of the world, even as I am not of the world. Sanctify them in the truth: Thy word is truth. As Thou didst send Me into the world, even so sent I them into the world. And for their sakes I sanctify Myself, that they themselves also may be sanctified in truth. Neither for these only do I pray, but for them also that believe on Me through their word; that they may all be one; even as Thou, Father, art in Me, and I in Thee, that they also may be in Us: that the world may believe that Thou didst send Me. And the glory which Thou hast given Me I have given unto them; that they may be one, even as We are one; I in them, and Thou in Me, that they may be perfected into one; that the world may know that Thou didst send Me, and lovedst them, even as Thou lovedst Me"

(Jn. 17:14-23).

Having prayed for the preservation of His disciples' own

faith, the Lord Jesus then prayed for their mission in the world as a result of which many more would come to faith in Him, and the world would have to recognize that God had sent Him. We can lay out the contents of this section of the prayer very simply thus:

A. 18:14-19: *The disciples' mission in the world:* "As Thou didst send Me into the world, even so I have sent them into the world" (17:18).

B. 17:20-23: *The effect of the disciples' mission:* "neither for these only do I pray, but for them also that believe on Me through their word" (17:20).

So let us investigate these two parts of the prayer in order: First Part A in this chapter, and then Part B in the next.

THE DISCIPLES' MISSION IN THE WORLD

Once more the prayer is very carefully ordered:

1. (a) *The situation:* "the world has hated them" (17:14).
   (b) *Petition:* "...keep them from the evil one" (17:15).
2. (a) *The situation:* "they are not of the world even as I am not of the world" (17:16).
   (b) *Petition:* "sanctify them in the truth" (17:17).
3. (a) *The situation:* "as Thou didst send Me into the world, even so I have sent them into the world" (17:18).
   (b) *Provision:* "and for their sakes I sanctify Myself that they also may be sanctified in truth" (17:19).

THE FIRST SITUATION—THE WORLD'S HOSTILITY

"I have given them Thy word; and the world hated them, because they are not of the world, even as I am not of the world" (17:14).

The world can be a very hostile place, as we all know too well. It is full of bitter hatreds engendered by nationalism, racism, class-struggle, religious wars, and individuals' greed and aggressiveness. But the hostility our Lord now refers to is a special hostility provoked in the world's heart through the word of God given by Christ to His disciples. That word always causes a fundamental division in the world's ranks (7:43; 9:16; 10:19). It exposes men's sin, calls on them to repent, to lay down their arms of rebellion against God and to be reconciled to Him. Naturally, those who accept the word and comply are felt by those who reject it to have gone over to the other side; and in consequence the world hates them, because they are no longer of the world, just as Jesus Himself was not of the world.

Strangely enough, it was not only Jesus' exposure and denunciation of the world's sin that provoked hostility: very often His message of mercy, forgiveness, and salvation had the same effect. When He taught, and demonstrated, that upon repentance and faith, a person can be forgiven, justified, have peace with God, and know it for certain, the religious teachers of the day objected strongly (Lk. 5:17-21; 7:49). When He taught that as the Judge of all mankind, He can give eternal life here and now to those who believe, so that they may be absolutely sure that they will never come into condemnation, the Jews sought to kill Him (Jn. 5:18-24). The fact is that, in spite of all their religious ceremonies and their attempts to keep God's law, these people had no assurance of salvation in their own hearts, and Christ's claim that He could give this assurance to His disciples filled them with unease, resentment, and hostility.

If, then, the world had been hostile to Christ when He preached God's word, so it would be to His disciples when they went out into the world to preach that very same word. And that is why, before our Lord mentioned in His prayer that He was going to send His disciples into the world, He first prayed (as we saw in the last chapter) for the preservation of their own faith; and why He let them overhear His request that the Father would keep them: for hearing that, they would be absolutely sure that the Father would let none of them be lost, and their hearts would be filled with joy (17:12-13). Without that assurance of salvation in their own hearts, how could they have gone out and preached the word to the world and endured its hostility? And what gospel would they have had to preach anyway?

THE FIRST PETITION

"I pray not that Thou shouldest take them from the world, but that Thou shouldest keep them from the evil one" (17:15).

But at the same time the Lord was aware of what the Evil One, the prince and god of this world, as the Bible calls him (14:30; 2 Cor. 4:4), would try to do to Christ's servants. He would not only oppose them by persecution, he would attempt to entice them into worldliness, compromise, and sin, in order to discredit their gospel if he could. That was serious; but our Lord was not frightened by it. He had no thought of praying that God would take His disciples out of the world, to avoid the enemy's attacks. Christ's confidence stood firm that His Father would guard His disciples from the Evil One; and to that end He prayed. Christians can never afford to think or speak lightly of Satan; and those who work actively to spread God's Word must expect to be the special targets of his counter-attacks. *"For our wrestling is not against flesh and blood, but against the principalities, against the powers, against the world-rulers of this darkness, against the spiritual hosts of wickedness in the heavenly places"* (Eph. 6:12).

But we do not go alone or unarmed into the conflict. The Father Himself protects and arms us; ours is to maintain humble dependence on Him at all times and to learn to use the armor He supplies. *"Be strong in the Lord, and in the strength of His might. Put on the whole armor of God, that ye may be able to stand against the wiles of the devil...Wherefore take up the whole armor of God, that ye may be able to withstand in the evil day, and, having done all, to stand. Stand therefore, having girded your loins with truth, and having put on the breastplate of righteousness, and having shod your feet with the preparation of the gospel of peace; withal taking up the shield of faith, wherewith ye shall be able to quench all the fiery darts of the evil one. And take the helmet of salvation, and the sword of the Spirit, which is the Word of God; with all prayer and supplication praying at all seasons in the Spirit, and watching thereunto in all perseverance and supplication for all the saints. And on my behalf, that utterance may be given unto me in opening my mouth, to make known with boldness the mystery of the gospel, for which I am an ambassador in chains; that in it I may speak boldly, as I ought to speak"* (Eph. 6:10-11, 13-20).

THE SECOND SITUATION

"They are not of the world, even as I am not of the world" (17:16).

When we hear our Lord say this, it might well seem to us at first that He was simply repeating word for word what He had just said in verse 14; and we might well ask: "Why the repetition?" The answer is that while it is, of course, a repetition, it is not simply a repetition. In verse 14, He was explaining the reason for the world's hatred, and it formed the basis of His prayer that His disciples should be kept from evil. Now to be kept from evil is the very negative side of practical holiness. But the negative side is not enough by itself: it needs to be supplemented by the positive side of holiness. And so our Lord now cites again the fact that His disciples are not of this world; but this time He makes it the basis of His petition for their positive sanctification.

THE SECOND PETITION

"Sanctify them in the truth: Thy word is truth" (17:17).

To illustrate the two sides to sanctification we may take as an example the sacred vessels used in the ancient Israelite temple. To be fit for the service of God, they had in the first place to be clean. No taint of defilement was allowed to soil such vessels; or if it did momentarily, it had immediately to be cleansed away. But it was not enough for such a vessel to be spotlessly clean. After all, there were many vessels in the kitchens of the Israelite housewives that were spotlessly clean. But they were not used in the temple. Why not? Because they had never been given over to the Lord's service; the housewives used them simply for their own purposes. For a vessel to be used in the service of God it had to be not only clean but totally devoted to the Lord. And so it is with Christ's disciples: to be used as witnesses to Christ in the world, they must be positively devoted to the Lord.

This principle applies not only to those who are called to spend all their time and energy in spiritual work; it applies equally to all believers in all walks of life. Christian workers in field, factory, shop, or wherever, are exhorted that whatever they do, they are to work heartily *as unto the Lord,* and not unto men, or they serve the Lord Christ (Col. 3:23-24). The Macedonian Christians are held up as an example in the New Testament (2 Cor. 8:5); for though very poor, when they were asked to make a contribution to a relief-fund to help their fellow-Christians who were suffering famine in Jerusalem, they gave an astonishingly large sum of money. And their secret was this: "They first gave themselves to the Lord"; and after that they found it easy to give their money when it was God's will they should. The norm for all true Christian living is stated as follows: *"For none of us liveth to himself, and none dieth to himself. For whether we live, we live unto the Lord; or whether we die, we die unto the Lord: whether we live therefore, or die, we are the Lord's. For to this end Christ died, and lived again, that He might be Lord of both the dead and the living"* (Rom. 14:7-9).

THE GROUNDS AND MEANS OF SANCTIFICATION

So let us now investigate: 1. The grounds on which Christ prayed for His disciples' sanctification; and then 2. The means by which that sanctification should be furthered and achieved.

The grounds were these: "They are not of the world, even as I am not of the world." How then did they become "not of this world?" They became so when, to use our Lord's words from chapter 3 of John's Gospel, they were "born from above," and received a new life that was not "of this world" any more than the Son of God was Himself of this world. That life was begotten in them directly by God, when first they received God's Son by faith (Jn. 1:11-13). That was the "new birth," the "washing of regeneration," the "bathing all over" of which we learned in our very first session of the school.

But granted that the disciples were no longer "of the world," they would need now to be positively devoted to God's service, and constantly maintained in that devotion. How and by what means could this be done? "Sanctify them by Thy truth," says Christ; "Thy word is truth."

As they went about their work of living and witnessing for Christ in the world, they would constantly be surrounded by the world's ideas, schemes, motives, and methods, and it would be an ever-present danger that the church would stray from its devotion to Christ and adopt the world's outlook and tactics. All too often in the course of the centuries Christianity has become part of the reigning political systems of the time in the various countries and empires of the world; and far from being a pure virgin betrothed to Christ and to none other as her Lord and Head (Eph. 1:11; Col. 1:18; 2 Cor. 11:2-3), has allowed the head of the worldly political power to usurp the place of Christ, and so compromise the Church's loyalty and devotion to the Lord. It is the simple, yet sorry, fact of history that from the fourth century onwards the Church built up huge ecclesiastical structures modeled on the autocratic imperial structures of the Roman Empire; and those structures fast became the occasion of worldly, scandalous power-struggles, and much international strife, on the part of ambitious ecclesiastics and politicians. In every age churches have found it perilously easy to identify the Christian gospel with whatever political philosophy was currently in favor, whether monarchy, or feudalism, democracy or socialism, Marxism or liberation theology, until the gospel itself has become confused in people's minds, and Third World countries have thought missionaries to be agents of their colonizing governments.

And it would be a question of keeping Christ's servants and their witness not only from being confused with the world's politics, but also from getting itself all mixed up with the world's alien standards of morality, philosophies, and commercialism. It has often been a public scandal that the Christian religion has appeared to be a great money-making machine, with all the sales techniques of the day being employed to bring in the dollars. And it has been an equal, if not greater, disaster that for the last two hundred years, particularly in the West, the academic study of the Bible has often been based on rationalist philosophies. Unbelief being the initial presupposition, the end product has not surprisingly been unbelief that has undermined the faith of generations of students.

How then could Christ's servants be kept as pure and clean vessels fit for the Master's use, uncompromised by the world, and free from their own vices and lusts (2 Tim. 2:14-26)?

"By God's truth," says Christ. But what is truth? "God's Word is truth," says Christ. Centuries before, the Psalmist had asked: "Wherewithal shall a young man cleanse his way?" And the answer he gave was this: "By taking heed thereto according to Thy Word" (Ps. 119:9). That answer remains true for young and old, individuals and churches, at all times and in all countries. The key to ongoing sanctification, and, when necessary, to the recovery of sanctification, is diligent study of, obedience to, and practice of, God's Word. For it is by His Word that God sanctifies His people; and those who have been bathed all over once and for all, need constantly to allow the Lord to rinse their feet by the washing of water through the Word if they are to enjoy practical fellowship with Him in His service, and rightly witness for Him in the world.

THE THIRD SITUATION

"As Thou didst send Me into the world, even so have I sent them into the world" (17:18).

Living among the world, then, would have its very real dangers for Christ's disciples, and both their faith and their holiness would need to be protected. But true Christian holiness was not to mean withdrawing the disciples from the world and building walls around them so that they never came in contact with the world. Here Christ is once more an example. The Father, in His love for mankind, sent Him into the world: He came to seek and to save that which was lost. He was not content simply to preach in the synagogues; He mixed freely with all kinds of people, so much so that He was prepared to show personal friendship and hospitality even to notorious sinners, and in turn to accept their hospitality (Lk. 15:1-2; 19:7). The Pharisees bitterly criticized Him for this, as if He were reducing God's standards of holiness and condoning sinful behavior. But His reply to His critics was unanswerable: "People who are well do not need a doctor, but those who are sick do...I have not come to call the righteous, but sinners to repentance" (Lk. 5:30-33). A doctor who visits and treats people who are ill in hospital with dangerously infectious diseases is not saying that disease does not matter: he is trying to cure it. And so it was whenever Christ mixed with sinful people. Everyone present always knew what His purpose was: He was out to save them; while He Himself remained utterly untainted by their sin Himself.

"But would it not be dangerous for His disciples to do that kind of thing?" says someone. Yes, of course; and practical wisdom suggests that you don't send a young person who has just escaped from drugs back into the dens of the drug-pushers, any more than you would send an inexperienced, untrained teenager to deal with a case of small-pox. But in general all Christ's disciples are sent out into the world, and the world at all its levels is a dangerous place. Yet Christ who sends them out has foreseen the dangers and has made provision to meet them.

THE PROVISION

"And for their sakes I sanctify Myself, that they themselves also may be sanctified in truth" (17:19).

Our Lord Jesus was never tainted with sin. Throughout His whole life He was holy, harmless, and undefiled. There was no sin in Him. He knew no sin. He did no sin (Heb. 7:26; 1 Jn. 3:5; 2 Cor. 5:21; 1 Pet. 2:22). How then could He talk about sanctifying Himself?

Well, not in the sense of cleansing Himself, for He needed no cleansing. But in the other sense of the word, He could speak of setting Himself apart for the work to which God had called Him.

An example will help. When God instructed Israel to build Him an earthly tabernacle so that He could come and dwell among them, He appointed a man named Aaron to be their High Priest. His noble office was to enter this tabernacle and to meet God as His people's representative; and for this special task he had to be sanctified, that is, set apart from all else for this purpose.

Now God has long ago done away with that earthly tabernacle and with all earthly high priests. Today there is only one divinely appointed High Priest and that is Christ (Heb. 7). He ministers, moreover, as the Representative of all His people, not in some earthly tabernacle but in heaven itself (Heb. 8:1-2; 9:24).

So when He stood praying with His disciples here on earth and talked about sanctifying Himself so that they also might be truly sanctified, He was referring to the fact that He was now going to leave them—and this world—in order to set Himself apart for, and devote Himself to, the two great tasks to which God had called Him. Those tasks were:

1. To give Himself as a sacrifice for sin on the cross that He might cleanse and sanctify all His people; and

2. To act as their High Priest, Representative and Advocate before God in heaven.

These two almighty tasks we may describe in the words of Scripture itself; and as we do so, it will become apparent how these two ministries of our Lord are relevant to the initial sanctification of His people, and then to guarding and maintaining them as they go out into the world to live and testify for Him.

THE SANCTIFYING EFFECT OF HIS DEATH

a) Heb. 10:6-10: *"In whole burnt offerings and sacrifices for sin Thou hadst no pleasure: Then said I, Lo, I am come (in the roll of the book it is written of Me) to do Thy will, O God. Saying above, Sacrifices and offerings and whole burnt offerings and sacrifices for sin Thou wouldest not, neither hadst pleasure therein (the which are offered according to the law), then hath He said, Lo, I am come to do Thy will. He taketh away the first, that He may establish the second.*

By which will we have been sanctified through the offering of the body of Jesus Christ once for all."

b) Heb. 13:12-14: *"Wherefore Jesus also, that He might sanctify the people through His own blood, suffered without the gate. Let us therefore go forth unto Him without the camp, bearing His reproach. For we have not here an abiding city, but we seek after the city which is to come."*

THE EFFECTS OF HIS
HIGH-PRIESTHOOD AND ADVOCACY

a) In supporting and strengthening His people in times of trial and temptation: *"Wherefore it behooved Him in all things to be made like unto His brethren, that He might be a merciful and faithful high priest in things pertaining to God, to make propitiation for the sins of the people. For in that He Himself hath suffered being tempted, He is able to succor them that are tempted...Having then a great high priest, who hath passed through the heavens, Jesus the Son of God, let us hold fast our confession. For we have not a high priest that cannot be touched with the feeling of our infirmities; but One that hath been in all points tempted like as we are, yet without sin. Let us therefore draw near with boldness unto the throne of grace, that we may receive mercy, and may find grace to help us in time of need"* (Heb. 2:17-18; 4:14-16).

b) In interceding for them when they fall and sin: *"My little children, these things write I unto you, that ye may not sin. And if any man sin, we have an Advocate with the Father, Jesus Christ the right-eous: and He is the propitiation for our sins; and not for ours only, but also for the whole world....Simon, Simon, behold, Satan asked to have you, that he might sift you as wheat: but I made supplication for thee, that thy faith fail not: and do thou, when once thou hast turned again, stablish thy brethren"* (1 Jn. 2:1-2; Lk. 22:31-32).

c) In His being able to save His people to the uttermost and bring them through all their difficulties home to God: *"Which hope we have as an anchor of the soul, a hope both sure and steadfast and entering into that which is within the veil; whither as a forerunner Jesus entered for us, having become a high priest forever after the order of Melchizedek...But He, because He abideth forever, hath His priest-hood unchangeable. Wherefore also He is able to save to the uttermost them that draw near unto God through Him, seeing He ever liveth to make intercession for them..." "Who is he that shall condemn? It is*

Christ Jesus that died, yea rather, that was raised from the dead, who is at the right hand of God, who also maketh intercession for us. Who shall separate us from the love of Christ? Shall tribulation, or anguish, or persecution, or famine, or nakedness, or peril, or sword? Even as it is written, For Thy sake we are killed all the day long; we were accounted as sheep for the slaughter. Nay, in all these things we are more than conquerors through Him that loved us. For I am persuaded, that neither death, nor life, nor angels, nor principalities, nor things present, nor things to come, nor powers, nor height, nor depth, or any other creature, shall be able to separate us from the love of God, which is in Christ Jesus our Lord" (Heb. 6:19-20; 7:24-25; Rom. 8:34-39).

32

The Son Prays for the Effects of His Disciples' Mission in the World

In this part of His prayer, our Lord makes a request from His Father, which He then follows by a statement of the provision which He has Himself made.

THE REQUEST

"Neither for these only do I pray, but for them also that believe on Me through their word; that they may all be one; even as Thou, Father, art in Me, and I in Thee, that they also may be in Us: that the world may believe that Thou didst send Me" (Jn. 17:20-21).

At this point in His prayer our Lord looked down the many succeeding centuries and saw in His mind's eye the ever increasing number of men and women that would come to believe in Him as an immediate or long-term result of the original witness of the apostles. And He prayed for them that they all might be one.

This was no vague prayer based on undefined idealism; for our Lord immediately specified what kind of oneness He had in mind and how it should be brought about: "that they all might be one, even as Thou, Father, art in Me and I in Thee, that they also may be in Us" (17:21).

This oneness of all believers of all time, then, was going to depend on all believers being equally in Christ and in the Father. To understand why Christ should need to petition the Father to bring this kind of oneness about, we must once more be good historians and place ourselves in imagination beside Jesus and His eleven disciples as they stood on the threshold of the Garden of Gethsemane.

At this point in history, the disciples were not yet in Christ. Obviously not; He stood external to them, physically by their side. Indeed, it would not be possible for them to be incorporated in Him until after His death, resurrection, and ascension, and the coming of the Holy Spirit at Pentecost. Until this time the disciples had been kept together as one band of men simply by their common interest in, and love for, the Lord Jesus. Like an army following a trusted general, or a group of school-children clustered round a loved teacher, they were a more or less closely-knit band of individuals; but as yet nothing more.

But soon another infinitely superior kind of oneness was going to be formed. In answer to this very prayer that the Lord Jesus was now praying, God would give to the Lord Jesus the "promise of the Father" and the Lord Jesus would pour out the Holy Spirit upon His disciples (Acts 2:33). The startlingly wonderful result would be that the disciples (and all subsequent believers in Christ) would be placed *in* Christ, be incorporated in Him and in God the Father.

WHAT IT MEANS TO BE IN CHRIST

But what does such language mean? Some religions talk of the individual's soul being eventually merged into the Universal Soul like a drop of water merging into the ocean. But in that case, the drop of water would completely lose its separate identity. That is not what the Bible means when it talks of the believer being *in* Christ. The Bible's illustration is that of a body and its members (1 Cor. 12:12-31). In a human body each member, be it hand, eye, or foot, retains its own distinctive individuality. And yet the body is not just a collection of separate items. Each member is an integral part of the body; and all the members are members of each other. This comes about because each member is in the body, and the life of the body courses through every member alike, holding all the members together.

This then is how it has been with every believer in the Lord Jesus since Pentecost; for then the risen Christ baptized all His people in the Holy Spirit and incorporated them into Himself. Read the New Testament and you will find the early Christians constantly referring to the fact that they are now "in Christ." Here are but a few examples out of many:

"There is therefore now no condemnation to those who are in Christ" (Rom. 8:1).

"If anyone is in Christ, *he is a new creature"* (2 Cor. 5:17).

"...the Son of God has come and given us an understanding that we know Him that is true (God), and we are in Him that is true, even in His Son Jesus Christ" (1 Jn. 5:20).

"Paul and Silvanus and Timothy, unto the church of the Thessalonians in God the Father and the Lord Jesus Christ" (1 Thess. 1:1).

Being "in Christ" distinguishes believers from unbelievers. It is a distinction and a reality that not even physical death can destroy; for when Christ returns, says Paul, "the dead *in Christ* shall rise first" (1 Thess. 4:16).

THE HISTORICAL UNIQUENESS OF CHRIST

Now historically, this is a very striking thing. There were many ardent followers of the ancient philosophers, Socrates and Plato, for instance. But none of them ever described himself as being "in Socrates" or "in Plato." It wouldn't have made sense for them, of course, to talk like that, for Socrates and Plato, brilliant though they were, were at best mere men. But Jesus is not a mere man. He is the Second Adam, the Son of Man, able to incorporate into Himself all who trust Him. And, as we remarked above, it is a striking and highly significant thing that a few years after Christ's resurrection we find the early Christians talking quite naturally of being "in Christ." It shows that from the earliest times they realized who and what Jesus really was.

But it is an equally important thing for each one of us to ask ourselves the practical, personal question: "Am I in Christ?" All the believers in Christ know instinctively that they are in Him. Like Noah and his family knew they were in the ark and safe from the Flood, so every believer instinctively realizes that he or she is eternally saved and secure because he or she is "in Christ, not having a righteousness of his own, produced by keeping the law, but that which is through faith in Christ" (Phil. 3:9). But it is all too possible to be just a nominal Christian, without any experience of what it means to be in Christ. Hence the need to ask ourselves the question squarely: "Am I in Christ?"

How Does One Get to Be "In Christ"?

Simply by believing in Christ! Christ is here talking explicitly about those who "believe on Me through their (the apostles') word." Being "in Christ" is not some advanced spiritual state into which some specially holy Christians manage to enter after years of spiritual discipline. All believers are "in Christ" from the very first moment that, in true repentance and faith, they put their trust in Christ. And it is God who puts them in Christ: "It is of God," says Paul, "that you are in Christ Jesus, who has become for us wisdom from God, namely righteousness, sanctification, and redemption" (1 Cor. 1:30). And not only are all believers in Christ from the moment that they put their trust in Him, but they are all equally in Christ. It is not a matter of degree: none is in Christ to a greater extent than another. Moreover being in Christ for salvation removes all other distinctions: "There is neither Jew nor Greek, neither slave nor free, neither male nor female; for you are all one in Christ Jesus" (Gal. 3:28).

Evidence that Convinces the Word

In asking His Father that all those who believe in Him should be one, our Lord had a further objective in view. It was that "the world may believe that Thou didst send Me" (17:21). Now it has become quite clear that the oneness our Lord was talking about was the oneness produced by the fact that every believer is in Him and in the Father. He was not thinking about the great— and small—organizational structures that have arisen within Christendom in the course of the centuries. Christendom certainly has produced from time to time and in different parts of the world some vast monolithic organizations as well as myriad other smaller ones. But the organizational unities are not what demonstrates that Jesus Christ was sent by God. The various forms of Marxist communism achieved vast organizational unities, kept together by the most rigorous intellectual and physical coercion, that ruthlessly suppressed any deviation or revisionism. But such unities did not prove that Marx was sent by God, or even that his doctrine was right.

What our Lord intended, what would impress the world, was this: as people came in contact with and observed individual true believers, whether rich or poor, educated or uneducated, they would find that they all had one striking and pre-eminent thing in common: Jesus Christ was real to them! They would not talk of Jesus as a merely historical figure, nor as a remote figure in some distant heaven. They would speak of Him as someone they knew, as a baby knows its parents. They would describe themselves as being "in Christ" and "in God the Father." Whatever denominational label they might carry (or none at all) they would not tell the world that they had to join the church to be saved, nor try to convince the world that their church was the only true church. They would preach Christ, and Christ alone, for salvation. For them Christ was all and in all. They would of course explain Christian doctrines. But those doctrines themselves would make clear that it is not the doctrines that save, but Christ. We must come each one directly to Him, not to some intermediary—trust Him, receive Him and be received by Him, to enter through Him as the door into salvation, like sheep enter into a fold, and to be in Him for now and forever. Only then would it be appropriate for them to join a Christian church.

THE STUMBLING-BLOCK OF DENOMINATIONAL LABELS

It is the regrettable fact that denominational labels have often obscured this unity that exists between all true believers. For some reason or other, Christians have shown a perverse (and biblically forbidden) tendency to advertise themselves publicly under a whole array of different labels. They have named their churches after countries or cities; after prominent Christian leaders (in defiance of 1 Cor. 1-4); after particular Christian doctrines or practices; after various theories and methods of church-government; sometimes to the complete exclusion from the label of the one Name that should alone be on it: the name of Christ. It is a scandal and a dishonor to Christ of which all Christians should everywhere and speedily repent.

But in spite of that scandal, the unity of all true believers, brought about by the fact that all true believers are in Christ and in the Father (in spite of their denominational labels), remains. It is indestructible. And it points the world to Christ as the present living Lord sent by God for mankind's salvation.

THE PROVISION

"And the glory which Thou hast given Me I have given unto them; that they may be one, even as We are one; I in them, and Thou in Me, that they may be perfected into one; that the world may know that Thou didst send Me, and lovedst them, even as Thou lovedst Me" (Jn. 17:22-23).

At first sight this provision seems simply to repeat the request word for word. But though there are similarities there are significant differences.

First, Christ no longer speaks simply of their being one, but of their being perfected into one. Here is a oneness that can be developed and increased.

Secondly, He does not speak here of believers being "in Christ" and "in the Father" ("in us," v. 21), but the opposite way round, of His being "in the believers" and the Father "in Him," and thus also "in the believers" ("I in them and Thou in Me," v. 23).

Both things are true of the believer, of course, simultaneously: the believer is in Christ and Christ is in the believer (see Col. 1:27; 2 Cor. 13:5). A fish, to be alive, must be in the water and the water in it. A human being, to remain alive physically, must be in the air, and the air in him, simultaneously. Life cannot exist if only one of these conditions is met. So a believer's eternal, spiritual life depends on his being in Christ and Christ in him simultaneously.

Thirdly, Christ here describes what He has done to bring this about: "the glory which Thou hast given Me I have given them." The glory which the Father gave to Jesus was the glory of the Father dwelling in Him (14:10). Now our Lord announces His resolve (hence the past tense, "I have given") to come and dwell in each one of His people. And since the Father dwells in Him, when the Lord Jesus dwells in His people, the Father dwells in them, too.

But fourthly, we should notice an important difference. All believers are in Christ, and that is not a matter of degree, some more, some less; all are in Him equally. Similarly Christ is in all believers. But here there are degrees. He dwells more fully, more extensively, in some of His people than in others. It is like it is with a house. An owner of a house might invite you to stay in his house. On your arrival he might admit you to just one room and bar all the other rooms to you. Or he might admit you to two rooms or to all three. Christ dwells in all His people; but sometimes there are areas of our hearts that are so full of other things that there is no room for Christ in them; and sometimes we keep the door to other areas shut to Him. That is why the Apostle Paul was in the habit of praying for his converts that they might be strengthened so that Christ might take up His residence without reserve in the home of their hearts. Here is his prayer: we do well to pray it for ourselves.

"For this cause I bow my knees unto the Father, from whom every family in heaven and earth is named, that He would grant you, according to the riches of His glory, that ye may be strengthened with power through His Spirit in the inward man; that Christ may dwell in your hearts through faith; to the end that ye, being rooted and grounded in love, may be strong to apprehend with all the saints what is the breadth and length and height and depth, and to know the love of Christ which passeth knowledge, that ye may be filled unto all the fullness of God. Now unto Him that is able to do exceeding abundantly above all that we ask or think, according to the power that worketh in us; unto Him be the glory in the church and in Christ Jesus unto all generations for ever and ever. Amen" (Eph. 3:14-21).

It is, then, as Christ dwells ever more fully in our hearts that we find ourselves led ever more deeply into the enjoyment of our union with every other believer: we are "perfected into one."

And finally, as this process develops, there will arise in our hearts an ever deepening sense of being loved by God, that God loves us in the same way and to the same extent as He loves His Son. And people in this loveless, hopeless, hate-filled, insecure, and restless world will sense it; they will come to see that our joy and peace and security spring not from our merit nor from our strength of personality, nor from our circumstances, but from this: that Christ dwells in us and we are loved by God.

33

The Son Prays for All His People All the Way Home to Glory

"Father, that which Thou hast given Me, I will that, where I am, they also may be with Me; that they may behold My glory, which Thou hast given Me: for Thou lovedst Me before the foundation of the world. O righteous Father, the world knew Thee not, but I knew Thee; and these knew that Thou didst send Me; and I made known unto them Thy name, and will make it known; that the love wherewith Thou lovedst Me may be in them, and I in them" (Jn. 17:24-26).

In the course of His prayer, the Lord Jesus had prayed for His disciples and for their progress in sanctification, ordering His petitions in logical steps. He had first rehearsed the way by which, at the beginning of their spiritual pilgrimage, He had brought them to faith, and nurtured and developed that faith throughout His earthly ministry while He was still with them. Then He had prayed for the preservation of their faith during His absence. Next He had covered with His prayer their mission in the world and their need for continuing sanctification. After that, He had prayed for the effectiveness of their witness as generation after generation of people all down the centuries would come to faith through their word. And now, as He came to the end of His prayer, He looked forward to the great consummation, when all His people should arrive in the glory of His eternal presence, their holiness complete. And for this too He prayed, that He might render its achievement secure. He who had begun the good work in them would complete it. He would not begin with His preaching what He could not complete through His prayers.

THE CONSUMMATION OF HOLINESS

He prays now therefore for the consummation of His people's holiness. Notice how He describes it. He does not pray for them to be taken to heaven, though of course that is implied. He prays: "Father, that which Thou hast given Me, I will that, where I am, they also may be with Me." Not simply 'that where I am they also may be.' Divine love could not leave it so vague as that. It must specify: "that where I am they also may be *with Me.*" Christ's love will not be content until every one of His people is with Him for ever.

This is the authentic Christian note: "Today shalt thou be *with Me* in paradise," said Christ to the dying thief (Lk. 23:43). "To be absent from the body, to be at home *with the Lord*," says Paul (2 Cor. 5:8); and adds elsewhere, "I have the desire to depart and be *with Christ*, for it is very far better" (Phil. 1:23).

THE ADDITIONAL OBJECTIVE

But in praying that His people may all eventually be with Him, Christ has an additional objective: "that they may behold My glory that Thou hast given Me." That is the glory to which our Lord had referred at the beginning of His prayer, the glory which He had with the Father before the world was created (17:5). The sight of that glory—to us as yet unimaginable—will bring home to us what now we see only dimly: the wealth which He had, being rich, and then left, in order to become poor for our sakes that we through His poverty might be enriched (2 Cor. 8:9).

But in praying that we be brought to see His pre-creation glory, our Lord's thought is travelling in a slightly different direction. That glory was the expression and the measure of the Father's love for Him. We must be brought to see that glory, therefore, for in seeing that immeasurable glory we shall begin to grasp the infinite extent of the Father's love for the Son. And then—but before He proceeds to the climax of His thought's flow, He interjects a solemn note: "O righteous Father, the world did not know Thee." O sad, sad ignorance! The world in its alienation and foolish independence and rebellion, did not recognize the Father's Son, and would not humble themselves as little children in order to be taught by God, to have the love of God and the love of His Son revealed to them. Instead they consigned God's Son to the shame of a cross. Now, in the justice of God, they will forever forfeit not only the blessings of creation and redemption but participation in the glory of the Creator and Redeemer.

But with deeper gratitude against that somber background, we hear our Lord proceed: "But I knew Thee and these knew that Thou didst send Me."

But how, we ask, did they come to know this? Not through any superior strength of intellect, and certainly not through their own merit. They were what our Lord described as little children (Lk. 10:21-24); only, they were prepared to take the position of little children. That Name on the knowledge of which their whole salvation, their eternal life and their everlasting glory depended—that Name was made known to them by the divine skill of their divine Teacher. "I have made known to them Thy Name," said Christ. And already as little spiritual children, taught by the Son Himself, if they understood little else, they knew the Father, as all little children in God's family do (1 Jn. 2:13).

But God's Name, that is God's character, is infinite in its wealth and glory. God's people, therefore, must not remain spiritual infants. They must grow into the knowledge of God, becoming His mature sons, and always increasing in their understanding of the Father and the Son. To that end therefore Christ now pledges Himself with a promise of never-ending revelation: "*I have made known to them Thy Name and will make it known.*"

True to that promise, Christ constantly makes known the Father's Name to His people here on earth as they can bear it, using God's Word and the education and discipline of life's experience. Few people have had a near-perfect human father;

some have been emotionally dented or even scarred by the distorted interpretations of fatherhood given them (unintentionally) by their parents. It can take a lifetime for Christ to correct these false impressions and to inform the mind and, more importantly, to impress the heart with the perfect care, nurture, sympathy, patience, and mercy of the Father's love, and to convince us that it is all more wonderful than we dare dream of. Similarly, it can take Christ a long time to make us aware of the Father's insatiable ambition for His people's growth in holiness to the point where it matches His own, cost what it may (Heb. 12:5-11).

But hear the climax to which Christ's prayer has been progressing. He plans to take His people at last to be with Him where He is. There He will show them the inexhaustible riches that were His before creation was summoned into being. And the purpose of that never-ending display will be that they shall explore ever more profoundly the infinite extent of the glory given to Him by the Father, and in doing so, perceive with ever increasing wonder the Father's love of the Son. And then above the music of their adoration of the Father's love for the Son, shall be heard the voice of the Son revealing always more of the Father's Name. Wave after wave of ecstatic wonder and joy shall then fill them in turn as they realize again and again, each time as though it were something completely new and fresh, that the Father loves them too, as fully and as richly and as infinitely as He loves the Son. And the love of God shall be in them, and the Son of God shall be in them, eternally.